With love
For Sarah and Stephanie

Contents

List of Tables

List of Figures

Preface

I must stress that my knowledge of tax evasion and the black economy is strictly academic. I have absolutely no practical experience of either subject. My interest was first aroused during the course of writing *The Economics of Crime and Law Enforcement* nearly ten years ago. Whilst I was engaged on that project I read a fascinating paper by Michael Allingham and Agnar Sandmo entitled 'Income Tax Evasion: A Theoretical Analysis' and made a mental note to give the subject some more detailed study.

When I did begin to read more widely around the subject I became acutely aware that a huge gulf existed in the literature. On the one side there were several books and many articles written for the layman, often by the layman, which were full of rather anecdotal material on the problems of the black economy. On the other side was a substantial literature written by professional economists but which could not be easily understood by the general public and seemed largely unknown even to much of the economics profession. It was then that I decided to try to write a book that would bridge that chasm. This book represents the result of the attempt to review and summarise the rather obscure academic debate in a manner that could inform popular and political debate. Whether I have been successful only time and the market-place can tell!

I find writing books to be a long, lonely and sometimes harrowing experience. At the end one is only too aware of the faults which remain. However, I hope that those who read this book will find it of value in introducing them to, what I find to be, a fascinating literature.

I would like to thank Professor Sir Alan Peacock and The David Hume Institute for commissioning me to write a study of tax evasion, which was published in 1987. The time spent in writing that work helped enormously to organise my thoughts. The income – which was all declared to the Inland Revenue I should add – was also very useful. Early versions of Chapter 5, 6, 7 and 8 were read by both Alan Peacock and George Norman and I am grateful to them for the time they devoted to trying to understand my arguments. I must absolve them from blame for any errors which may alas have re-entered during the redrafting process. I am also extremely grateful to my publishing editor, Tim Farmiloe, who has left me alone whilst I struggled with my thoughts. His patience deserves better reward than I fear he has received. And thanks, too, go to Elizabeth Black and Keith Povey for an excellent job in copy-editing the typescript. Finally, I would like to thank Sarah Mason and Julie Neat who have typed the final version of the book with great care. Their ability to decipher my handwriting is remarkable in itself.

Leicester   D.J.P.

1 Introduction

Recently *The Times* in the UK ran an article under the headline 'Revenue Steps up Moonlight Hunt'. This followed a decision by the Inland Revenue to deploy another 850 staff to work specifically on tracking down moonlighters, who, so the article claimed, are 'part of Britain's thriving black economy'.

The terms *black economy* and *moonlighting* are now widely used to indicate those activities which are concealed from the tax authorities in an attempt to evade paying tax. In the past few years there has been considerable Press and public interest in these activities. For example, another lengthy article on the subject in the *Daily Mail*, entitled 'The Artful Dodgers Who Cheat Us All', listed a number of ways in which individuals evade paying their taxes and the supposed effect that this has upon the honest taxpayer.

Politicians have also become concerned about the problem. Every year the UK's Public Accounts Committee quizzes the Inland Revenue on what it is doing about moonlighting and tax evasion. Also recently, we have seen the publication in the UK of the Report of the Committee on Enforcement Powers of the Revenue Departments. Although this Report was not primarily concerned with evasion, it was inevitable that the subject would feature in the deliberations of the Committee. The Report claims that the tax-revenue losses through evasion may be in excess of £4 billion per annum, enough to enable income taxes to be cut by 3p in the £.

Of course, interest in tax evasion and the black economy is not confined to the UK. Indeed, there is much evidence to indicate that press and political attention in the UK came much later than in many other countries. For example, Simon and Witte (1982) document press interest in the USA as arising in the late 1970s stimulated, it would seem, by the work of Peter Gutmann concerning the size of the black economy. This article was published in the *Financial Analysts Journal* in 1977. It sparked off considerable public, political and academic inquisitiveness and debate, some of which is discussed below. Gutmann's estimates suggested that the USA's black economy accounted for some 10 per cent of GNP. Subsequent work by Edgar Feige produced estimates more than three times larger!

Simon and Witte state 'an increasing number of American financial magazines and journals carried stories describing the surprising

1

growth of the underground economy in the United States'.[1] At about
the same time the US federal government set about deriving its own
estimates of the size of the black economy. These were subsequently
published in a report by the Internal Revenue Service entitled *Estimates of Income Unreported on Individual Income Tax Returns*. This
study lent considerable support to the notion of the existence of a
sizeable black economy.

In many ways work on the black economy in the USA was a
forerunner for other countries. Awareness of the existence of the
black economy, its size and growth and the examination of the
reasons for involvement in it all began in America. However, since
then both academic and general interest in the subject has spread
worldwide. Occasionally the public debate on the subject has tended
to become rather hysterical. In some countries – for example, Italy
(where tax evasion is thought to amount to some £13 billion a year),
evasion has been said to be reaching epidemic proportions and the
tax-collection system is in danger of collapse.

The objective of this book is to see what light can be shed upon
the subject of evasion and its effects by economic analysis. While
some economists have been interested in the analysis of evasion for
rather longer than it has been at the forefront of public discussion,
much of their work dates from 1980 onwards. The number of economists working in this area is still relatively small and their work is
probably unknown even to much of the economics profession. The
primary purpose of this book is, therefore, to review and evaluate the
work on the black economy carried out by economists. It is hoped
that the end product will be intelligible both to the general reader and
to those economists who, while not specialists in the area, would like
to find out something about the subject.

1.1 DEFINING TERMS

What precisely do the terms black economy and tax evasion mean? In
this section I propose to explain how I have defined these concepts.

It is common in reading the literature in this area to encounter a
host of terms which seem to be used almost interchangeably. For
example, one often finds reference to the submerged economy, the
hidden economy, the underground economy, the subterranean economy and so on. However, on a closer inspection it becomes clear that
different authors do not always mean the same thing when using

these different terms. Even worse, they sometimes use the same term to mean somewhat different things.

Fortunately, the term black economy now has a reasonably standardised definition. The black economy refers to all those perfectly legitimate activities, resulting in transactions (either in kind or for payment) between individuals, which are then hidden from the authorities, principally the tax authorities. Activities in the black economy are, therefore, primarily undertaken with a view to evading the payment of various direct and indirect taxes which their notification to the tax authority would normally imply. This definition, therefore, does *not* include illegal activities such as drug-pushing, prostitution or the takings of illegal gambling dens. Neither does it include activities such as DIY, growing your own vegetables or doing your own car repairs.

Some authors (e.g. Smith, 1986) include criminal, marketed activities within the definition of the black economy. Also, it is true that some attempts at estimating the size of the so-called black economy have included estimates of the market value of criminal activity (Kenadjian, 1982). However, it is also apparent that much of the work on the black economy – e.g. that concerning participation, economic consequences, policy and indeed even much of the work on size and measurement – equates the black economy with legitimate activity undertaken with the primary objective of evading payment of tax, i.e. it excludes criminal activity.

It is, then, convenient to define the black economy as being synonymous with tax evasion and we follow this definition throughout this book. Apart from a few minor exceptions this presents no real difficulty. The exceptions all relate to the measurement of the black economy. However, it is true to say that those engaged in the business of measurement have rarely been explicit about precisely what activities they have included in their estimate of the black economy. This needs to be borne in mind when reading Chapters 2–4 of this book.

What kinds of activity are involved, then? Really any legitimate activity upon which tax, whether it be income tax, sales tax, customs duty or whatever, should be paid, but is not. Some typical examples may aid understanding. For example, if individual *A* (a university professor) works as a gardener in his spare time, but fails to declare to the Inland Revenue the income which (s)he obtains from this work, then (s)he is guilty of tax evasion. The gardening work is defined as black economic activity. In fact individual *A* would be referred to, by the authorities, as a moonlighter. A moonlighter is technically someone who has a full-time job in which (s)he pays income tax and a part-time job in which (s)he does not because (s)he fails to declare the income (s)he obtains there. In addition to moonlighters there are also people known as 'ghosts'. Ghosts do not exist as far as the tax authorities are concerned. That is they do not have any income upon which they pay income tax. In other words they are full-time specialists in black economic activity. If, for example, individual *A* quit his/her job as a university professor to concentrate his/her energies on his/her gardening activities then (s)he would become a ghost.

The kinds of people who are supposed to be most heavily involved in the black economy are (i) self-employed business people of all kinds, (ii) odd-job persons, e.g. gardeners, window cleaners, bricklayers, and (iii) domestic help. On the fringes are people who earn small amounts of income from which income tax is not deducted and who conveniently 'forget' to declare this income to the tax authority at the end of the year.

From what we have said it should be clear that tax evasion means hiding part of one's income from the income tax authority (evasion can just as easily be applied to other taxes, e.g. VAT, motor vehicle licences, import duties and so on). Evasion as such is an illegal activity, although it should be emphasised that the activities which generated the income need not be illegal. Indeed in terms of our definitions of the black economy they are certainly not illegal.

Tax *evasion* needs, therefore, to be distinguished from tax *avoidance*, which is the entirely legitimate use of tax loopholes in order to minimize one's (income) tax burden. Again, a simple example might help to make the point. If I fail to declare any royalties that I might obtain from writing this book, then I would be guilty of tax evasion and, if caught, possibly subjected to a heavy fine. However, suppose that I declare my royalties, but also claim tax relief (which I do not actually!) for various expenses incurred in writing the book, e.g. the costs of typing, biros, etc., I would then be behaving perfectly legitimately in trying to reduce my income tax burden. In other words, I would engage in tax avoidance.

This distinction may seem rather minor, but it is all important. Of course, we need to stress that claiming larger expenses than one is entitled to is also evasion *not* avoidance. Tax evasion implies reducing one's tax payments by illegal means, whatever these might be. Tax avoidance means behaving quite legitimately, although in some cases perhaps cynically, in order to reduce one's tax payments. Of course, at the margins, it might be quite difficult to distinguish between some forms of evasion and avoidance.

1.2 THE MAIN ISSUES

This book examines four main issues relating to the black economy. This should not be interpreted to imply that there are no other issues worthy of discussion. It simply reflects my perhaps rather idiosyncratic categorisation of economic research on the topic. The four areas I have identified are:

(i) size and measurement;
(ii) participation;
(iii) economic consequences;
(iv) policy.

Some economists have devoted a great deal of attention to trying to measure the size of the black economy. Much of the early work on this front was undertaken in the USA by Gutmann, Feige and Tanzi. However, interest in measurement has spread to other countries, so that now (early 1988) it is possible to report estimates for most of the advanced, industrialised countries of Europe and North America. Some of this work is examined and reported in Chapters 2, 3 and 4.

To most people the question 'how big is the black economy?' seems absolutely fundamental to further analysis of the topic. After all, *if* it is large, then surely it poses a threat to the legitimate economy, whereas if it is small it can be safely ignored. Unfortunately, as we shall see, there are considerable obstacles preventing exact measurement. Obviously, tax evasion and participation in the black economy tend to be carefully concealed from the tax authorities. Accordingly such activities are largely unrecorded in official statistics of output and employment (although in some countries national income statisticians do add an assumed amount of tax-evaded activity to measures of GDP. See below).

If one wants to measure the size of the black economy, then one has to think up some fairly ingenious means of measurement. Economists have been nothing if not inventive on this front. We can identify two broad approaches, which we can label as the direct and indirect methods. The direct approach relies largely upon the rigorous examination of a random sample of taxpayers' income-tax returns. This method has been used in the USA by a study team set up by the Commissioner of the Internal Revenue Service. In that study extensive use was made of data drawn up by the Taxpayer Compliance Measurement Programme (TCMP). Here some 50 000 randomly selected individual tax returns were subjected to detailed scrutiny by auditors. This analysis should then give a fairly accurate approximation of the amount of undisclosed income of tax-return filers.

However, other sorts of undisclosed income may be more difficult to discover. For example, the income of those who have not filed a tax return or income from various illegal activities such as drugs or prostitution. Of course, we would not wish to measure the amount of illegal activity. The IRS study team undertook various special investigations to estimate the amount of such activity. In total they estimated unreported income in 1976 to be between $75 billion and $100 billion or 6.5 to 8.5 per cent of income reported from legal sources. Of this nearly one half was unearthed by analysis of the TCMP data.

In other countries there has been much less use of so-called direct methods and in particular of random audits of tax returns. A few surveys of household participation in the black economy have been carried out in other countries, e.g. Italy and Norway and are considered in Chapter 4. However, the use of indirect methods, and in particular monetary approaches, has been much more popular.

The indirect approaches rely upon discovering the traces which the black economy leaves in its wake. For example, some economists argue that black economy transactions are primarily paid for by cash in an attempt to avoid detection. A large (growing) black economy should therefore manifest itself in terms of a large (growing) demand for cash, they claim. This has led to numerous studies of the demand for currency, from which attempts are made to infer the size of the black economy.[2] These studies are examined and assessed in detail in Chapters 2 and 3 and so we shall not discusss them in any depth here. Briefly, they try to answer the question 'what would be the amount of currency in circulation if there were no black economy?' The difference between this figure and the actual amount of currency in circulation is assumed to be funding illicit transactions in the black economy. The amount of such activity can then be estimated if we know how much activity can be sustained by each dollar/pound sterling of currency, i.e. if we know the income velocity of circulation. Clearly this is a rather difficult problem to solve. It requires either some fairly heroic assumptions about the determinants of the black economy and how they influence the demand for cash or an ability to identify a period when there was little or no black economic activity. Even in the latter case one still needs to know how the demand for currency has changed between the bench-mark period and now. These issues are explored more fully in Chapter 2.

There are some economists who would question whether cash is the sole medium of transactions in the black economy. As we shall see in Chapter 2 there is some evidence to suggest that other methods of payments are perfectly acceptable. Recognition of this possibility has led other economists to develop alternative monetary methods for estimating the size of the black economy. Feige, for example, has invented the so-called *transactions method* which is loosely based upon Fisher's equation of exchange. Here, the idea is to attempt to measure the total value of transactions undertaken in the economy (including transactions in the black economy). The ratio of transactions to GDP or GNP is used to estimate the size of the black economy, provided that once again a bench-mark can be found when the black economy either did not exist or at least was fairly small. Clearly there are some interesting problems raised by this approach too and these are also examined in Chapter 2.

The various monetary approaches, which were all developed in the USA, have been applied (sometimes in an amended form) throughout much of the industrialised part of the world. In Chapter 3 I survey and comment upon some of these applications. Unfortunately, space precludes an exhaustive survey, but I hope that I have been able to include a fairly representative sample of studies and countries.

For various reasons some economists have voiced dissatisfaction with the monetary approaches and have sought other means of estimating the size of the black economy. For example, surveys of labour-force participation show that there are, in fact, many more people engaged in economic activity than can be accounted for by official statistics. These surveys can also be used to estimate the extent of such activity. Some of these studies are examined in Chapter 4.

Other indirect approaches have been developed as a result of concern with the monetary methods of estimation. One alternative relies upon uncovering discrepancies between household expenditure and income. This, too, makes use of survey data. Households whose declared income is below their expenditure *may* be concealing a part of their income. Of course, one must be careful to isolate other reasons for excess expenditure, e.g. deliberate dissaving generated by life-cycle factors or by periods of temporary misfortune. Chapter 4 considers several attempts to estimate the UK's black economy which make use of such discrepancies.

If households conceal part of their income, but declare all their expenditure, then might it not be possible to use the discrepancy between national income and expenditure to estimate the size of the black economy? In principal the income and expenditure methods of calculating GDP/GNP should give exactly the same answer. However, in practice they do not, because they use quite different data sources. In the UK, for example, the income measure is based upon income-tax returns made to the Inland Revenue whilst the expenditure measure is obtained from various household and industrial surveys. If households conceal their income, but expenditures are declared truthfully then the residual discrepancy could give some indication of the extent of income concealment. Studies using this approach are examined in Chapter 4.

Finally, there is a kind of 'black box' approach to estimation which is advocated by Professor Bruno Frey. This approach relies upon identifying a number of factors contributing to the growth of the black economy, e.g. increases in taxation, regulation, etc., and a number of indicators of the extent of the black economy, e.g., a falling labour-force participation ratio. The approach then uses the statistical theory of unobserved variables to make inferences about the relative size of the black economy. This approach is also discussed in Chapter 4.

The second main area of research activity I will examine concerns individuals' decisions to participate in the black economy, either as suppliers of goods and services or as buyers, and consequently their decision to engage in tax evasion. These issues are examined in Chapters 5 and 6. Chapter 5 concentrates upon theoretical analysis, whilst Chapter 6 examines empirical studies.

Participating in the black economy is, to some degree, a risky activity. It is also illegal. One can, after all, be caught and punished. Economists who have attempted to model the individual's decision-making process have, therefore, borrowed fairly extensively from the literature on the economics of crime (see Pyle, 1983).

Initial attempts – e.g., by Allingham and Sandmo – treated the individual as if (s)he were simply gambling with a portion of his/her income in each time period, by deciding not to declare a part of it to the tax authority. Whilst models of this type were able to provide some interesting predictions about the effect upon tax evasion of changes in certain law-enforcement variables, there were still some weaknesses. For example, the effects of changes in the rate of income tax could not be predicted by such a model. Later contributors were able to solve this particular problem, but a much more fundamental criticism remained. This was that the formulation was, for many cases, rather unrealistic. The decision to evade paying tax was not in those situations a portfolio decision, but a labour-supply decision. In order to get away with evading income taxes, one had to work in the black economy. It was not just a matter of 'forgetting' to declare an amount of income on a tax return. Realisation of this fact has generated a number of models in which evasion and labour supply are jointly determined. These models are, of course, considerably more complicated than the portfolio models discussed earlier. Readers with a limited mathematical background may find this section rather heavy going. For them it is not essential that they attempt this particular section. The results of this type of modelling are summarised in the conclusions to Chapter 5.

One of the principal conclusions of more elaborate model-building is that it is very difficult for economists to make clear, unambiguous predictions about the effect upon participation in the black economy of almost any variable affecting that decision, e.g. income-tax rates, penalties, detection rates and so on! Whilst economists would not really be surprised by this, others might find that rather disappointing. The reasons why this is so are discussed in detail in Chapter 5.

Most theorising, by economists, about tax evasion treats individuals as if they are perfectly amoral. They act solely to maximise their own well-being and if that involves tax dodging then so be it. Whilst some people might think that this is a perfectly accurate description of how most people do in fact conduct their lives, there are others (perhaps the majority) who hold a rather less cynical view of the rest of humanity. Recently several economists have tried to take these objections into account by constructing models which incorporate so-called stigma costs. Their argument is that engaging in tax evasion causes individuals considerable discomfort in terms of lost utility. They would, therefore, be willing to become involved only if the potential monetary rewards were sufficient to outweigh the likely stigma of being caught and branded as an evader. Indeed in many cases they need not be caught in order to suffer the pangs of guilt and remorse! Models incorporating stigma costs are presented in Chapter 5, where it is shown that they have some interesting properties. In particular they are able to explain why an increase in the income-tax rate might, in the aggregate, cause an increase in the amount of income-tax evasion.

Whilst theoretical analysis can provide some interesting insights into the decision-making process it can provide little information on the precise impact of a change in an exogenous variable or parameter. For example, suppose that we want to know what the impact of say, a 10 per cent increase in penalties would be upon the amount of undeclared income. To answer such a question requires empirical evidence.

It should be clear from the foregoing discussion that empirical work in the area of tax evasion is going to be very difficult to carry out. However, economists have attempted to gather information on decisions to evade taxes from several different sources. One method relies upon questionnaires/interviews concerning individuals' attitudes to taxation and tax evasion. A second approach is to play tax evasion 'games' which simulate real-life situations. In these simulations individuals are provided with information on penalties, detection rates, income and so on and then asked to file a tax return. The third approach uses TCMP data (largely) to estimate the extent of under-recording and then tries to relate this to objective measures of certainty and severity of punishment and income-tax rates. Studies using these three kinds of approach are examined in Chapter 6.

Each of the approaches makes some use of econometric methods to try to established the effect upon tax evasion of different contributory factors. These results are reported briefly in Chapter 6, which also examines some of the limitations and problems surrounding these particular methods.

The third major area of research activity is concerned with establishing the economic consequences of the existence of a black economy and the consequent tax evasion. These issues are examined in Chapter 7. Broadly speaking the consequences can be labelled as being (i) microeconomic, e.g. upon the way resources are allocated; and (ii) macroeconomic, e.g. upon the levels of national income and prices, etc.

There are in fact a number of interesting questions to be analysed here. For example, does tax evasion mean that tax revenues are reduced? If they are, does it matter? Does the existence of a black economy mean that the level of national output is higher than it would otherwise be? Further, how is the government's ability to operate stabilisation policy affected? One interesting aspect of this is the impact which undeclared economic activity has upon the reliability of various macroeconomic indicators, e.g. is unemployment overstated? Is the real level of economic activity much larger?

It turns out that tax evasion also has an effect upon the allocation of resources. The coexistence of a taxed and an untaxed (i.e. black) sector means that some resources are diverted into the untaxed sector when they would be more efficiently used in the taxed sector. This misallocation of resources imposes a welfare cost upon society. There is now a small developing literature which tries to estimate the welfare costs of tax evasion. The limited amount of evidence shows that this may be quite considerable.

The final area of research activity examined in this book covers policy towards tax evasion. This inevitably raises the question whether evasion is inherently bad or serves a useful social function in terms of raising output and employment. To some extent the literature examined in Chapter 7 shows that evasion can produce some fairly harmful economic consequences, particularly in terms of its effect upon economic efficiency. However, whether on balance it is a harmful activity depends upon the form of society's welfare function. If a utilitarian stance is adopted then it may indeed be optimal to allow some evasion to take place.

Of course, there may be other reasons for refraining from adopting Draconian policies aimed at completely eliminating tax evasion. Enforcement can be costly and so an economically efficient enforcement policy should balance benefits against costs at the margin. Only in the most unusual situations would an efficient solution involve complete enforcement. Even if the extreme view is taken, that punishment by fines has a zero social cost, it is most unlikely that punishment could be raised to levels that would be large enough to deter all acts of evasion. A sensible criminal justice policy imposes upper limits on penalties for tax evasion. All these issues are explored in detail in Chapter 8.

Finally in Chapter 9 some broad conclusions are presented about the achievement of economic research in the area of tax evasion and the black economy. There are also some suggestions for future research in these areas and indications where it seems that further research would offer little hope of success. The black economy is a relatively new topic for economic research, but already a great deal of work has been done and much has been learned. However, it would be wrong to think that all the questions can be answered satisfactorily. Still, it is an exciting subject which is likely to attract increasing attention from both academics and the general public.

2 Measuring the Size of the Black Economy: Monetary Approaches

Of all the various direct and indirect methods used to estimate the size of the so-called black economy, the ones that are most frequently used are those based upon monetary indicators, and in particular the amount of currency in circulation.

The justification for this is the assertion that transactions in the black economy are funded largely by cash in order to reduce the chances of detection. As will be shown later, there are grounds for questioning the underlying presumption that cash is the major medium of transactions in the black economy.

Certainly the amounts of currency in circulation with the public are large and seem to be well above what one might regard as reasonable for legitimate transactions purposes. For example, in the UK in 1985 the amount of notes and coin in circulation with the public was £12 732 million or about £225 per person.[1] Admittedly some of this cash is held by companies, some is circulating abroad and some may even be lost or destroyed! Even so, these figures suggest that per capita currency holdings in 1985 may be of the order of £200.

It is difficult to believe that such sums are needed for legitimate transactions purposes, when average per capita living expenses are in the region of £60 per week (*Family Expenditure Survey*, 1985). How else can one explain this desire on the part of the public to hold large sums of cash? It is hard to believe that cash offers a particularly good return as a form of asset holding, even though inflation in UK in 1987 had fallen below 5 per cent per annum. Given the incredible growth of different forms of bank accounts, building society accounts and so on all offering positive real rates of return and instant access, cash balances represent a poor way of holding one's liquid assets. One is forced to conclude that currency is being held either to finance various kinds of illegal activities or as a means of storing the proceeds of one's ill-gotten gains. It is very much this kind of logic that underlies the use of monetary statistics as a way of estimating the size of the black economy.

There are, in fact, several monetary approaches to estimation discernible in the literature. The first focuses upon the ratio of currency in circulation with the public either to bank deposits or to some measure of the money supply. This ratio is often referred to as the *currency ratio*. Within this broad approach there are several variants. One treats the *desired* currency ratio in the legitimate economy as a constant and ascribes any changes in the ratio to changes in the size of the black economy. Another tries to account for variations in the currency ratio attributable to various factors including black economy factors, e.g. an increase in taxation.

The second monetary approach, based loosely upon the original quantity theory of money, concentrates upon the relationship between the total value of transactions and recorded GNP (the transactions ratio). An increase in the transactions ratio is attributed to an increase in the black economy. In order to measure total transactions the identity $MV \equiv PT$ is utilised. So that the value of transactions is measured by the money supply multiplied by the transactions velocity of circulation. Money is further subdivided into currency in circulation with public, and bank deposits. These in turn are multiplied by their respective velocities of circulation.

The third monetary approach concentrates upon the use of large-denomination banknotes, the so-called 'big bill phenomenon'. An increase in the relative importance of high-denomination banknotes as part of the total amount of currency in circulation is believed by some to indicate an increase in black-economy activity.

The following sections elaborate upon each of these methods in turn and the following chapter summarises the results of attempts to apply these estimation methods in various OECD economies. However, before beginning, one minor issue should perhaps be clarified. This concerns currency losses – i.e. currency that is irretrievably lost, destroyed, in collections, and so on. No readily available statistics exist on the amount of currency that has been lost. However, careful research by Laurent for the USA suggests that '. . . as of 1971 . . . approximately 3.4% of the amount listed in circulation, was irretrievably lost.' (Laurent, 1974, p. 222). He was able to conclude that 'the general disregard by economists for currency irretrievably lost has probably *not* had a significant impact upon empirical studies utilizing currency figures' (ibid, p. 224, my emphasis).

All the methods examined below make use of currency statistics that have *not* been adjusted for currency losses. However, given Laurent's researches, the bias that this omission will introduce into estimates of the size of the black economy would appear to be small.

Intuition would suggest that it is probably small in comparison with biases caused by other rather more fundamental omissions.

2.1   THE CURRENCY RATIO

The changing relationship between currency and demand deposits (the currency ratio) was used by Gutmann (1977) to estimate the size of the black economy in the USA in 1976 at $176 billion.[2] Gutmann's method has subsequently been applied in both its original and modified forms to a number of other countries and time periods (see Chapter 3).

Gutmann's method is fairly straightforward but rests on a number of crucial assumptions. The first of these is that '(w)e take the pre-World War II period (i.e. 1937–41), prior to steep income taxes, as normal' (Gutmann, 1977, p. 27). In other words, Gutmann assumes that during the period 1937–41 there was effectively no black economy in the USA. During that period the average ratio of currency to demand deposits was 0.217 – i.e. $217 of currency per $1000 of demand deposits. By 1976 the currency ratio had risen, somewhat unevenly, to 0.344. The increase in this ratio was taken by Gutmann 'as a measure of the amount of currency held for illegal purposes' (ibid, p. 27). To illustrate, in 1976 the total volume of demand deposits in the USA was $226.2 billion. Gutmann argues that in the absence of any black-economy activity a proportion (0.217) of this – i.e. approximately $49.1 billion – would be needed for entirely legitimate pursuits (note that he is implicitly assuming no change in the 'legitimate' currency ratio since 1937–41. See below). In fact, the amount of currency in circulation with the public in 1976 was about $77.8 billion. According to the logic of Gutmann's analysis this must imply that some $28.7 billion of currency was being held to finance illegal transactions.

How does Gutmann then proceed to estimate the size of the black economy? The method is as follows. He argues that the $226.2 billion of demand deposits and $49.1 billion of legitimate cash (i.e. $275.3 billion of 'legitimate' money supply in total) was used to 'produce' a legitimate GNP of $1693 billion in 1976 – i.e. each dollar of money supply generated slightly more that $6 of GNP. Gutmann then assumes that the income velocity of circulation in both the legitimate and black economies is the same. So, the $28.7 billion of currency held for illegal transactions is argued to have generated a black economy of about $176 billion in 1976 (or 10 per cent of the USA's GNP in that year).

Gutmann, himself, argues that the income velocity even in the legitimate sector might have been rather higher than his calculations suggest, because some of the currency and demand deposits are not being held for transactions purposes. This would suggest that his estimate for the USA's black economy was an underestimate. However, against this it must be remembered that the US dollar has a role as an international currency, so some of the increase in the currency ratio could be explained, not by the increasing importance of the black economy, but by an increase in the number of dollars held outside the USA in order, for example, to finance international trade.

Appealing though Gutmann's method is, there are a number of critical assumptions which must cast (considerable) doubt upon the validity of the technique. The first of these is the assumption that currency is the sole medium of transactions in the black economy. Smith (1986), for example, argues that 'there is little reason to believe that black economy transactions are made exclusively in cash' (Smith, 1986, p. 88).[3] He points to the use of barter or payments-in-kind as means of engaging in the black economy without leaving easily identifiable traces for the tax man. For example, individual A might offer to teach individual B mathematics. Rather than accept a cash payment, A might prefer that B (an experienced gardener, say) provides advice on garden design or even landscapes A's overgrown garden. Alternatively, A might happily accept a gift of a gold-plated fountain pen. Clearly whilst these services are part of GNP and should be counted, as long as cash does not change hands there is an element of ambiguity, at least in the participants' eyes, as to whether they should be declared to the tax authority. After all, one good turn deserves another!

Further, as Smith points out, a request for payment in cash might very well be made to the wrong person, so that active black-economy traders might feel there is less risk of detection if they accept a cheque than if they insist on cash. After all, the trader might reason that it is unlikely that the Inland Revenue would closely scrutinise his/her bank account, especially if (s)he was careful enough to declare a 'reasonable' amount of his/her income.

So, the claim that cash is *the* medium of transactions in the black economy seems on closer inspection to be of rather dubious credibility. Accordingly, any estimate of the size of the black economy that relies upon such an assumption must be of questionable accuracy. The second crucial assumption of Gutmann's analysis is that there was no black economy in the period between 1937 and 1941. This assumption would seem to be less important than the first, although it still seems to be of questionable validity. Despite the wealth of evidence that during the 1930s there was a great deal of underworld activity in the USA, it has been common to assume the absence of any black economy on the eve of the Second World War (see, also, the discussion of Feige's method below).

This problem arises from the attempt to obtain a precise estimate of the absolute size of the black economy. To do so it is essential to identify a bench-mark, i.e. a period when the size of the black economy was actually known. Of course, no such bench-mark exists. The response seems to have been to claim that such activity did not exist at a particular point in time. If instead one simply wishes to measure the *increase* in the black economy between two time-periods then it is not necessary to measure its absolute size in the first period. For example, using Gutmann's technique and data one might instead conclude that there was $176 billion *more* black economy activity in 1976 than there was in 1937–41, but one would leave the exact amount of such activity in both 1937–41 and 1976 as unknown.

The third crucial assumption of Gutmann's method is the assumption that the income velocity of circulation in both the legitimate and black economies is identical. Various authors (e.g. Feige, 1979, and O 'Higgins, 1980) have questioned this assumption. One can find *a priori* arguments in favour of both a lower and higher velocity of circulation in the black economy and it is not clear which, if either, view is correct. On the face of it, it may be safest to adopt a neutral stance on this particular issue.

The fourth crucial assumption is that in the absence of a growing black economy the ratio of currency to bank deposits observed during the bench-mark period (i.e. 1937–41) would have remained unchanged. This seems to be a fairly strong assumption to sustain over a period of observation lasting nearly forty years. As Gutmann himself points out, '(a)s an economy develops, ever more transactions are typically carried out with checking accounts, and demand deposits grow more rapidly than currency' (Gutmann, 1977, p. 26). Indeed his own figures show that between 1892 and 1941 the ratio of currency to bank deposits fell from 0.352 to just 0.219. The period since 1941 has seen widespread financial innovation (e.g. introduction of credit cards) and the spread of banking habits throughout a much larger proportion of the population. Using the logic of Gutmann's analysis it would appear then that the 'legitimate' currency ratio in 1976 would be even less than the 1937–41 average of 0.217. If this were the case then his estimates of the size of the black economy would need to be revised upwards.

One further criticism of the currency ratio method should also be mentioned at this stage. A rise in the currency ratio could come from a fall in bank deposits just as easily as from an increase in currency in circulation with the public. Gutmann's measure of bank deposits is *demand* deposits. It is possible to conceive of a situation in which the public switches out of demand deposits into time deposits, say because interest rates are rising. As a result one might observe a fall in the ratio of cash to demand deposits, but no change whatsover to the ratio of cash to demand plus time deposits. Estimates of the black economy based upon a rise in the ratio of cash to demand deposits would be entirely incorrect. Bowsher claimed that in the USA over the period 1939–79 the ratio of currency to total deposits has 'changed little' (Bowsher, 1980, p. 13), whilst Laurent argues that 'currency declined relative to total bank deposits from 1939 through 1976'. (Laurent, 1979, p. 4).

Garcia and Pak (1979) acknowledge that the rise in the currency/ demand-deposit ratio can be attributed to a fall in demand deposits rather than a rise in cash holdings. However, they further show that the fall in demand deposits is itself largely a statistical illusion brought about by mismeasurement of the demand deposit series. Simply put, this arises because the volume of demand deposits is measured at the close of bank business. However, this is after for example some of these deposits have been invested overnight in Treasury bills and other securities. The following morning, of course, the transaction is reversed. Garcia and Pak argue that the sums invested in this way are *during the day* available as transactions media, but because they are measured *at night* they are excluded from the definition of demand deposits. When these sums, known as Immediately Available Funds purchases or IAFs, are included the increase in the currency/deposit ratio is much less marked than indicated by the unadjusted figures.

On the other hand, Laurent supports Gutmann's use of the currency/demand deposit ratio on the grounds that 'currency and demand deposits are the only components of any money measure that can be immediately transferred for goods and services' (Laurent, 1979, p. 4). However, he further argues that '*transfers* of currency and demand deposits would be more indicative of economic activity than the *stocks* of currency and demand deposits' (ibid, p. 4; my emphases).

Laurent then attempts to see what happened to the ratio of currency transfers to demand deposit transfers between 1937–41 and 1976. To do this he requires information on turnover rates for both currency and demand deposits. Information on the latter is published and shows that turnover rates increased substantially during the period. The currency turnover rate has to be inferred – indeed Laurent only measures changes in this relative to its unknown 1939 level – from changes in the length of life of currency (see the discussion of the transactions approach for a more ingenious means of calculating turnover rates for currency). Of course, this assumes that the number of transactions/transfers that can be accomplished by a unit of currency during its lifetime does not change. As we shall see later there are very strong grounds for doubting this assumption.

Laurent then calculates the ratio of currency to demand-deposit transfers and concludes that this has *fallen* substantially between 1937–41 and 1976. This is quite different from what happened to the currency stock/demand deposit stock ratio calculated by Gutmann, which grew over the same period. He is led to conclude, therefore, that 'the proportion of total economic activity associated with currency has declined substantially over the past 40 years. Thus, it seems unlikely that the subterranean economy could presently account for a tenth of reported GNP' (Laurent, 1979, p.6).

One must conclude that Gutmann's method is rather unsystematic and lacking in rigour. There are potentially many factors at work that could affect the currency ratio – e.g. interest rates, income-tax rates, etc. If Gutmann's method is to produce meaningful results these factors have to be controlled for in a much more systematic fashion. A number of investigators have tried to do this and their efforts are discussed in the next subsection.

2.2 THE MODIFIED CURRENCY RATIO

The attempt to refine the estimates of the black economy using the currency ratio owes much to the work of Tanzi ([1980, 1983) which in turn is based upon an earlier insight by Cagan (1958).

Cagan was interested in explaining the long-run behaviour of the currency ratio (defined by Cagan as currency relative to the *money supply*) over the period from 1875 to 1955. He identified a number of factors that he expected to influence this ratio. These were:

(i) the opportunity cost of holding currency;
(ii) expected real income per capita;[4]
(iii) the volume of retail trade (cash being more acceptable in retail transactions!);
(iv) the volume of travel per capita (cash being more acceptable in transactions between strangers);
(v) the degree of urbanisation;
(vi) the rate of tax on transactions.

It is this last variable that provides the link between the currency ratio and the extent of tax evasion. As Cagan argues 'some people evade taxes by making as many transactions as possible with currency and not reporting them to the tax collector' (Cagan, 1958, p. 312). However, 'evasion will occur on a large scale only if the tax rate is high enough to create sufficient incentive' (ibid, p. 312). He therefore postulates a direct, positive relation between income tax rates and the currency ratio.[5] This hypothesis was confirmed using multiple regression analysis for the period 1919–55. Here the dependent variable was the ratio of currency to the M2 definition of the money supply,[6] and the independent variables were:

(i) the interest rate paid on bank deposits;
(ii) expected real income per capita (based on previous income levels with exponentially declining weights);
(iii) the annual percentage of personal income collected for income taxes.

The estimated regression equation was:

$$\log \frac{C}{M2} = \text{constant} - \underset{(0.02)}{0.21} \ \log(\text{interest rate}) - \underset{(0.21)}{1.16} \ \log(\text{real income})$$
$$+ \underset{(0.04)}{0.22} \ \log(\text{income tax rate})$$
$$R^2 = 0.89$$

Figures in parentheses represent standard errors for the estimated regression coefficients. It is clear that all the coefficients are statistically significant and have their expected signs.

Tanzi (1980) adopted this idea linking the currency ratio to tax rates and used it to drive alternative estimates of the size of the black economy in the USA. Tanzi's procedure was as follows. He hypothesised that the redefined currency ratio ($C/M2$) was a function of:

(i) the tax rate (T);
(ii) the share of wages and salaries in personal income (W);
(iii) real per capita income (Y) – either permanent or measured;
(iv) the interest rate on time deposits (R).

Tanzi uses per capita real income to proxy all the developments such as the introduction and increasing use of credit cards, urbanisation, travel per capita, the spread of branches of banks, etc. He postulates that 'increases in real per capita income would bring about falls in the currency ratio' (Tanzi, 1980, p. 435). The share of wages and salaries in personal income is used because many wage payments are still made in currency. (Unfortunately Tanzi was unable to separate the shares of wages from salaries.) In consequence a positive relationship with the currency ratio was posited. The presence of the interest rate and tax rate are self-explanatory. However, the choice of a measure to proxy the tax rate posed problems and Tanzi eventually used three different measures:

(i) the ratio of personal taxes to personal income net of transfers;
(ii) the top-bracket statutory tax rate;
(iii) the weighted average tax rate on interest income.

The regression equation was estimated in log-linear form using annual data for the USA over the period 1929–76. Tanzi's preferred regression equations are:

$$\ln \frac{C}{M2} = -5.3751 + \underset{(4.54)}{0.3395} \ln T - \underset{(6.98)}{0.2181} \ln R \qquad (2.1)$$
$$\underset{(8.31)}{}$$

$$+ \underset{(6.01)}{1.7059} \ln W - \underset{(1.31)}{0.0849} \ln Y$$

$$\bar{R}^2 = 0.968 \qquad D.W = 1.793$$

and

$$\ln \frac{C}{M2} = -5.2163 + \underset{(6.62)}{0.2618} \ln T - \underset{(5.39)}{0.1715} \ln R \qquad (2.2)$$
$$\underset{(5.13)}{}$$

$$+ \underset{(6.53)}{1.5989} \ln W - \underset{(1.64)}{0.0955} \ln Y + \underset{(2.98)}{0.2042} \ln \left(\frac{C}{M2} \right)_{-1}$$

$$\bar{R}^2 = 0.971 \qquad H = 0.932$$

Figures in parentheses are *t*-statistics. The tax-rate variable in both cases is the weighted average tax rate on interest income.[7] In equation (2.2) the lagged dependent variable has been added to take account of any lags in the adjustment of the actual currency ratio to its desired level. However, given that Tanzi is working with annual data it is hard to justify the presence of this variable. It is difficult to believe that individuals take a year to adjust their cash holdings to their desired levels. All the coefficients have their expected signs and most are significant, the only exception being the income variable. This conclusion was not affected by the choice of income measure.

How does Tanzi use his results to obtain an estimate of the size of the USA's black economy in 1976? The underlying idea is basically that used by Gutmann. One must first of all obtain an estimate of the amount of money that is being used for illegal purposes. From there one can multiply this figure by the ratio of GNP to 'legal' money.[8] The first stage then is to determine how much money is being used in the black economy. The procedure adopted by Tanzi is as follows.

The first step is to calculate a *predicted* value for the currency ratio in 1976, using the regression equations reported above. Given the value of $M2$ in 1976 this is then converted into a predicted value for C ($\hat{C}$). Not unexpectedly the value of C is very close to $\hat{C}$. For example C is \$77.8 billion. Using equation (2.1) the predicted value of C ($\hat{C}$) is \$78.3 billion and $\hat{C}$ from equation (2.2) is \$78 billion. Tanzi then uses equations (2.1) and (2.2) above to predict what the level of C would have been (a) if the tax rate took its lowest value over the period 1929–76 ($\bar{C}$) and (b) if the tax rate were zero (C'). These results are represented in Table 2.1.

Table 2.1   Actual and predicted values for currency in the USA, 1976
($ billions)

Equation used	Actual C	$\hat{C}$	Predicted $\bar{C}$	C'
(2.1)	77.8	78.3	63.8	46.8
(2.2)	77.8	78.0	68.1	55.5

Tanzi argues that the difference between $\hat{C}$ and C' indicates how much currency is being used in the black economy as a result of having the 1976 level of taxation rather than having no income taxes at all. This amounts to between \$22.5 billion and \$31.5 billion depending upon which of the regression equations has been used to predict it.

The difference between $\hat{C}$ and $\bar{C}$ is taken to indicate how much *extra* currency is being channelled into the black economy because the 1976 taxation level is higher than the lowest rates that had been operative during the 1929–76 period. Of course this is a much smaller sum, being between $9.9 billion and $14.5 billion.

Tanzi uses these figures to divide up the total money supply for 1976 ($304.3 billion) between 'legal' and 'illegal' money and to calculate an income velocity to circulation for 'legal' money. Finally, this is used to determine the size of black-economy GNP in 1976. Tanzi's estimates of the USA's black economy are given in Table 2.2.

Table 2.2   Tanzi's estimates of the black economy of the USA, 1976

Equation used	With zero taxes		With lowest taxes	
	$bn	%GNP	$bn	%GNP
(2.1)	198.8	11.7	86.1	5.1
(2.2)	137.5	8.1	57.9	3.4

As can be seen from Table 2.2 Tanzi's estimate for the overall size of the black economy in the USA in 1976 lies between $137.5 billion and $198.8 billion or between 8.1 per cent and 11.7 per cent of GNP. It is interesting to note that despite the considerable refinements in Tanzi's estimation procedure his overall conclusion is not markedly different from that reached by Gutmann, who estimated the USA's black economy at $176 billion (10 per cent of GNP) in 1976.

Tanzi (1983) has subsequently used his method to derive two sets of annual estimates of the black economy in the USA between 1930 and 1980. These estimates differ quite substantially depending whether the weighted average tax rate on interest income or the ratio of total income tax payments to adjusted gross income is used to measure the tax rate. For example, for 1976 Tanzi estimates the USA's black economy to have been $94.3 billion ($\approx$5 per cent of GNP) if the weighted average tax rate is used, but only $61.1 billion ($\approx$3.6 per cent of GNP) if the alternative tax measure is employed instead. Both these estimates are somewhat removed from his earlier estimate which put the black economy between $137.5 billion and $198.8 billion (or 8.1–11.7 per cent of GNP).

Tanzi's time-series estimates, for what they are worth, suggest that during much of the post-war period the black economy's 'share' of GNP was fairly static, being around either $2\frac{1}{2}$ per cent or 4 per cent depending upon which tax rate was being used to derive estimates. However from the late 1960s or early 1970s the black economy began to grow, so that by 1980 its share had risen quite appreciably, i.e. to 4.5 per cent or 6.1 per cent depending upon which tax rate was being used.

It is disturbing that Tanzi's procedure should have generated such radically different estimates for the black economy in a single year (1976) by the addition of only four extra observations, i.e. 1977–80. Careful scrutiny of Tanzi's tables shows that in his 1980 paper he predicted that 'illegal' currency in circulation in 1976 was some $31.5 billion. By 1983 he had revised this estimate to approximately $15.8 billion. The reason for this may be that the coefficients of his estimated currency ratio equations are unstable. Certainly they are different in the equation for 1929–76 compared with that for 1929–80.[9] However Tanzi does not perform a rigorous test of stability. The answer may simply be that he has made an error in predicting currency holdings in the absence of taxes in one or other of the papers.

What general criticisms can be made of Tanzi's approach? Some of these have already been encountered in the previous discussion of Gutmann's approach. For example, it relies upon a presumption that:

(i) black economy transactions are paid for in cash;
(ii) the income velocity of circulation in the formal and black economies is identical.

As has already been suggested, there are grounds for doubting the validity of these assertions.

Tanzi's approach is undoubtedly more sophisticated than that adopted by Gutmann. For example, by using both demand and time deposits in the denominator it avoids the problems posed for Gutmann's methods by switches from demand to time deposits. In addition Tanzi's method takes into account the influence upon the currency ratio of factors such as interest rates, income and so on, all of which could have influenced the currency ratio without implying anything about the size of the black economy. Gutmann's approach would have unquestioningly ascribed such changes to the black economy. Despite that, Tanzi's approach does have its limitations. For example, it focuses upon the tax rate alone as the determinant of the size of the black economy and consequently upon the holdings of currency relative to the total money supply. It is surely somewhat naive to believe that the level of taxes is the sole cause of a movement of resources away from the formal and into the black economy. Indeed, as will be shown in Chapter 5 the link between income-tax rates and involvement in tax evasion is far from being the established 'fact' that many investigators believe it to be. Further, there are other variables which one would expect to influence the degree of involvement in the black economy which have been ignored by Tanzi, e.g. penalties for being caught, the probability of detection, the amount of government regulation of economic activity and so on. By the logic of Tanzi's approach these factors should be included in the currency/money supply equation. It is difficult to justify their exclusion on the grounds that they were either probably constant throughout the period or behaved in such a manner as to off-set one another completely. This may have been the case, but only detailed investigation could reveal whether or not it was the case.[10]

There is a potentially worrying flaw in Tanzi's analysis and this concerns his calculation of the income velocity of circulation (Acharya, 1983). In his concluding remarks, Tanzi states 'The estimates attempt to measure the incomes that were generated through excessive use of currency and that *presumably* were not reported to the tax authorities. Whether these incomes were or were not measured by the national income accounts authorities cannot be determined' (Tanzi, 1983, p. 303; my emphasis). Now, it is rather important for Tanzi's method that these incomes were *not* included in GNP. This is because Tanzi uses the ratio of measured GNP to 'legal' money in order to calculate the income velocity of circulation. This measure is in turn applied to 'illegal' money in order to calculate the amount of black economy activity. If, as is possible, some of the black-economy activity has already been included in recorded GNP then two things immediately follow. First, the estimate of the velocity of circulation of 'legal' money is wrong; and second, not *all* the estimated size of the black economy can be added to measure GNP.

Whilst admitting the logic of Acharya's argument on this point, Tanzi claims that it 'is not empirically important' (ibid, p. 749). His argument seems to be that as his latest estimates of the size of the

USA's black economy were between 4 and 6 per cent of GNP at the most, then in calculating the size of the income velocity of circulation it matters very little whether none, some or all of this amount is included in the numerator – i.e. the effect on the estimates of the size of the black economy is small in relation to the margins of error of the estimates in any case.

The final word on Tanzi's approach is probably best left to himself:

> The 'Tanzi method' was applied to the US case – where income taxes have been universally blamed for sending some activities underground; where other taxes have not played much of a role; and where; because of the absence of banking secrecy, it seems reasonable to assume that most underground transactions are made in cash. It was explicitly stated in my work that non-tax-related causes (such as criminal activities) that may generate underground incomes are not captured by my method. I would certainly not apply, without major modifications, the 'Tanzi method' to situations quite different from the case I examined. The study of underground economic activities is in its infancy. Our methods must be refined and the quality of our estimates im-proved. But let us not fall into the trap of believing that, at this juncture, we can generate estimates that indicate more than orders of magnitude. (Tanzi, 1983, p. 750).

The next chapter examines some of the attempts to apply the Gutmann and Tanzi methods to other countries. However, the next section considers Feige's attempt to estimate the size of the black economy using the so-called transactions method.

2.3   THE TRANSACTIONS METHOD

The transactions approach was devised by Feige (1979) in response to the work of Gutmann on the currency/demand deposit ratio. Feige was particularly concerned by one of Gutmann's assumptions. He felt that the assumption that the black economy uses currency as its sole medium of exchange was highly dubious. This was an important influence upon his development of the transactions approach, which allows bank deposits to be used in 'irregular' purchases. Whilst he was also concerned about Gutmann's assumptions of a fixed currency ratio (in the absence of any irregular activity) and an equal income velocity of circulation in both sectors, these were obviously less important factors influencing his choice of the transactions approach. Indeed, Feige like Gutmann before him also assumes that the income velocity of circulation in both sectors is identical!

The basis of Feige's contribution is the relationship between the total value of transactions and measured income in an economy.[11] According to Feige any change in that ratio is attributable to a change in the size of the black economy. If, like Gutmann, one can identify a period in which the black economy did not exist, then a bench-mark total transactions/GNP ratio can be established. Dividing this ratio into observed total transactions for any later year gives us an estimate of the income level generated by the official and black economies in that year. It is then a simple matter to arrive at an estimate of black economy activity by substracting measured GNP from this total.

The justification for Feige's approach is as follows. He focuses upon the ratio

$$\frac{P\,T}{p^i y}$$

where P is the average price of a transaction, T is the total number of transactions undertaken in any time period, p^i is the price index of goods included in GNP and y is real GNP.

He argues that there are three possible causes of a change in this ratio. These are:

(i) a change in the price ratio $\dfrac{P}{p^i}$,

(ii) a structural change in the economy which alters the ratio $\dfrac{T}{y}$,

(iii) a change in the scale of transactions in the black economy.

It is Feige's contention that over the period since 1939 changes in the ratios $\dfrac{P}{p^i}$ and $\dfrac{T}{y}$ have been basically in the same direction and such that the transactions ratio $\dfrac{P\,T}{p^i y}$ should have fallen. If it transpires that the transactions ratio has actually risen, then this must be due to an increase in the size of the black economy.

However, Feige's tests are neither exhaustive nor rigorous on this point. He tests what has been happening to $\dfrac{P}{p^i}$ by comparing first, the consumer price index to the GNP deflator for three years and second, the wholesale price index to the GNP deflator for two years. The second ratio shows virtually no change, although the first does indeed fall. However, the consumer price index is hardly a comprehensive measure of the price of all goods and services being traded in the economy.

The tests of the trend in the ratio $\dfrac{T}{y}$ are even more superficial. He openly admits that '(t)he volume of gross financial transactions is . . . not readily identifiable' (Feige, 1979, p. 8). However, he was able to conclude that 'the ratio of intermediate to final goods . . . has fallen'. This conclusion was reached as a result of comparing two sets of unpublished input–output tables for 1948 and 1973 with a not directly comparable input–output table for 1939! The ratio of intermediate to final transactions was 1.88 in 1939, 0.84 in 1948 and 0.80 in 1973. The main evidence for Feige's conclusion obviously lies in the fall in this ratio between 1939 and 1948. This fall looks suspiciously large and even Feige admits that the tables for those years are 'not strictly comparable' (ibid, p. 8). Certainly the change between 1948 and 1973 is minimal.

A major problem in using the transactions method is the absence of readily available data upon the total value of transactions undertaken in an economy during a particular time-period. Here, however, Feige makes use of the well-known Fisherian identity that:

$$MV \equiv PT$$

where M is the stock of money, V is the transactions velocity of circulation, P is the average price of a transaction and T is the total number of transactions undertaken in any time period. Clearly, Feige is interested in the magnitude of PT. However, in the absence of data on this he must use MV. Unfortunately, even here his passage is not completely smooth. As we have already seen, most definitions of the money supply include currency in circulation with the public *and* bank deposits, either sight deposits only or sight plus time deposits. Feige adopts a narrow definition of the supply of money and so includes only currency and sight (or demand) deposits. The next step is to obtain estimates of the transactions velocity of circulation of money. Whilst this is readily available for demand deposits, it is not so for currency and so Feige has to make rather ingenious assumptions at this point.

The main problem in calculating the total value of transactions is to calculate turnover figures for currency. Feige estimates this by taking a figure produced by Laurent (1979) for the number of times a unit of currency can be used before it is retired from circulation (125) and dividing it by the estimated average lifetime of currency (based upon published statistics of currency redeemed each year). Turnover rates for demand deposits are published annually for the USA.

To summarise, Feige's method rests on the following set of assumptions. First, the relationship between the total value of transactions and measured GNP in 1939 was 'normal'. Second, any increase in that ratio can be attributed entirely to an increase in the size of the black economy. Third, the total value of transactions in any period is given by the stock of demand deposits multiplied by the average turnover of demand deposits plus the stock of currency multiplied by the average turnover of currency.

Feige, therefore, estimates the total value of transactions in 1939 as $934.9 billion, compared with a measured GNP of $90.8 billion. This gives a transaction ratio of 10.3. Feige then estimates that the total value of transactions undertaken in 1976 was some $19 899.4 billion. He then divides this total by the 1939 transactions ratio. This gives a sum of $1932 billion. This compares with a measured GNP of only some $1706.5 billion. The difference ($225.5 billion or about 13 per cent of GNP) is Feige's approximation of the size of the black economy of the USA in 1976. A similar calculation for 1978 produces a black economy of about $542 billion (or nearly 26 per cent of measured GNP)!

Feige produced a second set of estimates that were even larger. These indicated that the black economy was about $369 billion in 1976 (22 per cent of GNP) and $704 billion in 1978 (33 per cent of GNP). These estimates arose from altering the estimate of the average number of transactions a unit of currency can perform before it disintegrates, from 125 to 225.[12]

It is evident that Feige's estimates of the size of the black economy are much larger that those produced by either Gutmann or Tanzi. It is true that Feige was not immensely confident about the precision of his estimates. Indeed he was prepared to admit that 'estimates of the irregular economy based upon these methods could vary within a rage of several hundred billion dollars' (Feige, 1979, p. 10). His estimates are quite sensitive to alternative assumptions about the length of life of currency. He lists a number of other factors which could either reduce or increase his estimates of the size of the black economy. Among these influences were:

(i) the assumed size of the black economy in 1939;
(ii) the assumption that the income velocity of money is the same in the black economy as in the formal economy;
(iii) the exclusion of barter transactions;
(iv) the role of increased credit market activity on demand deposit turnover, and so on.

Feige's estimates are quite sensitive to changes in some of these assumptions.

There are obviously a number of question marks hanging over Feige's method. It is worrying, for example, that his estimates are so sensitive to changes in some of his assumptions. A more robust technique would be preferable. It is also slightly disturbing that Feige's estimates should show what appear to be quite implausible increases in the size of the black economy between 1976 and 1978. Depending upon which of the assumptions about currency life one accepts, Feige's estimates indicate that the black economy grew either from $225.5 billion in 1976 to $541.7 billion in 1978 or from $369.1 billion to $704.4 billion over the same period. Whilst these estimates are in money terms as distinct from real terms, they suggest a growth of the black economy of between 90 per cent and 140 per cent over the two-year period. This needs to be compared with a growth in measured GNP over the same period of only 23 per cent. Whilst growth of this magnitude is possible – after all almost anything is – it does *not* look credible. Between 1976 and 1978 consumer prices in the USA rose by about 14 per cent (Gordon, 1981, p. 271). If prices in the black economy rose by the same amount, this would suggest an average real growth rate for the black economy of at least 37 per cent per annum compared with 4.5 per cent per annum for the official economy. This seems to be beyond the capacity of the economic system to produce and were it to be true would suggest that there was immense under-utilisation of capacity in the years 1976–8. Certainly, careful research by Denison (1982) fails to reveal any drastic changes in the ratio of employment to population during this time that would lend credence to Feige's findings.

Frey and Pommerehne claim that 'the choice of the base year is crucial [to Feige's calculations]. The transactions method gives a negative hidden economy for the whole period between 1939 and

1968, and it suggests a falling underground economy during World War II, when casual observations suggest a strongly rising trend' (Frey and Pommerehne, 1984, p. 11). Findings like this, they claim, led Feige to revise some of his assumptions, particularly concerning the life of paper currency. Feige's modified estimate of the size of the black economy was 27 per cent of GNP in 1979 (Feige, 1980).

2.4 CURRENCY HOLDINGS AND THE 'BIG BILL' PHENOMENON

As was said at the beginning of this chapter one of the reasons why people became interested in using currency statistics to measure the size of the black economy was the apparently large amount of currency in circulation with the public. One aspect of that phenomenon has been the ever-increasing popularity of large denomination bank-notes, which seem to form an ever-increasing proportion of currency in circulation.[13] How is this supposed to be related to the size of the black economy? For example, between 1965 and 1985 in the UK the total value of currency held by the public rose by nearly fourfold. However, when inflation is taken into account this increase is largely illusory.[14] The real value of currency in circulation is actually less than it was twenty years ago. Bowsher (1980) also shows that in the USA the ratio of currency to GNP has *fallen* steadily over the period from 1939 to 1979.

It would seem then that currency holdings *per se* are an unpromising indicator. Despite this, economists are still attracted to the notion that black economy transactions are being fuelled by large holdings of cash. We have already encountered some of these theories in relation to the currency ratio. A perhaps rather less reputable theory is based upon the observation that the numbers of high-denomination banknotes have increased more rapidly than currency in general, so that an increasing proportion of the currency in circulation is made up of so-called 'big bills'. This has been observed in the USA by Ross (1978) and in the UK by Freud (1979). In other words it is not so much the amount of currency in general that is an indicator of the size of the black economy, but the amount that is being held in large-denomination notes. For example, Ross states that 'Kenadjian, the chief economist of the IRS task force . . . set up to refute Gutmann . . . believes that one compelling piece if evidence (on the size of the black economy) is the increased circulation of large-denomination currency' (Ross, 1978, p. 93).

He further goes on to argue that:

> Between the end of 1967 and June 30, 1978 the value of $100 bills
> in circulation rose by more than 250 per cent, to $32.9 billion.
> (During this period, the total value of currency in circulation rose
> by only 125 per cent). The ratio of $100 bills to GNP final sales
> increased sharply during the same time. In mid-1977, there was an
> excess of $7.35 billion in $100 bills outstanding beyond what would
> have been the case had the 1967 ratio held. Some of the excess may
> be due to the fact that, with inflation, large bills are employed
> more often in ordinary transactions, but this usage is probably
> minimal (Ross, 1978, p. 93).

Similar kinds of calculation have been undertaken by Freud for the
UK. His calculations show that:

> between 1972 and 1978 the aggregate value of £10 and £20 notes in
> circulation grew by 470 per cent, while the growth in the aggregate
> value of all British notes rose by only 110 per cent. Inflation and
> increased consumer spending account for only a small proportion
> of the increase, for over the same six years, consumer expenditure
> at current prices rose by only 140 per cent (Freud, 1979, p. 16).

Whilst this is all very interesting it is not clear that it tells us
anything at all about the size of the black economy. All the methods
discussed earlier – i.e. the currency ratio (modified or otherwise) and
the transactions ratio – do at least have some underlying rationale,
despite their various faults. The *raison d'être* for the big-bill phenomenon remains shrouded in mystery. The only possible – and it has
so far remained implicit – explanation is a belief by its proponents
that black-economy transactions are paid for by using large-
denomination notes, i.e. $100 bills in the USA and £10 and £20 notes
in the UK. But why should this be? Admittedly it may be convenient
to pay for some large black-economy transactions (e.g. drug deals)
with a smaller number of notes. However, much black-economy
activity involves small sums of money, e.g. household cleaning,
plumbing, window-cleaning, etc. It is not obvious that payments for
these services need to be made with large-denomination notes.
Indeed, given the recent scare stories in the UK concerning the
forging of £20 and £50 notes it is likely that recipients would prefer
payment in notes of smaller denomination.

Tanzi (1982) has claimed that many of the $100 bills are not even held *inside* the USA. The reasons for this are many, but perhaps one of the most important is currency substitution. In countries with high inflation rates, e.g. Brazil, Israel, Argentina, etc., US dollars have replaced some of the domestic currency. In those countries holdings of US dollars are a hedge against inflation and it is convenient to hold them in fairly large denominations, even if only to reduce storage and handling costs.

So the grounds for believing in the so-called 'big-bill' phenomenon do not look promising. They look even worse when one realises that the whole phenomenon may just be a sympton of a ' "substitution effect" of inflation on currency holdings' (O'Higgins, 1980, p. 18).

Inflation has an effect not just upon the level of currency holdings but also upon their composition and it is this latter effect that is relevant here. In a time of rising prices, *ceteris paribus*, individuals will need to hold more currency to finance the same amount of transactions. They can do this by simply holding more notes and coin in the same proportions as previously or they can switch, partially or totally, out of small denominations into larger denominations. Given that people are restricted in terms of the size of their wallets, it is likely that they will engage in some form of substitution away from low-denomination notes and coin into higher denominations.

O'Higgins illustrates this quite well for the UK. Over the period from 1972 to 1978 when the aggregate value of notes in circulation rose by 110 per cent, 'the *number* of £1, £5, £10 and £20 notes in circulation increased by only 29 per cent, (O'Higgins, 1980, p. 18). This clearly came about because of a switch from low- to high-denomination notes. This can be seen clearly in Table 2.3, where we give the proportion of currency held in different denominations of notes in both 1972 and 1978.

Table 2.3 Proportions of notes of different denominations, UK, 1972 and 1978

	1972	1978
£1	0.66	0.44
£5	0.30	0.40
£10	0.03	0.13
£20	0.01	0.03

The consequence is that the consumer can 'hold' the additional 110 per cent of currency needed to finance transactions by carrying only an extra 29 per cent more notes. As a result the aggregate values of £10 and £20 notes increases by nearly 500 per cent, but this is not necessarily a sinister development.

Overall, there is little to be said in favour of the 'big-bill' phenomenon as a means of indicating anything about the black economy let alone measuring its size.

2.5 CONCLUSIONS

This chapter has examined in some detail the various monetary approaches to measuring the size of the so-called black economy. These are the currency ratio, the modified currency ratio, the transactions method and the 'big-bill' phenomenon. Of these, the least promising is the big-bill phenomenon and this will not be discussed any further. All the other methods have disadvantages too and these have been explained in some detail. It should be clear from that discussion that monetary approaches to estimating the size of the black economy rest upon some rather crucial assumptions that are difficult to justify in practice. It would seem sensible then to treat the estimates obtained by Gutmann, Tanzi and Feige for the size of the black economy in the USA with a fair degree of scepticism. The margins of error in their predictions appear to be large relative to the estimate, even by the standards of economics, e.g. their estimates could be several hundred billions of dollars out! (Feige, 1979).

So far, this book has only considered the methods themselves and how their inventors have applied them to estimate the USA's black economy. These methods suggest a black economy in the mid- to late-1970s of anywhere between 3.6 per cent and 33 per cent of GNP. Of course, these methods (and variants on them) have also been applied in other countries and it is interesting to see what results have been obtained in these other studies. This will be the subject of the next chapter. Of course, many (if not all) of the reservations expressed about the various monetary approaches will also apply to these studies undertaken in other countries.

3 Monetary Statistics and the Black Economy: Some Evidence

Chapter 2 examined four basic approaches to the estimation of the size of the black economy, all of which were based upon the use of various monetary statistics/indicators. Chapter 4 will examine in detail various other methods of measurement that have been proposed. These methods are based upon the use of national accounts statistics, labour-force participation rates, surveys of household income and expenditure, tax audits and so on. Before these other methods are considered in detail some time will be spent examining the results of various attempts to use monetary indicators to estimate the size of the black economy.

As Chapter 2 shows much of this work was developed in the USA. However, the methods have since been applied in a number of other countries. This chapter will examine some of these applications in detail. Of necessity the survey cannot be exhaustive and I apologise to those authors whose studies have not been included. I have attempted to survey only a representative sample of the kind of work that has been undertaken.

One immediate difficulty presents itself and that is how to present the results. Two obvious solutions to this problem suggest themselves. These involve grouping the studies either by method of approach or by the country/region of the investigation. The latter approach has been adopted here for the following reasons. First, some studies estimate the size of the black economy by several of the monetary methods, not just one. In order to save space, duplication and irritating cross-referencing it was decided to deal with these studies in one place. Second, some studies have modified the approaches outlined in Chapter 2 and so do not fit neatly into one or other of the categories listed there. It was thought sensible to avoid forcing these into a particular category of approach. At the same time we wanted also to avoid having a rag-bag of miscellaneous approaches listed at the end of the chapter.

The procedure then has been to split the studies roughly into two groups. First, those covering North America, i.e. Canada and the

34

USA, and second, those covering Western Europe, i.e. UK, West Germany, Italy, the Scandinavian countries and Ireland. In the former group are also included references to studies in Australia. Australia's presence in North America may surprise some readers, but there did not seem to be any other logical place to put it! I hope that Australians (and Americans!) reading this can find it in their hearts to forgive my insensitivity.

3.1 THE BLACK ECONOMIES OF NORTH AMERICA

Porter and Bayer (1984) present estimates of the black economy of the USA based upon each of the methods advocated by Gutmann,

Table 3.1   Porter and Bayer's estimates of the USA's black economy ($ billion, and as % of GNP)

Year	Currency ratio	Modified* currency ratio	Transactions ratio**
1950	15.9 (5.6)***	14.5 (5.1)	27.6 (9.6)
1955	14.7 (3.7)	12.8 (3.2)	1.7 (0.4)
1960	17.3 (3.4)	20.7 (4.1)	–3.4 (–0.7)
1965	31.6 (4.6)	26.3 (3.8)	9.6 (1.4)
1970	62.4 (6.3)	45.6 (4.6)	101.0 (10.2)
1975	150.8 (9.7)	77.0 (5.0)	467.3 (30.2)
1980	372.8 (14.2)	159.9 (6.1)	1095.6 (41.6)

* The figures in the column headed 'modified currency ratio' are not the same as those in the column with the same heading in Porter and Bayer's paper. Some explanation is required. I have used the term 'modified currency ratio' to summarise the amendments to the technique suggested by Tanzi (1980). Porter and Bayer use the same term to refer to an amendment to Gutmann's technique suggested by Feige (1980). The figures which appear in the column headed 'modified currency ratio' in Table 3.1 appear in Porter and Bayer's Table 1 under the heading 'Tanzi's model of the ratio of currency to M_2 (*TW*)'. These estimates have been obtained from regressions using a weighted average tax rate on interest income.

** Estimates for the transaction ratio method are those reported by Porter and Bayer based upon a 1939 bench-mark.

*** Figures in parentheses show the black economy as a percentage of recorded GNP.

Tanzi and Feige. They generate time-series estimates covering the period from 1950 to 1982. A selected summary of their results showing the size of the black economy in both absolute terms ($ billion) and as a percentage of GNP is given in Table 3.1.

The estimates obtained using the currency ratio use essentially the same technique suggested by Gutmann. They do make one minor modification and this is to calculate the currency ratio as the proportion of currency to checkable deposits, i.e. deposits that can be accessed by means of a cheque. This compares with Gutmann's definition of the currency ratio as the ratio of currency to demand deposits. Porter and Bayer's modification here is an attempt to take into account the growth in new forms of bank deposits which are direct substitutes for demand deposits.[1] It is not clear from Porter and Bayer's paper precisely what they have chosen as the bench-mark period, but one presumes that it must have been 1937-41.

Porter and Bayer's estimates using the currency ratio indicate that until the early 1970s the black economy was a fairly small and stable share of recorded GNP. After 1975 the black economy seemed to grow much more rapidly than the formal economy with the result that as a percentage of GNP, it grew to nearly 15 per cent by 1982.

However, the results obtained using the modified currency ratio (as suggested by Tanzi) are in marked contrast. This gives results similar to those obtained using the currency ratio for the period up to about 1965. After that, whilst they indicate a slightly rising 'share' for the black economy, they show nothing like the acceleration in the size indicated by the estimates based upon the simple currency ratio. By this method, the black economy as a percentage of GNP in 1980 is little more than 6 per cent. This conclusion is not changed when the tax measure is replaced by the ratio of total net tax payments to adjusted gross income. Indeed, estimates using this tax measure suggest a somewhat smaller black economy, i.e. 4.4 per cent of GNP in 1980, although the trend is still slightly upwards. By far the largest estimates are obtained by using Feige's method based upon the transactions ratio. Using a bench-mark of 1939 (also used by Feige) Porter and Bayer estimate that by 1981 the black economy, expressed as a percentage of recorded GNP, was nearly as high as 60 per cent! The figures in Table 3.1 also indicate that Feige's 1939 bench-mark may be wrong (see discussion in previous chapter), because the estimated black economy in 1960 is *minus* $3.4 billion. Porter and Bayer recalculated these estimates assuming that the black economy was 5 per cent of GNP in 1964. This removes the possible embarrassment of a negative black economy, but produces an estimate for the USA's black economy in 1981 of nearly $2000 billion or 68 per cent of GNP! These figures look ridiculously large. It is unlikely that illegal activity on that kind of scale could be hidden from the tax authorities for long.

Mirus and Smith (1981) report the results of a similar exercise using data for Canada. However, unlike Porter and Bayer, theirs is an estimate for a single year (1976), rather than for a number of years. A summary of Mirus and Smith's results for 1976 are given in Table 3.2.

Table 3.2 Mirus and Smith's estimates of Canada's black economy in 1976***

	$ billion	as % of total economic activity*
Currency ratio	31.3	14 (16.3)
Modified currency ratio**	9.6–14.9	4.8–7.2 (5–7.8)
Transactions ratio	53.7	21.9 (28)

 * Figures in parentheses express black economy activity as a percentage of GNP.
 ** Mirus and Smith use the ratio of currency to demand deposits *not* the ratio of currency to the M2 definition of the money supply.
 *** The base years chosen are 1937–9 (currency ratio); 1936 (modified currency ratio); and 1939 (transactions ratio).

A few comments on Mirus and Smith's techniques are called for. In calculating the currency ratio they have followed Gutmann and taken the ratio of currency to *demand* deposits only. It is clear that this ratio has risen sharply – from 0.33 in 1937–9 to 0.53 in 1944 and to more than 0.56 in 1980. What is not clear is whether this was caused by a switch from demand to time deposits rather than an increase in currency. The estimates based upon the currency ratio are sensitive to choice of base period. For example, using the period 1950–2 as the bench-mark produces an estimate of the size of the black economy of 8.4 per cent of total economic activity (or about 9.2 per cent of GNP).

In view of the well-known sensitivity of estimates based upon the currency ratio to choice of base year and doubts over how precisely the currency ratio should be calculated, it would be wrong to try to draw too many comparisons between the estimates of the black economies of the USA and Canada obtained by using it. Mirus and

Smith claim that their estimates 'are slightly higher for the Canadian case, possibly reflecting the more generous unemployment insurance provisions and somewhat higher average level of income and profit taxes in Canada' (Mirus and Smith, 1981, p. 448). However, their estimates using the transactions ratio produce quite the opposite conclusion, i.e. Canada's black economy is smaller than that of the USA. They *seem* to dismiss the transactions method on the grounds that the estimates it produces will 'no doubt . . . strike many as shockingly large, just as Feige's estimates for the irregular economy appeared too high to many observers' (ibid, p. 449). In view of the uncertainties surrounding all the monetary approaches it would seem wisest to refrain from attempting inter-country comparisons at this stage.

Mirus and Smith's attempt to produce an estimate of the black economy based upon the 'Tanzi method' is the most peculiar of all. First of all, they measure the currency ratio as the ratio of currency to demand deposits and not as currency relative to the M2 definition of the money supply. Apparently this is done for 'consistency with Gutmann's and Feige's approaches' (ibid, p. 449, fn 17). It is not clear to me what 'consistency with Feige' – who does not use a currency ratio – means here. Whilst use of the currency-demand deposit ratio may be consistent with Gutmann, whatever that means, it is certainly *not* consistent with Tanzi! Second, Mirus and Smith's reported regressions of the currency ratio on the tax rate (T),[2] the share of wages and salaries in personal income (W) and real per capita income (Y) are poor.[3] The signs of two of the coefficients are wrong. Tanzi 'predicts' that the wage variable will have a positive coefficient, because many wage payments are still made in currency. Mirus and Smith's estimated equation produces a negative coefficient for this variable. Further, Tanzi hypothesises that the income variable will have a negative coefficient (for a detailed explanation of why, see previous chapter). Yet, Mirus and Smith's estimated equation has a positive coefficient on the income variable. Third, and finally, Mirus and Smith use the estimated equations 'to predict what the [currency] ratio would have been had the tax burden remained *at its historical low for the period*' (ibid, p. 449; my emphasis). By the logic of Tanzi's method (see previous chapter) this does not generate an estimate of the size of the black economy *unless* the historically low level of taxation had actually been zero or had been so low that no black-economy activity existed during the period. What Mirus and Smith have calculated is the *extra* black economy activity in 1976 generated by having the 1976 level of taxation rather than the lowest tax rate during the period of observation, i.e. 1936–77.

Finally this section reports some estimates of the size of the black economy in Australia. These have been derived using broadly the approaches outlined in the previous chapter.

Tucker (1982) uses the Gutmann approach to estimate a black economy for 1978–9 at about $10.7 billion (about 10.6 per cent of officially recorded GDP). In deriving this estimate Tucker assumes that the 'normal' currency ratio (currency relative to current deposits in checking accounts) was that which prevailed 'throughout the late 1950s and the 1960s'. Had this ratio been maintained until 1978–9 then currency in circulation with the public would have been some $1.2 billion less than it actually was. It is this currency that Tucker claims is financing the black economy. In 1978–9 $11.2 billion of 'legitimate' currency and demand deposits 'financed' some $101.2 billion of GDP, so that the income velocity of circulation was approximately 9.03. Assuming the same income velocity of circulation in the black economy as in the legitimate economy, the extra $1.2 billion of currency produces a further $10.7 billion of output.

Carter (1984) briefly reports two unpublished studies for Australia which apparently used the Tanzi method. One by Evans and Renehan (undated) obtained estimates that, in the view of Carter, were comparable to Tanzi's estimates for the USA (Tanzi, 1980; see discussion in previous chapter). The second, by Norman (1982), estimated the size of the black economy in Australia at 13.4 per cent of GDP in 1981–2. However, as it was not possible to obtain copies of either of these papers it would be unwise to attempt to draw too much by way of conclusion from these estimates. The Australian studies seem to be subject to much the same kind of criticism that has been raised in the previous chapter. For example whilst 'there has been a marked increase in the ratio of currency to demand deposits in Australia in recent years . . . this has been brought about by a reduction in demand deposits rather than an increase in currency holdings' (Carter, 1984, p. 213). Further, in real terms per capita currency holdings in Australia are now lower than they were some thirty years ago. This does not add up to a convincing picture of a large and rapidly expanding black economy based upon cash transactions.

3.2　THE BLACK ECONOMIES OF EUROPE

European studies using monetary statistics have *not* usually been straightforward replications of the approaches of either Gutmann, Tanzi or Feige. At various points investigators have adapted those models in subtle and sometimes significant ways. I will endeavour to illustrate those deviations in the course of this survey.

One exception to that general rule is the work of O'Higgins (1981) who attempted to replicate the work of Gutmann for the UK. O'Higgins offered two measures of the currency ratio – currency expressed as a percentage of (i) the $M1$ and (ii) an approximation to the £$M3$ (M^*) measures of the money supply.[4,5]

Unfortunately, O'Higgins's data series was bedevilled by problems, e.g. no data on the $M1$ measure of the money supply exist before 1963 and there were breaks in both the $M1$ and £$M3$ series in 1967, 1972 and 1975. In view of these difficulties it would be wrong to read too precise a significance into O'Higgins's findings. Using 1974 as a base year, he calculated that the UK's black economy was between £4.1 bn and £7.6 bn in 1978 (or between 2.9 per cent and 5.4 per cent of GDP). The precise result here depends upon whether the income velocity of circulation is calculated by the ratio of $\frac{GDP}{M1}$ or $\frac{GDP}{M^*}$.

Matthews (1982) uses an adaptation of the Tanzi method to derive estimates for the UK's black economy in 1979. His calculations suggest that the black economy may lie in the range between 5.8 per cent and 7.1 per cent of GDP. The lower figure is obtained when the currency ratio is proxied by the ratio of $M1$ to total time deposits $M1/TD$. The upper bound is obtained when the currency ratio is instead measured by the ratio of notes and coin in circulation to £$M3$ less notes and coin, i.e. both sight and time deposits (C/D).

Matthews's procedure is to estimate a regression equation in which the dependent variable is the currency ratio as defined above. The explanatory variables are disposable income, the interest rate on bank deposits, the expected inflation rate, a household income-tax rate, the employers' rate of national insurance contributions, a lagged value of the dependent variable (to allow for speed of adjustment to the desired currency ratio) and a time trend. The time trend is included in order to capture 'advancement in the efficiency of the payments mechanism and the growth of intermediation' (Matthews, 1982, p. 10). The regression equations are estimated by two-stage least squares for quarterly data for the period from 1971(3) to 1979(4). Different lags were tried for the tax variables, although Matthews claims that lags of one quarter performed best 'under standard statistical criteria' (ibid, p. 12).

Matthews's 'best' equations (selected using the predication criterion of Amemiya (1980)) are as follows:

$$\log \frac{C}{D} = 3.45 - 0.114 \log R - 0.336 \log P^i - 0.484 \log Y \quad \text{(i)}$$
$$\qquad (1.33) \quad (0.38) \qquad\qquad (2.26) \qquad\qquad (1.82)$$

$$+ \ 0.0002 \ T + \ 1.279 \ T_{y_{-1}} + \ 1.739 \ T_{e-1}$$
$$\quad (0.12) \qquad\quad (2.5) \qquad\qquad (4.43)$$

$$+ \ 0.474 \log \left(\frac{C}{D} \right)_{-1}$$
$$\quad (4.51)$$

and

$$\log \frac{M1}{TD} = 3.02 - 0.973 \log R - 0.055 \log P^i - 0.365 \log Y \quad \text{(ii)}$$
$$\qquad\quad (1.02) \quad (2.79) \qquad\qquad (0.31) \qquad\qquad (1.21)$$

$$- \ 0.0004 \ T + \ 1.292 \ T_{y_{-1}} + \ 3.191 \ T_{e-1}$$
$$\quad (0.22) \qquad\quad (2.16) \qquad\qquad (5.36)$$

$$+ \ 0.612 \log \left(\frac{M1}{TD} \right)_{-1}$$
$$\quad (8.47)$$

Figures in parentheses are t-statistics. Subscripts attaching to variables indicate time-lags of one period (quarter) duration. R represents the seven-day rate of interest on bank deposits, P^i is the expected rate of inflation 'obtained as an instrument' (Matthews, 1982, p. 11), Y is real disposable income, T is a time trend, T_y is an income-tax rate and T_e is the employer's national insurance contribution expressed as a percentage of gross average earnings.

Coefficients normally have their expected signs although they are not always statistically significant e.g. R, Y and T in equation (i) and P^i, Y and T in equation (ii).

Generally, the most important explanatory variable is the lagged dependent variable. Even with quarterly data it is hard to accept that adjustment towards equilibrium currency ratios has not been achieved within the time-period. The tax variables are usually significant and have their expected effects.

Matthews proceeds to estimate the size of the black economy along similar lines to those used by Tanzi. We can use a simplified version of equation (i) to illustrate this. We can write equation (i) as follows:

$$\log \frac{C}{D} = Q + \pi_1 \log Y + \pi_2 T_{y_{-1}} + \pi_3 T_{e_{-1}} + \pi_4 \log \left(\frac{C}{D} \right)_{-1}$$

where Q represents the combined effects of all the other exogenous variables. In equilibrium

$$\frac{C}{D} = \left(\frac{C}{D} \right)_{-1}, \ T_y = T_{y_{-1}} \text{ and } T_e = T_{e_{-1}}$$

and so

$$\log \frac{C}{D} = Q' + \frac{\pi_1}{1 - \pi_4} \log Y + \frac{\pi_2}{1 - \pi_4} T_y + \frac{\pi_3}{1 - \pi_4} T_e \qquad (3.1)$$

where

$$Q' = \frac{Q}{1 - \pi_4}$$

Now, if tax rates were zero there would not be a need for a black economy. Indeed, Matthews hypothesises that K, the ratio of black economy activity to disposable income, will be given by:

$$K = \alpha T_y + \beta T_e \qquad \alpha, \beta > 0$$

when $K = 0$, i.e. when $T_y = T_e = 0$, the currency ratio will be

$$\log \frac{\bar{C}}{D} = Q' + \frac{\pi_1}{1 - \pi_4} \log Y \qquad (3.2)$$

subtracting (3.2) from (3.1) we obtain:

$$\log \frac{C}{\bar{C}} = \frac{\pi_2}{1 - \pi_4} T_y + \frac{\pi_3}{1 - \pi_4} . T_e$$

It can be fairly easily shown, although it takes rather a long time, that:

$$\frac{\pi_2}{1 - \pi_4} = \eta\alpha \quad \text{and} \quad \frac{\pi_3}{1 - \pi_4} = \eta\beta$$

Matthews further assumes that $\eta = 1$.[6]
So that:

$$\frac{\pi_2}{1 - \pi_4} \Delta T_y + \frac{\pi_3}{1 - \pi_4} \Delta T_e = \Delta K$$

It is then a simple matter to calculate the change in the size of the black economy between any two points in time. By assuming that the black economy was about 0.5 per cent of GDP prior to 1971, Matthews then calculates its absolute size in 1979 as either 5.8 per cent or 7.1 per cent.

There has been a great deal of interest in the application of monetary approaches in Scandinavia. For example, the papers by Klovland (1984), Isachsen and Strøm (1985), Schneider and Lundager (1986) and Schneider (1986) have applied the monetary approach to Norway, Sweden, and Denmark. In order to save space this discussion will consider only the papers by Klovland and Schneider and Lundager.[7]

Klovland's starting-point is to assume a relationship between the stock of currency held by the public (C); the price level (P); household disposable income (Y); the rate of interest (R), and 'Some tax rate, T, as a proxy variable for hidden economic activity' (Klovland, 1984, p. 427). Further, by assuming a price-level elasticity of unity and that all variables except T enter as natural logarithms, the basic estimating equation can be written as:

$$c - p = \alpha_0 + \alpha_1 y + \alpha_2 r + \alpha_3 T \tag{3.3}$$

where lower-case letters denote natural logarithms.

Klovland modifies equation (3.3) to allow for the now standard assumption of lags in the adjustment of actual to desired cash holdings. As Klovland eventually estimates the cash demand equation using annual data this modification seems difficult to justify. The modified estimating equation is:

$$\Delta(c-p) = \alpha_0 + \beta_1\Delta y + \beta_2\Delta r + \beta_3\Delta r_{-1} + \beta_4\Delta p + \beta_5\Delta^2 p + \beta_6\Delta T$$
$$+ \alpha_1(c - p - y)_{-1} + \alpha_2 y_{-1} + \alpha_3 r_{-2} + \alpha_4 T_{-1} \qquad (3.4)$$

where a Δ preceding a variable indicates a change in that variable. The subscripts attaching to variables denote time lags. Equation (3.4) was estimated using annual data for 1953–78 for both Norway and Sweden. Separate estimates were reported for several different measures of the tax rate.[8]

The reported regression results show that the tax variable is singularly unsuccessful in explaining cash holdings in Norway. In most cases this variable's coefficient has the wrong sign (i.e. negative), but is in any case statistically insignificant. In the case of Sweden the tax variable performs rather better. At least its coefficient is of the right sign (i.e. positive) and in some cases it is statistically significant.

Klovland concludes that 'the tax variables did not directly contribute to explaining the demand for currency in Norway . . . In the case of Sweden, there is some expirical evidence that part of the total demand for currency is derived from the use of cash in fuelling hidden economic activity' (Klovland, 1984, p. 433).

In view of this Klovland does not attempt to use his regression equations to generate an estimate of the size of Norway's black economy. This is done, however, for Sweden and follows almost exactly the procedure suggested by Tanzi (1980).

Klovland assumes that in 1953 there was no black economy in Sweden. He, therefore, uses his estimated cash demand equation to predict what the demand for cash would have been had taxes in 1982 been at their 1953 levels. The difference between this and the level of cash that was actually in circulation in 1982 represents the amount of currency that is circulating in the black economy. If this is then multipled by the income velocity of circulation it produces an estimate of the scale of black-economy activity.

Klovland estimates the amount of 'black' currency in 1982 to be between 9369 million and 17 499 million Swedish krone (depending upon which tax rate is chosen). He suggests that the income velocity of circulation may be somewhere between 2 and 7. Combining these predictions yields a black economy anywhere between 3 per cent and 20 per cent of Sweden's GDP in 1982. Perhaps not surprisingly he concludes that 'the uncertainly involved in applying the currency approach is so great as to make it hazardous to rely on such estimates. Other methods are obviously necessary in order to obtain more than an obscure glimpse of the hidden economy' (ibid, p. 437).

Schneider and Lundager (1986) follow the approach suggested by Klovland and attempt to estimate a currency-demand equation. The basic form of this equation is as follows:

$$\log\left(\frac{C}{P}\right) = \alpha_0 + \alpha_1 \log Y_{-i} + \alpha_2 \log R_{-i} + \alpha_3 \log T_{-i}$$
$$+ \alpha_4 \log\left(\frac{C}{P}\right)_{-i} \qquad (3.5)$$

where C is the stock of currency held by the public; P is the price level; Y represents the volume of transactions in the official economy; R is an after-tax interest rate used to proxy the opportunity cost of holding currency, and T is a measure of the marginal tax rate. The i subscripts attaching to variables denote time-lags which can differ both between variables and across countries.

Equation (3.5) is a somewhat simplified version of Klovland's currency-demand equation (see equation (3.4)). In other words it has not been 'Hendrified' or, at least, not entirely. The variable Y above was in practice proxied by two measures – the *change* in private consumption as a share of GNP and the yearly *growth rate* of real per capita GNP. Like Klovland, Schneider and Lundager experimented with three different tax variables. The simplest was a marginal income tax rate for those on average taxable income.[9] A second measure added employers' contributions to social security schemes to this. The most comprehensive measure incorporated the indirect tax rate. The final modification to equation (3.5) was to add dummy variables for both Denmark and Norway to capture structural changes in banking practices and financial regulations respectively.

The currency demand equations were estimated separately for Denmark, Norway and Sweden using annual data for the period 1954 to 1982 by means of a Cochrane–Orcutt estimation procedure. All of the tax variables were incorporated with a *two year lag*. All the variables are statistically significant, except for the interest rate in the currency equations for both Denmark and Norway. In particular *all* the tax variables are significant and have their predicted positive coefficients. This result is in stark contrast with Klovland's previously reported findings for Norway (see earlier).[10] It is difficult to understand the reasons for this quite significant disagreement. It could be due to a change in the specification of the relationship, a slightly different period of observation (and somewhat different measurement of the variables). However, it should *not* be of much comfort to economists working in this area that such 'minor' changes should generate such diametrically opposed results. Differences so easily generated must cast some suspicion upon the reliability of the estimates.

Schneider and Lundager use their estimated currency demand equations to calculate the size of the black economies of Denmark, Norway and Sweden between 1954 and 1982. The procedure should now be familiar. First, they simulate what currency holdings would have been had taxes remained at their 1954 levels, which were the lowest levels observed between 1954 and 1982.[11] The difference between this simulated demand for currency and actual currency holdings is attributed to black-economy dealings. The size of the black economy is then calculated by multiplying this 'black-economy cash' by the income velocity of legal currency and sight deposits in the officially recorded economy. By this process Schneider and Lundager generate time-series estimates of the development of the black economies of the three countries, which are then expressed as a percentage of GNP.

These estimates suggest that Denmark's black economy had by 1982 grown to between 6.8 per cent and 7.1 per cent of its GNP depending upon which currency demand equation was used to predict 'illegal' cash holdings. Norway's black economy is estimated to be between 9.0 per cent and 9.6 per cent of GNP in 1982. Finally, Sweden's black economy is claimed to be between 11.6 per cent and 13.1 per cent of GNP in the same year.

The time-series results indicate that, in all of the countries, the black economy's 'share' of GNP rose steadily from 1954 until about 1977. Since then the share has stabilised. However, given the reservations already expressed about the method in general, it would be unwise to invest too much faith in these estimates. It would certainly be wrong to conclude, as Schneider and Lundager do, that because their results 'fit nicely into the results obtained by the same method for countries like Germany, Switzerland and the USA . . . [then] . . . these estimates seem to lie within a plausible range' (Schneider and Lundager, 1986, p. 22). First, their method is *not* exactly the same as that used by Tanzi for the USA. Second, *all* these studies could be using entirely incorrect methods. Third, Schneider and Lundager's results are *not* consistent with those of Klovland for Norway which is the most directly comparable study.

Estimates of the size of the black economy of West Germany using both the modified currency ratio and cash demand approaches has been made by Kirchgässner (1983). He rejects Gutmann's method on the grounds that the ratio of currency to demand deposits has fallen continuously in West Germany (from 0.87 in 1950 to 0.50 in 1975 and has stabilised at that level since then). Rather than argue that this might constitute evidence that West Germany has a falling black economy (relative to GDP), he argues that the currency ratio is a poor indicator of its extent and goes in search of other methods that might reveal its existence. This raises an interesting point of scientific methodology. It would have been interesting to see what Kirchgässner would have made of Gutmann's method had the West German currency ratio been rising rather than falling.

Kirchgässner's paper reports the results of applications of the methods proposed by Tanzi (1980) and Klovland (1980).[12] As with most of the Europeans, Kirchgässner has not been content to undertake a straightforward application of Tanzi's method. He, in fact, uses a number of different measures of the currency ratio:

(i) the ratio of currency to demand deposits;
(ii) the ratio of currency to the $M1$ measure of the money supply;
(iii) the ratio of currency to the $M2$ measure of the money supply.[13]

Fortunately, 'significantly better results were reached for $\frac{C}{M2}$ than for $\frac{C}{D}$ or $\frac{C}{M1}$, (Kirchgässner, 1983, p. 203). Tanzi, of course, measures the currency ratio as $\frac{C}{M2}$, so that provided that the West German and US measures of $M2$ are broadly the same then the results reported by Kirchgässner relate to roughly the same measure used by Tanzi.

Kirchgässner also altered Tanzi's specification of the estimating equation by regressing the ratio $\frac{C}{M2}$ upon real per capita GNP(Y), the interest rate on time deposits (R), the inflation rate (P^i) measured by the percentage change in the GNP deflator, the marginal tax rate of the average wage earner lagged two years (T) and the lagged value (one year) of the dependent variable. The main change from Tanzi, apart from the specification of the tax variable, is the inclusion of the inflation rate as an explanatory variable.

Kirchgässner's estimates of the currency ratio use annual data for the period 1952–80. He claims that 'all the coefficients have the expected sign, and all are significantly different from zero' (ibid, p. 203). Yet, it is not clear to me why the coefficient of the inflation variable should be positive. Why should an increase in the inflation rate encourage individuals to move away from bank deposits (including time deposits) and into currency? Admittedly with inflation the real return on bank deposits falls, thus possibly reducing their attractiveness, but both forms of asset holding would be less attractive in comparison with other forms of wealth holding e.g. equities, physical capital, etc. It is, *a priori*, difficult to see that out of all this switching, currency's popularity should rise relative to bank deposits.

Kirchgässner's preferred equation is:

$$\ln \frac{C}{M2} = -0.014 + 0.802 \ln \left(\frac{C}{M2} \right)_{-1} - 0.16 \ln Y \qquad (3.6)$$
$$\qquad\quad (0.33) \quad (10.74) \qquad\qquad\qquad (4.19)$$
$$+ 0.468 \ T_{-2} + 1.301 \ P^i - 1.78 \ R$$
$$\quad (3.29) \qquad\quad (3.46) \qquad (5.15)$$

Figures in parentheses are absolute values of the *t*-statistic and subscripts are time lags.

Equation (3.6) is then used, in the now familiar way, to estimate the amount of cash used in black economy transactions. Kirchgässner makes one minor modification to this process and that is to assume 'that there would be no shadow economy, if the marginal tax rate was 0.16, which is the value it had in 1957 and is its historical minimum from 1952 until to-day' (ibid, p. 203). Using this assumption Kirchgässner 'predicts' the amount of currency that would be in circulation in the absence of a black economy. The difference between this figure and the actual amount in circulation is attributed to black-economy transactions. The extent of these transactions is then estimated by multiplying the amount of 'illegal' cash by the income velocity of circulation in the 'official' economy. This produces time-series estimates for the black economy in West Germany. These indicate that until about 1975 the black economy was a fairly small and stable 'share' of GNP (about 3–4 per cent). However, after 1975 Kirchgässner's results indicate substantial growth in the black economy to around 10.3 per cent of GNP (about DM 155 billion) by 1980.[14]

Kirchgässner also estimates a currency demand equation for West Germany using the data described above. The estimated equation is:

$$\ln \frac{C}{P} = -1.262 + 0.787 \ \ln \left(\frac{C}{P} \right)_{-1} + 0.044 \ \ln Y + 0.468 \ T_{-1}$$
$$\qquad\quad (3.17) \quad (13.79) \qquad\qquad\qquad (0.81) \qquad\qquad (5.35)$$
$$- 0.079 \ P - 0.616R$$
$$\quad (0.35) \qquad (2.98)$$

Again, figures in parentheses are absolute values of *t*-statistics, and subscripts indicate time lags. All the variables are as defined above, except for *P* which is the GNP deflator and *C* is measured in per capita terms. Note that the tax variable enters now with only a one-year lag. This equation is used to predict what the real per capita demand for currency would have been if the tax rate had remained at its historically low level of 16 per cent. Again, an estimate of cash used for black-economy transactions is obtained and this is then converted into a volume of black-economy transactions by means of an assumed income velocity of circulation (see previous discussion).

The estimates produced are very similar to those generated by Tanzi's method and show that the black economy grew from about 2 per cent of GNP in 1960 to about 11 per cent by 1980. Again, much of the expansion of the black economy seems to have occurred since 1975. At least, that is what is suggested by these estimates.

Kirchgässner dates the 'take-off' of the black economy as the oil crisis of 1973–4, although he claims that there had been a mini-boom in black-economy activity in the late 1960s.

There must be one major additional doubt hanging over Kirch-gässner's estimates based as they are upon the use of currency statistics. The emergence of a substantial black economy found by Kirchgässner coincides with the emergence of West Germany as a major industrial nation and the Deutschmark as a strong inter-national currency. As a consequence of Germany's economic success there was an upsurge in demand for Deutschmarks. Much of this demand would have been from outside West Germany, e.g. by international traders, foreign-exchange speculators and so on. In addition, even Kirchgässner has to admit that 'there was a growing demand for DM in the GDR (East Germany) as a second currency . . . so that part of the growth of the shadow economy measured here is the growth of the shadow economy of the GDR' (Kirchgässner, 1983, pp. 206–7). It is difficult to know precisely how much currency is/was being held outside West Germany. In view of this, Kirchgässner's estimates must over-estimate (perhaps consider-ably) the extent to which currency was being held to fund black-economy activity.

Boyle (1984) has used a kind of monetary approach to produce time-series estimates of Ireland's black economy between 1970 and 1983. His estimates suggest that in Ireland the black economy was negligible (1 per cent or less of GDP) prior to 1977. However, since then it has grown steadily so that by 1983 the black economy amounted to some £1.5 billion or 11 per cent of GDP.

By comparison with some of those discussed earlier in the chapter, the approach used by Boyle was rather unsophisticated. He rejected the currency ratio on the grounds that 'the stock of current accounts is a poor indicator of the use of a current account' (Boyle, 1984, p. 35). He argued that a rise in the currency ratio, which has in fact occurred in Ireland during the 1970s and 1980s, is not necessarily an unambiguous indicator of the rise of a black economy. Instead, Boyle preferred to estimate a cash-demand equation.

However, unlike the rather complicated formulations suggested by Klovland, Boyle simply regresses the logarithm of nominal currency holdings upon the logarithm of nominal consumer expenditure for the period 1960 to 1969.[15] This relationship is then used to predict what the demand for currency would have been in each of the years 1970–83 had the relationship still been valid. Any 'excess' cash is assumed to be being used to fuel black-economy transactions. Black-economy income is then estimated by multiplying the excess cash by the observed income velocity of circulation in the official economy.

There are some obvious weaknesses with Boyle's approach. First – a common weakness of monetary approaches – is the identification of a bench-mark period when the black economy did not exist. Boyle asserts that in Ireland this was between 1960 and 1969. This may be true, but when combined with his method of calculating normal cash holdings, it indicates that in 1974 excess cash holdings and, by implication, the black economy were negative! Second, there are several variables which could be expected to influence currency holdings and these have been ignored by Boyle. For example, interest rates, real income and prices.[16]

Boyle also uses Feige's transaction method to estimate a relationship between total transactions and GDP. However, whilst he was able to show that this ratio had risen, and by implication that the black economy had grown, he did not use the method to produce predictions about the size of Ireland's black economy.

Martino (1981) has shown that in Italy between 1958 and 1978 the ratio of money supply (whether defined to include only sight deposits or both sight and time deposits) to GDP rose substantially. For example, the ratio $\frac{M1}{GDP}$ increased from 0.29 in 1958 to 0.51 in 1978. At the same time the ratio $\frac{M2}{GDP}$ increased from 0.58 to 0.97.

In other countries examined by Martino (USA, UK, France and West Germany) the ratio of narrow money to GDP had fallen during this time-period. It is also notable that Italy had a much higher $\frac{M1}{GDP}$ ratio than any of the other countries.[17] Further, whilst the ratio of narrow money to broad money had fallen in all the other countries, it had actually risen in Italy.

Now, of course, this is all rather suggestive. However, it is no more than data in search of a theory. No doubt one could find all kinds of explanations for the unusual behaviour of Italy's monetary statistics. For example, there has been considerably more political uncertainty in Italy than in the other countries listed. This might cause individuals to hold a much larger proportion of their assets in liquid form. Martino, himself, refers to the lack of options open to small savers in Italy. 'Time deposits' he argues 'might be the only option available to small savers because the stock market is negligible' (Martino, 1981, p. 93). One other factor is that in Italy, banks pay interest on demand deposits too, which is quite different from the practice adopted in most other countries.

Despite this, Martino was convinced that Italy's high and growing money/income ratio was largely to be explained by the emergence of a substantial black economy. However, it must be stated that there was no formal testing of this conjecture. Accordingly Martino's claim that 'it would be surprising if official income statistics were, say, 30 per cent below the mark' (ibid, p. 95) must be treated with even more circumspection than other black-economy estimates based upon monetary statistics.[18]

Admittedly, Martino does cite evidence to show that the Italian Central Institute of Statistics established a committee in 1979 which eventually revised upwards by almost 10 per cent its previous estimates of GNP. He also points to the suspiciously low and falling labour-force participation rate in Italy as support for his hypothesis of a thriving black economy. However, these are other issues and do not directly relate to the estimation of the size of the black economy using monetary statistics. (See the next chapter for a discussion of these other approaches.)

To conclude, Martino's study can only really be suggestive of a possibly large and growing black economy in Italy. Of all the studies so far encountered in this chapter it is the least sophisticated.

The results of a number of studies in other European countries have been reported by Schneider and Hofreither (1986–7). These include studies in Austria, Belgium, France, Spain and Switzerland. Unfortunately these estimates have been contained either in unpublished papers or papers published in either French or German. It has not been possible to scrutinise these papers carefully so as to determine precisely the methods adopted. In view of this I have refrained from reporting the estimates obtained in these studies.

3.3   CONCLUSIONS

In the last two chapters I have examined a number of studies which have attempted to estimate the size of the so-called black economy. The common characteristic of these studies is that they have all used information about the money supply (and, in particular, the amount of currency in circulation) to obtain their estimates. In all, fifteen studies covering ten countries within the OECD region have been considered. A summary of the results obtained in these studies is contained in Table 3.3.

These studies have already been discussed in detail, so this concluding section merely summarises some main points of that discussion and adds a few more observations about the approach in general.

It should be clear from the discussion of the last two chapters that the currency-demand approach is now a very popular way of estimating the amount of black-economy activity. There is one obvious reason why this should be so. This is that monetary statistics are readily available at low cost and, as far as is known, they are relatively accurate. In this respect monetary statistics have definite advantages over other methods of estimating the size of the black economy. Other methods, for example, require the collection of sample data on household incomes and expenditure (see next chapter). Such exercises are potentially expensive and have to be repeated at regular intervals. They are also potentially hazardous in such a sensitive area of human activity, e.g. would respondents answer truthfully, would they even participate, etc.? However, convenience and cheapness should not blind us to the problems involved in (i) using monetary statistics to measure the size of the black economy, and (ii) interpreting the results from studies based upon this approach. In what follows some of the major deficiencies of the currency demand and transactions approaches are re-emphasised.

The basic presumption of the currency-demand approach is that payments in the black economy are made in cash, so that an increase in the amount of currency circulating in the economy (relative to the volume of bank deposits) is *prima facie* evidence of a growing black

Table 3.3 Estimates of the black economy using monetary approaches (as % of GDP/GNP)

Country	Author	1970	1975	1976	1978	1979	1980	1981	1982	1983
USA	Gutmann (1977)			10						
	Feige (1979)			13–22	25–33					
	Tanzi (1980)			8.1–11.7						
	Tanzi (1983)	2.2–4.6	3.8–5	3.6–5.5			4.5–6.1			
	Porter and Bayer (1984)	4.6–10.2	5–30.2				6.1–41.6			
Canada	Mirus and Smith (1981)			5–28						
Australia	Tucker (1982)					10.6 (1978–9)				
	Norman (1982)								13.4 (1981–2)	
UK	O'Higgins (1981)				2.9–5.4					
	Matthews (1982)					5.8–7.1				
Sweden	Klovland (1984)								3–19.7	
	Schneider and Lundager (1986)	6.8–7.8	10.2–11.3				11.2–12.4		11.6–13.1	
Norway	Schneider and Lundager (1986)	6.2–6.9	7.8–8.2				9.9–10.4		9–9.6	
Denmark	Schneider and Lundager (1986)	5.9	6.4–6.6				6.8–7.2		6.8– 7.1	
West Germany	Kirchgässner (1983)	2.7–3.1	5.5–6				10.3–11.2			
Ireland	Boyle (1984)	1	1				8			11
Italy	Martino (1981)						30?			

economy. Both this presumption and the deduction following from it have an intuitive appeal, but there are reasons for questioning whether they are valid. For example, evidence suggests that cash payments are no more frequent in the black economy than they are in the official economy, so that a substantial volume of black-economy transactions are paid for by cheque. Second, there is a potential ambiguity in the interpretation of a rising currency ratio. It could be due to an increase in currency, but more likely it is due to a fall in demand deposits. Further, there is much evidence to suggest that in many countries the real value of currency in circulation is now less than it was twenty or more years ago.

Clearly changes in the currency ratio are caused by many influences. An objection to the simplistic approach of Gutmann is that it ascribes all the change in the currency ratio to the black economy. Even the more sophisticated approaches of Tanzi and others include only tax rates to proxy the effects of black-economy activity upon the demand for currency. In addition, it is not clear how financial innovation, which clearly does affect the demand for currency, has been taken into account.

Another difficulty with the currency-demand approach is the selection of a base year in which it is assumed that either the black economy did not exist or its size was known with a fair degree of certainty. This problem is plainly exacerbated by the observation that the results obtained are quite sensitive to the particular choice of base period (see Frey and Pommerehne, 1984, p. 9). No really satisfactory solution to this problem seems to have been found. Presumably if tax rates were zero, then there would be no need to engage in tax evasion and black-economy activity, but what is the trigger point at which people become willing to act illegally? Is it with a 5 per cent tax rate or 10 per cent or some even higher level of taxation? Unfortunately, theory does not offer any guidance on this particular question (see Chapter 5).

There are further difficulties with the currency-demand approach when it is applied to countries whose currencies are often held internationally. For example, both the US dollar and the Deutschmark are used for international trade and as second (dual) currencies in many countries. Accordingly, part of any increase in currency in circulation has nothing to do with the existence of a black economy. To ignore this fact leads obviously to an overstatement of the extent of black-economy activity. Unfortunately, the degree of overstatement cannot be determined, because it is simply not known how much of the currency is circulating *outside* the country.

The evidence in favour of the currency-demand approach rests upon a finding that taxes (normally income taxes) have a significant effect upon the demand for currency. However, tests performed on Tanzi's data (Tanzi, 1983) by Porter and Bayer (1984), suggest that the tax variable is only significant for years up to 1945. When Tanzi's currency-demand equation is re-estimated for the period 1946–80 the tax variable either proves to be statistically insignificant or has the wrong sign.[19] Indeed Porter and Bayer claim that the demand for currency in the USA can be perfectly well explained by standard empirical demand equations without the need to add tax variables to proxy black-economy activity.

Finally, the currency-demand approach assumes:

(i) equal income velocities of circulation in both the black economy and the official economy;

(ii) that existing GDP/GNP measures do not include any black economy activity.

Feige (1979) has argued that the first assumption is questionable and certainly it would be preferable to have a method of estimation which avoided having to make strong assumptions like that. On the second assumption, it is becoming clear that the tax authorities are increasingly including estimates of tax-evaded income in their statistics (see Chapter 4). If this is so, then GDP/GNP calculations based upon revenue statistics *will* include some, if not all, black-economy income.

On balance then the currency-demand approach does not look to be a very convincing method of estimation and one should be wary of placing too much reliance upon the results obtained by using it.

Feige's transaction method, whilst also relying upon monetary statistics, is an altogether different approach. It has some advantages over the currency-demand approach, but also some glaring weaknesses. Also, when it has been applied, e.g. in the USA and UK, it has produced some quite breathtaking, not to say unbelievable, results (see, for example, Porter and Bayer, 1984).

The advantages of the approach are:

(i) it does *not* assume that currency is the sole medium of exchange in the black economy;

(ii) it makes no assumptions about the relative income velocities of circulation of money in the official and black economies.

From what has been said earlier these are quite important advantages over the currency demand approach.

Against this must be set the disadvantages of the transactions method. The first of these is that there is absolutely no underlying theory of the relationship between the total volume of transactions and the level of GNP/GDP. The consequence of this is that any interpretation of a change in this relationship must be highly contentious. This would be bad enough, were it not for the fact that generally there are no readily available data on the volume of transactions in any case! This leads Feige and others to estimate the volume of transactions by use of Fisher's Identity. However, this in turn requires fairly bold assumptions about the turnover of currency, because once again data simply do not exist. As various investigators have shown, estimates of the size of the black economy are sensitive to different assumptions about currency turnover. So, the whole method is highly questionable. Not only is there no theory, but often there are no data.

Finally, the transactions approach shares with the currency-demand approach the problem of finding a base year in which the amount of black-economy activity was either negligible or known. On balance the transactions approach cannot be considered to offer any more reliable information about the extent of the black economy. Indeed, the estimates it produces suggest quite implausible growth rates of such activity.

The overwhelming conclusion must be that both the currency demand and transactions approaches suffer from serious defects. Indeed, these problems are so severe that one would be very unwise to place too much reliance upon estimates of the scale of the black economy derived by using these approaches.

4 Non-Monetary Approaches to Measuring the Black Economy

The last two chapters have examined various monetary approaches to measuring the size of the black economy, and have also surveyed some of the results of research using these approaches. Monetary approaches have been by far the most popular methods used in assessing the extent of black-economy activity. The principal reasons for this are (i) that monetary statistics are readily available and, (ii) a strong presumption in the literature that cash is the *modus operandi* of the black economy. However, other direct and indirect methods of assessment have been developed and it is the purpose of this chapter to review some of these alternative techniques. This chapter will concentrate on the indirect methods. (Direct methods, using tax audits, were briefly examined in Chapter 1).

One possible indicator of involvement in the black economy is evidence that a household's (or individual's) expenditure is (considerably) larger than its declared income – that is, if the discrepancy cannot be otherwise explained. Similarly, discrepancies between *national* income statistics, based upon income-tax data, and *national* expenditure statistics, drawn from household and industrial surveys, *may* be another potential source of information. These two methods are described as the income/expenditure approaches, and are examined in section 4.1.

A second discrepancy, which could be used to measure the extent of black-economy activity, is that between the official labour force and the actual labour force. This kind of approach, normally using labour-force-participation surveys, has been particularly popular amongst Italian economists. A low (compared with other countries) and/or falling participation rate may constitute evidence of a large or growing black economy. This approach is analysed in more detail in section 4.2.

Section 4.3 examines perhaps the most controversial method that has so far been devised to measure the size of the black economy. This is the so-called 'soft-modelling' approach, which has been pioneered by Frey and Weck (1983). This approach is based upon aggregating information upon the *presumed* determinants of involvement in the black economy into an index of irregular activity. However, this approach can *not* measure the absolute size of the black economy, unless it is possible to fix both a scale and a base point using one of the other methods. It has primarily been used to determine a rank ordering of countries' black economies.

Finally, section 4.4. draws some perhaps rather tentative conclusions about the quality of the various non-monetary approaches to measurement.

4.1 DIFFERENCES BETWEEN INCOME AND EXPENDITURE

(a) At the household level

It is often the case that a household's expenditure in a time-period exceeds its (declared) income during that same period. This *may* be because the household's actual income is somewhat higher than it has been prepared to reveal. In other words, members of the household have been involved in black-economy activity, the income from which has not been declared to the authorities.

However, there may be other much less sinister reasons for the existence of a discrepancy between income and expenditure. For example, a household may be experiencing a temporary fall in income below its 'normal' level caused, for example, by unemployment or illness. In that case, it is quite reasonable to expect current expenditure to exceed current income, the difference being funded by drawing upon past savings or borrowing from relatives, friends and from financial institutions.

In other cases households may consist of elderly, retired people who are deliberately financing an expenditure level which is above their current income by using up previous accumulations of wealth. Alternatively, a young household may spend more than its current income when, for example, it purchases consumer durable goods on credit. The 'excess' expenditure is not in these cases a sign that members of the household are acting illegally. It is simply that they are basing their expenditure on their expected lifetime income and not their current income.

Clearly then the mere fact that an individual's or household's expenditure exceeds its current income is insufficient reason to suggest the presence of undisclosed income. In order to use the discrepancy approach one has to find some means of eliminating all those households and/or individuals whose expenditure is quite legitimately in excess of their income.

The discrepancy approach was suggested by Dilnot and Morris (1981) and applied by them to a sample of households in the UK. The data used by Dilnot and Morris were drawn from the 1977 Family Expenditure Survey (FES), which records both incomes and expenditures for some 7200 households. In the FES each household is asked to record its income and expenditure during a particular time-period, usually two weeks.

Participation in the survey is entirely voluntary, which points to one immediate problem with using FES data on such a sensitive topic as black-economy activity. Would households which are engaged in such activity be prepared to participate in the survey? Non-participation in the survey would appear to be the safer option if one was at all worried about the possibility of being caught. It is unlikely, but of course not impossible, that such risk-averse individuals will be reassured by investigators' claims that responses will be treated in strictest confidence.

In fact, the response rate for the FES is about 70 per cent. If the missing 30 per cent are those who are most heavily involved in the black economy, then results using this sample will considerably underestimate the true extent of black-economy activity. There is, for example, some evidence (Kemsley, 1975) to indicate that the self-employed – a group with greater opportunities to engage in tax evasion – are underrepresented in the FES.

Indeed, to be at all useful the approach suggested by Dilnot and Morris requires tax evaders to participate in the sample to the same degree as non-evaders. Further, when they do respond, tax evaders must fail to declare their 'true' income to the investigators, i.e. they must not declare their black-economy earnings. This is because the *raison d'être* for the approach is the existence of a discrepancy between declared expenditure and declared income, which can only be explained by the existence of black-economy earnings. If, for example, evaders did believe that their responses were treated confidentially they might declare *all* their income, both legitimate and 'black'. If that were the case, discrepancies between income and expenditure would tend to disappear. On the other hand 'suspicious' evaders, who participated in the survey, might deliberately under-record their expenditure, thus keeping it in line with their under-recorded income.

To be successful the technique also requires the tax evaders to spend their moonlighting income. If they were to save it, e.g. by putting it into a Swiss or even British bank account, then their expenditure would not necessarily be in excess of their income and they would not show up in the FES as a potential black-economy household.

However, Dilnot and Morris argue that the discrepancy approach at the household level could be quite successful in identifying small-scale evasion activity. Their argument is that 'those with small amounts of moonlighting income . . . may not realise there is any-thing illegal . . . in their failure to seek out a tax inspector to whom to report their earnings' (Dilnot and Morris, 1981, p. 68). This seems to require belief in a remarkable degree of schizophrenia on the part of the evaders. First, they do not believe there is anything wrong with failing to declare all their earnings to the tax authority, but second, they are cautious enough not to reveal all their earnings to the FES survey. Such behaviour lacks credibility.

It seems unlikely then that large-scale evaders will participate and most small-scale evaders may 'doctor' their returns so as to minimise any obvious income–expenditure differences. It would appear that only the forgetful, the stupid and the brave could be caught by such a technique.

With these reservations in mind we now examine the procedure adopted by Dilnot and Morris. First, for each household in the sample, a comparison was made between its net income and its expenditure. This was done after having corrected for some of the more obvious deficiencies of the FES data.[1] Then, various house-holds were selected for more detailed analysis. These were house-holds whose expenditure was in excess of their declared income. At first only households whose expenditure exceeded income by at least 50 per cent were analysed, but this criterion was gradually relaxed until all households spending more than 20 per cent of their recorded income were included.[2]

Dilnot and Morris tried to remove from the above subsamples households whose expenditure exceeded declared income for reasons other than black-economy income. For example, those households which had made 'unusual' purchases,[3] those whose income was abnormally low perhaps because of sickness or unemployment and those living off capital were all excluded. Unless, that is, 'the trap might be too strong' in which case the households concerned were included in the lower-bound sample, but not the upper bound.[4]

There is an obvious danger in excluding such households. For example, periods of unemployment leading to lower-than-normal levels of income, might provide a strong incentive, not to say opportunity, to take up black-economy work. In that case part, at least, of such households' excess expenditure may be due to 'off the books' work. To exclude all such households would be to throw out the baby with the bath water. Similar arguments can be made, for example, about households whose primary source of income is a pension. The opportunities for black-economy work by such households may be substantial.

Dilnot and Morris excluded all such households in obtaining an upper-bound estimate of the amount of black-economy activity, but included them in obtaining a lower estimate. On this basis, they found that 14.8 per cent of the FES sample had expenditures which were at least 20 per cent (or £3, whichever is the greater) above their declared income level and 9.6 per cent had expenditures more than 50 per cent above their declared income. The average discrepancy between expenditure and income was £30 per week in the upper-bound sample and £31 per week in the lower-bound sample.[5]

These discrepancies were then 'grossed up' for the whole population and this produced estimates for tax-evaded, i.e. black-economy, income of between £3.2 billion and £4.2 billion per year or between 2.3 per cent and 3.0 per cent of GNP in 1977. It is noticeable that these estimates of the extent of the UK's black economy are considerably less than that obtained using the currency-demand approach – see Chapter 3. However, not too much should be read into such a comparison. As was argued in the earlier chapters, there are good grounds for doubting the accuracy of estimates based upon the monetary approach. Doubts have also been raised about the validity of Dilnot and Morris's estimates. It would be entirely inappropriate to regard one approach as generating a lower bound and the other an upper bound. Indeed they may even be measuring different things (see below).

Again, for what it is worth, Dilnot and Morris's analysis produces some evidence on the characteristics of those households thought to be most heavily involved in the black economy. This shows that some 22 per cent of the lower-bound sample classified themselves as self-employed. This should be compared with the number of self-employed households in the FES as a whole, which is approximately 7 per cent. Of course care should be exercised in interpreting this result, both in terms of validating Dilnot and Morris's analysis and as a finding in its own right.

There is a strong presumption that people who are self-employed are active in the black economy. They have, certainly, the best opportunities for concealing income from the tax authorities and there is some evidence from tax audits carried out in the USA which would support this view (US Internal Revenue Service, 1979).

Given this belief there is a temptation to argue that Dilnot and Morris's results are 'feasible'. For example, they themselves in ex-amining the lower-bound sample argue that 'the sample does in fact consist mainly of households where the occupation of the head would indicate, *a priori*, that black-economy activity is feasible' (Dilnot and Morris, 1981, p. 67). However, it is probably the case that the self-employed are underrepresented in the sample and that tax-evaders, whether self-employed or not, are likely to be grossly underrepresented (see the previous arguments on this). As a conse-quence, one cannot necessarily conclude that the self-employed are between two and three times as likely as full-time employees to be involved in the black economy (ibid, p. 69, Table 4).

Likewise, the mere fact that the characteristics of Dilnot and Morris's sample of supposed black-economy workers coincide with our beliefs about who is most likely to be working in the black economy, does not lend credence to their technique. The technique is only as strong as the reasoning behind it and the data which have gone into estimation. Both have been found wanting.

Certainly the self-employed do seem to have the best opportunities for hiding part of their income and it requires belief in a form of superhuman virtue not to think that some of them would abuse their position. O'Higgins (1980), for example, quotes the General Sec-retary of the (UK) Inland Revenue Staff Association as saying 'The low incomes to which the self-employed admit defy belief. Only 70 000 of them declare the average wage of £60 or more' (A. Christopher, 1976, pp. 210–11).

Despite their apparently low income, the self-employed appear to have a much higher standard of living than employee households when this is measured by ownership of consumer durables such as cars, washing machines and central heating (O'Higgins, 1980, p. 25). Further, evidence from the Family Expenditure Survey indicates that self-employed households spend a much larger proportion of their income than employee households (but are they merely trying to keep up with the proverbial Jones's?). O'Higgins produces some 'back of the envelope' calculations to suggest that 'about 18 per cent of self-employment income is not declared in the FES (and hence presumably not declared to the Inland Revenue)' (O'Higgins, 1980, p. 28). He calculates that this amounts to about £2.1 billion or 2 per cent of national income in 1977.

This estimate is obtained in a rather peculiar way. O'Higgins calculates from FES data, that the self-employed spent on average about 84 per cent their declared income over the period 1971–7. This compares with an expenditure–income ratio for clerical and manual households of about 77 per cent and for administrative and professional households of about 71 per cent. O'Higgins concludes '(g)iven their relative income levels a figure of about 75 per cent might have been expected for self-employed households, all other things being equal' (ibid, p. 26). From this, he concludes that the degree of understatement of income is about 12 per cent (84/75 = 1.12). Because earnings from self-employment constitute about two-thirds of household income for the self-employed, he argues that understatement of self-employment income might be as high as 18 per cent (this assumes that other sources of income are fully declared).

However, the apparent understatement of income by self-employed households may really only reflect the way that their income statistics are recorded in the FES. As we have said earlier, the FES measures self-employment income by asking what their income has been in the most recent twelve-month period. If incomes are rising, even if only because of inflation, the FES measure will underestimate current self-employment income.

O'Higgins attempted to adjust for this by expressing expenditure in one year as a proportion of income in the *following* year. When this was done 'the expenditure ratios for the self-employed differ little, on average, from similar ratios for all employed households' (ibid, p. 33). This is a rather rough-and-ready adjustment, but the difference it generates is sufficiently worrying to cause one to be cautious about interpreting raw FES data as implying too much about the precise extent of tax evasion and the size of the black economy.

A perhaps less significant worry has been voiced by Carter (1984). He argues that the average propensity to consume, which is calculated by O'Higgins, will be sensitive to economic conditions. The income of the self-employed is likely to be more variable than that of employee households, so that if the survey was undertaken at a time when self-employed households were doing relatively badly their expenditure–income ratio will be higher than it normally is. He suggests that one should use estimates of permanent income in order

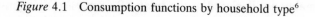

Figure 4.1   Consumption functions by household type[6]

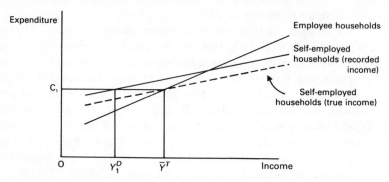

to calculate the average propensity to consume. However, as O'Higgins's estimate of the expenditure–income ratio is the average of seven years' observations, this criticism loses some of its force. Carter reports expenditure–income ratios for employee and self-employed households in Australia (in 1974–5 and 1975–6) which show remarkably little difference between the two types of households, even when no allowance is made for any possible difference between permanent and actual income.

Smith, Pissarides and Weber (1986) have also used the FES in a somewhat different way to obtain an estimate of the extent of income concealment by the self-employed. They claim that this may be of the order of 10–20 per cent of self-employment income.

The basis of their approach is the common claim that the self-employed are more likely to underdeclare their income than are employees. If this is true, then one would expect that self-employed households with declared incomes and other characteristics similar to those of employee households would have higher standards of living, i.e. they would spend more on housing, food, holidays, etc.

The way that this generates an estimate of concealed income can be most easily explained as follows. If we were to plot expenditure against income for employee households and self-employed household, Smith et al argue that we would obtain Figure 4.1.

The consumption function for self-employed households has a smaller slope, i.e. indicating a lower marginal propensity to consume, because such households probably have rather more variable incomes than do employee households. Therefore, they will not spend all their increased income in a good period and will supplement their reduced income in a bad one. In other words, the relationship between changes in income and changes in consumption will be rather weaker for these households than for employee households, which have a more stable income stream.

As it is thought that self-employed households conceal part of their income and employee households do not, there will be two consumption functions for self-employed households. One shows the relationship between spending and recorded income, the other shows the relationship between spending and true income. The latter will lie to the right of the former, simply because the self-employed household's true income exceeds its declared income. Clearly only the relationship between declared income and consumer spending can actually be estimated.

The next crucial stage in the argument is that the consumption expenditures of self-employed households at their *true average income* ($\bar{Y}^T$ in Figure 4.1) will be the same as employee households with the same characteristics at that same income level. This is the consumption level C_1. It is then a simple matter to calculate, from the estimated regression of consumption expenditure against recorded income-level for self-employment households, the average declared income (Y_1^D) corresponding to C_1.

The difference $\bar{Y}^T - Y_1^D$ gives an estimate of the extent of concealed income by self-employed households earning average self-employed incomes.

Smith *et al.* estimated consumption functions of the form:[7]

$$C = aZ + b_1X + (b_2 + b_3X)\,Y \tag{4.1}$$

where C is consumption expenditure

Z is a vector of household characteristics, e.g. age, composition of household, housing tenure and so on

Y is income, and

X is a dummy variable, which takes the value 1 if the household is of the self-employed type and 0 if it is an employee household.

The extent of income concealment can be obtained from equation (4.1) as follows. If the consumption level of self-employed households (C_1) at their *true* average income level ($\bar{Y}^T$) is the same as the consumption level of employee households with the same income level (and household characteristics) then from (4.1):

$$C_1 = a\bar{Z} + b_2\bar{Y}^T \tag{4.2}$$

where $\bar{Z}$ is the vector of household characteristics for self-employed households with average income.

However, equation (4.1) shows that the relationship between consumer spending and measured income for such households is:

$$C_1 = a\bar{Z} + b_1 + (b_2 + b_3)Y_1^D \tag{4.3}$$

where Y_1^D is the declared income of those self-employed households with average self-employment income.

From equations (4.2) and (4.3) it is clear that:

$$\bar{Y}^T - Y_1^D = \frac{b_1 + b_3 Y_1^D}{b_2} \tag{4.4}$$[8]

The extent of income concealment can be found from (4.4). All that is required are estimates of the parameters, b_1, b_2 and b_3 in equation (4.1) and Y_1^D, the declared income of those on average self-employment income.

Smith *et al.* estimated equation (4.1) for two kinds of occupational groupings:

 (i) white-collar workers, i.e. managerial, professional and clerical occupations;
 (ii) blue-collar workers, i.e. manual workers;

and for three principal categories of expenditure:

  (i) food, drink and tobacco;
 (ii) pre-commitments, i.e. rent, mortgage payments and rates;
(iii) other non-durables, e.g. fuel, travel, services, etc.

Their estimates of both excess consumption and income concealment for these different groupings are given in Table 4.1.

The results shown in Table 4.1 indicate that only in some areas do self-employed households spend significantly more than employee households with the same income and household characteristics. This is most noticeable for food, drink and tobacco. This is also confirmed by examining estimates of equation (4.1). Smith *et al.* estimate equation (4.1) for eight separate categories (occupational grouping by commodity grouping). In only three of these categories is the coefficient of the dummy variable representing self-employment status statistically significant.[10,11] Estimates of the modified version of

Table 4.1   Smith *et al.*'s estimates of concealed income by self-employed households[9]

	'Excess' consumption at average income %	*Concealed income* %
White-collar households		
food, drink and tobacco	11.1	36
food alone	9.6	34
pre-commitments	1.8	5
other non-durables	–3	–6
Blue-collar households		
food, drink and tobacco	8.9	30
pre-commitments	8.5	34
other non-durables	4.0	8

equation (4.1), in which b_3 is set equal to zero, perform hardly any better. Here four of the eight coefficients on the dummy variable are significant.[12]

The problem is that this generates estimates of concealed income which range from −6 per cent to +36 per cent, which seems distinctly unhelpful. After adjusting for the somewhat dated information on self-employment income in the FES, Smith *et al.* conclude that concealment of self-employment income could be in the range 10–20 per cent.

There seem to be several possible drawbacks to the analysis offered by Smith, Pissarides and Weber. One is that it rests on the assumption that employee households do not have any undeclared income. Without this it would be impossible to construct the employee-household-consumption function and so estimate concealed income.

Now who is to say that employee households do not engage in any moonlighting, i.e. have second jobs, the income from which is not declared to the tax authorities? (Evidence from various labour-market surveys suggests that second-job-holding can be quite common and that it is a major aspect of black-economy activity. (See the following subsection.)

Another objection to the procedure adopted by Smith *et al.* is that the estimates of the consumption function are not particularly impressive. Many coefficients, apart from those for the income variable, are statistically insignificant and some are quite sensitive to the specification of the consumption function. In addition, the regressions seem to fit the data quite poorly (R^2 is invariably less than 0.5). Further, estimates of the mpc for self-employed households show that it is actually larger than for employee households, which is quite the reverse of what the 'theory' suggests.

In conclusion, the work of Smith, Pissarides and Weber is potentially interesting, but it suffers from too many weaknesses for it to be usable as a reliable indicator of the extent of concealed income.

This conclusion really applies also to the work of Dilnot and Morris. The basic problem facing both studies is the dependability of the data source. Intuition would suggest that participants in a voluntary survey are unlikely to reveal incriminating evidence about their economic activities. If this reasoning is correct, research using the FES is unlikely to generate accurate estimates of the extent of black-economy activity.

(b)   At the national level

If the idea of measuring the size of the black economy by comparing household incomes and expenditures looks unpromising, how about comparing estimates of *national* income and expenditure? This approach has been used by Macafee (1980), who has claimed that the UK's black economy may have been about 3–3½ per cent of GDP in the late 1970s.

However, introductory economics texts tell us that national income and expenditure should be identical. Certainly they tell us that whilst there are three methods (or is it two or only one?) of calculating GDP (or GNP) they should all produce exactly the same answer. That is, it should not matter whether we calculate GDP by the expenditure method, the income method or the output method. Expenditure and output are, in any case, only the opposite sides of a transaction,[13] i.e. the value of the output produced (sold) is exactly matched by the amount expended in buying it. This is so, provided we remember to count things such as additions to stocks of finished goods as an expenditure on the part of the firm that produced them in the first place. Likewise, provided we treat profits as a residual between the value of output produced (sold) and the payments to all other factors of production, i.e. labour and land, then by definition the sum of factor incomes will exactly match the value of output.[14] By the logic of national accounting procedures all three methods should generate exactly the same answers for the size of GDP.

However, in practice the estimates of GDP obtained by the various methods often disagree. One reason why this happens is that all three methods derive their estimate from sample surveys, i.e. partial information about expenditure, income and output. This does not immediately seem relevant to our interest in measuring the scale of black-economy activity. Indeed, it is not so much sampling errors that are important here, but the possibility that one source of information about GDP is more reliable than an other. That is, it is systematic errors in one method of calculating GDP that could possibly reveal something about the size of the black economy. How can this be?

In the UK the estimates of the expenditure measure of GDP are based upon a range of industrial and household surveys (including the FES) and central and local government accounts. However, the main source of information for the income measure, is data compiled by the Inland Revenue during the process of tax collection.

Macafee contends that the expenditure measure is unbiased since there is little reason for respondents to the Family Expenditure Survey or other inquiries to disguise or exaggerate expenditure, except in the case of sensitive items of household expenditure such as alcoholic drink (Macafee, 1980, p. 81).[15] However, he argues, the income measure probably understates the true level of incomes earned because black-economy incomes are not declared to the Inland Revenue.

If the main difference between the income and expenditure estimates of GDP comes from the underreporting of factor incomes then a comparison of the two measures should show something of the extent of income concealment and the size of the black economy.[16]

The difference between the income and expenditure measures of GDP is referred to as the initial residual difference (IRD). Macafee found that between 1960 and 1978 the IRD had been consistently positive (see Figure 4.2) and that expressed as a percentage of the expenditure measure it had grown appreciably in the early 1970s. By 1974 the IRD was estimated to be about 4 per cent of GDP (expenditure measure). However after that it began to fall.

Since Macafee's work was published the IRD has continued to fall and by 1984 had in fact become negative, i.e. the income measure of GDP actually exceeded the expenditure measure (see Figure 4.3, which is taken from Smith, 1986).

The mere fact that the IRD can be negative must cast some doubt on the value of this measure as a means of assessing the extent of

Figure 4.2   The initial residual difference, 1960–78, UK

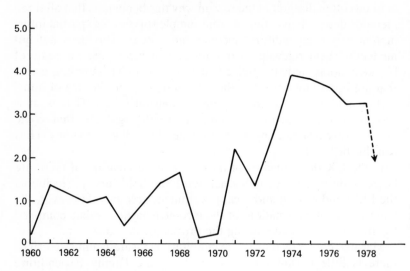

Source: Macafee (1980)

concealed income and the size of the black economy. The fact that it is negative in 1984 suggests that timing and sampling errors may be substantial and could perhaps just as easily have been substantially positive in earlier years.

It is inconceivable that there has been a dramatic decline in the scale of black-economy activity since 1976 (although see the later discussion of Matthews's attempt to relate the size of the IRD to tax rates, where Matthews claims that the fall in IRD after 1976 is closely related to a fall in the average tax-rate). Admittedly there have been changes in tax rates and social security contributions during the period, just as there have been changes in unemployment. (However, prior to 1988 the tax changes (cuts) that have occurred seem to be fairly marginal, and certainly insufficient to cause a flood of resources out of the black economy and back into the official economy. Against that there has been a massive increase in recorded unemployment which one would expect to provide both the incentive and the opportunity to work in the black economy.)

Smith (1986) argues that the change in the size of the IRD during the 1970s may have been caused by two quite different factors. First, the growth in alternative forms of remuneration such as payments-in-kind, which showed up in the expenditure statistics but not the

Figure 4.3   The initial residual difference, 1968–1984, UK

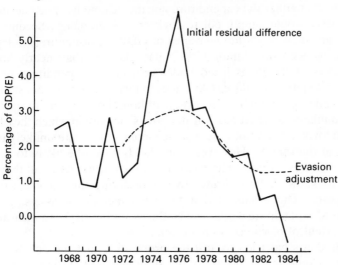

Source: Smith (1986)

income statistics. Second, changes in the rate of inflation which accentuate (diminish) the importance of timing discrepancies when the rate of inflation is rising (falling).

It is hard to accept the first of these explanations and Smith's argument on this point is singularly unconvincing. Besides, why should these forms of payment suddenly become much less important after 1976? The second explanation has more appeal. At a time when prices are rising rapidly (inflation in the mid-1970s reached 25 per cent per year) it may be quite important for the size of the IRD that the two sets of payments are recorded in the same time-period. The fall in inflation since then would explain the fall in the IRD, except that inflation did reach nearly 20 per cent in 1980 and the IRD showed no signs of a return to its 1974–5 levels.

Is the initial residual difference (IRD) a good measure of the size of the black economy? The answer to that question must be 'probably not'. Even if we ignore timing discrepancies and sampling errors there are two more reasons why. First, it ignores certain (potentially important) areas of black-economy activity. It concentrates solely on tax evasion, i.e. the failure to declare all one's earnings to the tax authorities. For example, the IRD does not pick up concealed expenditures on illegal goods and the incomes generated by selling them. As neither the expenditure nor the income has been declared, the IRD would simply fail to register a discrepancy. Second, the income and expenditure measures of GDP are not entirely independent assessments. Smith (1986) has claimed that nearly three-quarters of the items listed under consumers' expenditure by the Central Statistical Office (CSO) are, in fact, estimated from statistics of retail sales and not from surveys of household expenditure. Firms are unlikely to report any 'off-the-books' activity in which they have been involved and full-time black-economy 'firms' are unlikely to be part of the sample. However, households would be likely to report expenditures on items purchased from such firms. After all they are not to know that the firms are not declaring this income for tax purposes. The upshot is that the CSO method of assessing consumers' expenditure works against the use of the IRD as a measure of the extent of black-economy income.[17]

Matthews has tried to 'test the proposition that the "black economy" is reflected in the size of this discrepancy (IRD)' by regressing 'the IRD obtained from O'Higgins (1982) on the average tax rate for a married male manual worker with two children' (Matthews, 1984, p. 445) over the period from 1969 to 1980.

Various (six) forms of the regression equation are estimated, i.e. simple linear, semi-logarithmic and logarithmic functional forms using both the absolute size of the IRD and IRD expressed as a percentage of GDP (expenditure measure). To quote Matthews, '(a)ll six regressions point to a statistically significant relationship between the initial residual difference and the tax rate' (ibid, p. 446).

The significance of this result (economic rather than statistical) is rather more debatable. It requires first of all that the IRD is a good measure of the extent of black-economy activity. Leaving aside our reservations on this point, it should be stressed that the estimates of the black economy generated by the IRD are totally different from estimates obtained by Matthews himself using other means – see Chapter 3. At the very least the result requires that movements in the IRD reflect changes in the size of the black economy. Once again the data used by Matthews here are totally at variance with results he has published elsewhere (Matthews and Rastogi, 1985).[18] In addition the analysis rests on the assumption that an increase in the tax rate provides an incentive to switch resources into the black economy. As we shall see in Chapter 5 this is not an unambiguous prediction. It seems to come about in Matthews's analysis because he assumes a totally inelastic supply of labour in the economy. In that case, any increase in the tax rate simply diverts labour supply from the regular sector to the black economy.

In conclusion Matthews's result lends neither credence to the IRD as a measure of the black economy, nor support to a view that high tax rates lead to a large amount of irregular/informal economic activity.

The use of the national income/expenditure discrepancy as a means of calculating the size of the black economy has largely been confined to the UK, although Blades (1982) reports results for Sweden. These show 'undeclared legal production' amounting to about 3–4 per cent of GDP between 1970 and 1979.[19] The approach has been rather less common in other countries (possibly because in these countries the income and expenditure measures of GDP are not obtained from independent sources). However, something very like it has been used in the USA, West Germany and Denmark. This is the discrepancy between national accounts estimates of income and income reported to tax authorities.[20]

For example, Park (1979) compares estimates of income obtained from national accounts and tax returns for the USA and concludes, after some adjustment, that the discrepancy may show underrecording of income for tax purposes of about 4 per cent of GNP in 1977. This has declined from 5.5 per cent in 1968 and 9.4 per cent in 1948.

Likewise Petersen (1984) reports estimates of the discrepancy between income reported to the fiscal administration and national income accounts estimates of income for West Germany. This discrepancy, which amounted to 16 per cent of national income in 1961, had fallen to 4.8 per cent of national income by 1974. Frey and Pommerehne (1982) report similar studies for Denmark, Belgium and France.

Even where the method has been applied, e.g. in the UK, it is quite clear that there are other reasons for the discrepancy between income and expenditure measures of GDP, so that the measure may be a relatively poor indicator of the extent of black-economy activity – besides which the method really only works if the two estimates are obtained largely independently. As has been shown this is far from being the case for the UK.

4.2   LABOUR-MARKET STUDIES

It should be stressed that this section is concerned with the way that analysis of the labour market provides an indication of the extent of 'irregular' economic activity. Our interest is purely empirical and focused solely on the question 'How big is the black economy?'. We will *not*, therefore, be concerned with either theoretical or empirical analysis of decisions (i) to work in the black economy, or (ii) to engage in income tax evasion. These are the subjects of several of the following chapters.

The basis of the labour-market approach has been to try to estimate, by the means of surveys, the number of workers who are active in the black economy and/or the total number of hours worked. This is then converted into a monetary figure by multiplying hours worked by the average productivity of workers in the irregular market. From that brief description of the method it is clear that it is fraught with difficulties. How can one know accurately how many workers there are operating in the black economy and how long they work there? How can one estimate these workers' average productivity?

This method of attempting to estimate the size of the black economy has been used largely by Italian economists. One possible reason for this is that the measured labour-force-participation rate in Italy is considerably below that observed in other economically advanced countries.[21] Furthermore, Contini (1981) has argued that the measured participation rate in Italy fell from 44 per cent in 1959 to slightly less than 34 per cent in 1977. He contends that this drop in the participation rate merely reflects the fact that a growing number of people were actively engaged in the black economy and did not appear in official surveys of employment.

The basis of Contini's claim is that 'two *ad hoc* surveys on the non-working population estimated [the participation rate] as 42 per cent in 1971 [against an official participation of 36.2 per cent) and at 41.4 per cent in 1977 (against 33.7 per cent) (Contini, 1981, p. 404).

Contini's contention is that these surveys provide an accurate measure of the true participation rate in 1971 and 1977. He also argues that the measured participation rate in 1959 is the true one. Using these three observations as bench-marks he then interpolates the 'true' participation rate for years between 1959 and 1977. It is then a fairly simple matter to calculate the number of 'marginal' workers, i.e. those engaged in the black economy.[22] Unfortunately, Contini does not report the full time-series estimates of workers engaged in the irregular economy. He merely reports two point estimates, which show the irregular work-force to have been 1.6 million in 1962 rising to 3.8 million in 1972. He comments that after 1972 the number 'widely fluctuates. . . on a trend which is still moving upwards although at a slower pace' (Contini, 1981, p. 404), so that by 1977 the irregular workforce is claimed to amount to over 17 per cent of the total working population. This would imply a total irregular work-force of about 4 million workers in 1977, which Contini claims is 'undoubtedly a conservative estimate' (Contini, 1982, p. 202). The reasons for this are that whilst this figure includes some discouraged unemployed workers (who should *not* be counted) it ignores those who by 1959 were already working in the black economy and those who work part-time in that section whilst holding [full-time] jobs in the official economy. Contini estimates the number of multiple-job holders at 1.5 million in 1977.

How precisely he converts this estimate of jobs held in the black economy into a monetary figure is not altogether clear. All he will say is that '(d)epending on which source one is willing to accept (17 per cent of total labour force according to my own estimates, 20 per cent according to independent estimates. . .) and accounting for second jobs that may be excluded from either of these counts, one obtains a figure that varies between 14 and 20 per cent of the recorded gross national product for 1977' (Contini, 1982, p. 202).[23] The implicit assumption seems to be that output per head in the black economy is more or less the same as in the official economy.

The reliability of the method clearly depends upon the accuracy of the surveys of the non-working population in establishing a 'true' participation rate. In addition the conversion to a monetary figure is dependent upon assumptions about labour productivity. Unfortunately it is difficult to comment on the original surveys, because they are buried in inaccessible Italian official publications.[24] Certainly the method is novel and, providing interviewees can be persuaded to reveal possibly incriminating information about their work activities, it is potentially a much more direct and powerful technique than any we have so far encountered.

The results of a similar labour market survey carried out in Norway in 1980 are reported by Isachsen, Klovland and Strøm (1982). Isachsen and Strøm (1985) have also briefly reported some early results from an update to this survey. The original questionnaire was issued to approximately 1200 people, of whom 877 replied. The objective of the work was to try to establish how much work was carried out in the black economy and how much income and expenditure was generated by it.

Isachsen *et al.* found that some 37.5 per cent of their sample admitted to having either worked in the black economy or paid for black-economy services over the previous twelve months. Some 18 per cent of the sample actually admitted to having worked in the black economy, although the amount of work undertaken was, on average, quite small, i.e. 110 hours per year or about two hours per week.[25, 26] Not surprisingly, the monetary sums involved are quite small. For example, in 1980 the average income claimed to have been earned in the black economy was only 3735 krone (about £340) per year, whilst average expenditure on black-economy services was about 4575 krone (approximately £420).

Using these figures Isachsen *et al.* estimate that the monetary value of irregular economic activity may be between 0.85 per cent and 1.5 per cent of GNP.[27] However, it seems that prices charged for such work are only 40 per cent of the prices for similar work undertaken in the official or regular economy. Isachsen *et al.* revise their estimate of income received to 2.3 per cent of GNP by valuing the irregular work at official market-prices. Using the same approach on the 1983 survey results Isachsen and Strøm (1985, p. 27) claim that irregular economic activity in Norway accounted for 2 per cent of GDP.[28]

The 1983 survey shows that undeclared labour income is only about two-thirds of total undeclared income. In view of this and the possible downward bias in answers to the questionnaires, Isachsen and Strøm tentatively conclude that 'the present size of the hidden economy [is] between 4 and 6 per cent of GDP, of which labour income constitutes about half' (Isachsen and Strøm, 1985, p. 27).

Isachsen *et al.* (1982) use their survey material to test some hypotheses about participation in the black economy. However, these issues are not the immediate concern of this chapter. They will be discussed in Chapter 6.

Pestieau (1984) reports the results of a small survey of the involvement of Belgians in the black economy. The study interviewed 330 people living in the district of Liège. Pestieau found that some 47 per cent of his sample acknowledged having supplied labour to the black economy and 36 per cent had paid for services from that sector. Altogether some two-thirds of the sample had been active in the black economy. However, once again, amounts of time spent working in the black economy were not large, i.e. about 9 hours per individual per week, which Pestieau says is 14 per cent of reported hours worked. He does not convert this into a monetary equivalent or express it as a proportion of GDP. It is noticeable that Belgians claim to spend rather longer working in the black economy than do Norwegians. This result is also found by Frey and Weck-Hanneman (see section 4.3).

A telephone interview technique was used by Smith (1984) in an effort to establish the level of involvement in the black economy in USA. This involved contacting some 2100 households in the autumn of 1981. Respondents were asked to report amounts spent on various goods and services over the previous twelve months. The survey was more concerned with buyers of such services than with the suppliers of labour to the irregular sector. However, households were also asked about ways of making extra income, although they were not specifically asked as to whether these were 'black' or 'official' sources.

From the responses Smith estimates that the black economy in the USA amounted at most to $42 billion (although $10 billion of this may actually have been reported to the Internal Revenue Service). This would amount to less than 1½ per cent of GNP in that year.

The onus of deciding whether a supplier was legitimate or not rested with the household being interviewed. This is not an easy task and one can imagine that in these circumstances respondents would tend to underrecord their purchases from the irregular sector. Similarly, in asking questions about ways of earning extra income, it is clear that respondents were *not* asked to indicate only activity in the black economy. Not surprisingly over 20 per cent of respondents indicated ways of earning extra income, some of which may have little to do with irregular labour market activity.

On the whole one feels that there is little of substance to be gained from Smith's study. Because the questioning seemed to lack specific direction one can see why buyers may well have underestimated their purchases from the black economy and some suppliers were not supplying labour to the black economy in any case.

Del Boca and Forte briefly report a number of studies of the irregular labour market in Italy. These show that, especially in agricultural areas, 'off-the-books' activity may be very considerable and may even outweigh official labour supply. For example, they report a survey carried out by the Turin Chamber of Commerce in 1976 which showed that in one commune in a semi-rural area '53.7 per cent of work (in terms of hours) was done by unofficial workers' (Del Boca and Forte, 1982, p. 188). In another, industrial, area 'the percentage of unofficial hours was 19.2 per cent' (ibid, p. 188). Similarly another survey of industrial and agricultural areas in Fruili in 1979 showed that 'unofficial workers did 34 per cent of the working hours in the agricultural and 24.5 per cent of the hours in the industrial area' (ibid, p. 188).

Surveys of this kind are also useful in providing information on the characteristics of the irregular labour force. It seems, from the Italian studies referred to above, that in the agricultural sector irregular work is undertaken on a full-time basis by women and very young and elderly males. However, irregular work in industrial areas is carried out by males in the prime age groups who are holding two or more jobs.

However, we cannot comment too specifically on the quality of the results obtained in these surveys in view of our dependence upon a secondary source of information. One would expect that if anything, interviews and questionnaires would underestimate the extent of involvement in irregular economic activity. Yet the estimates obtained in the Italian studies listed above suggest a massive black economy. It may be that the areas sampled are not representative of Italy as a whole. Alternatively, it could be that the somewhat sensationalistic stories of Italy's black economy are indeed correct.[29] Del Boca and Forte (1982) provide evidence of a considerable 'underground' building industry in Italy. Between 1971 and 1979, according to official statistics, the number of new houses completed was approximately 1.5 million. However, the number of new household connections for electricity consumption in the same period, was in excess of 3.1 million. They argue that the difference cannot be explained by connecting existing housing to the electricity system, but reflects building activity that is simply not being recorded by the authorities.

Of course, Italy may be a special case, although research by Frey and Weck-Hanneman (reported below) indicates that Italy does *not* have the largest black economy even in Europe. Given the problems involved with using other techniques, e.g. the currency-demand approach, the income/expenditure discrepancy, etc., it may be that the interview technique will be increasingly used to elicit information about the scale of the black economy. The major disadvantages with the technique are its high cost and the need to keep updating by holding repeat interviews. The design of questions and the way that responses are interpreted are important too in reaching valid conclusions.

Figure 4.4   Modelling the black economy

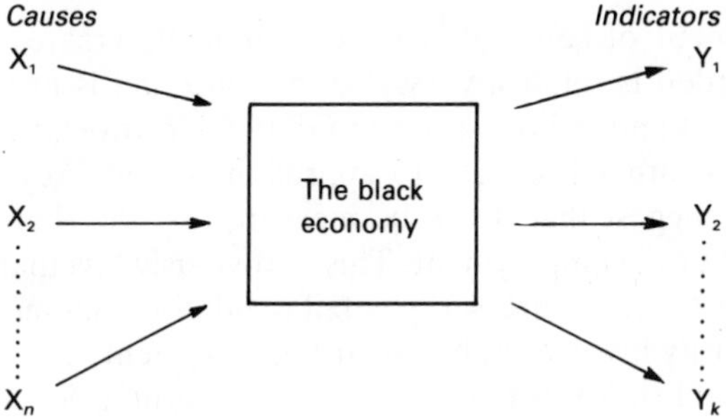

4.3   THE 'SOFT-MODELLING' APPROACH

The final approach considered in this chapter owes a great deal to the pioneering work of Frey and Weck-Hanneman (1982, 1983, 1984) and is based upon the statistical theory of unobserved variables. The approach treats the black (or hidden) economy as an unobservable variable. However, certain observable determinants or causes of black-economic activity are identified along with various observable indicators of such activity. Diagrammatically the process linking causes, indicators and the hidden economy can be seen in Figure 4.4.

Frey and Weck-Hanneman use the method to estimate the relative size and development of the black economies of seventeen OECD countries from 1960 to 1978. The method is obviously very different from those encountered previously in that it focuses upon *multiple* causes leading to the development of the black economy as well as the *multiple* effects (or indicators) of such activity. Previous methods have either totally ignored causes or at best concentrated upon one factor, e.g. taxation. Likewise, other approaches have usually concentrated upon one indicator – 'excess' cash holding, a discrepancy between declared income and expenditure or a falling labour-force-participation rate.

Frey and Weck-Hanneman (1984) distinguish four types of determinants of black-economic activity. These are:

(i) the burden placed upon individuals by the public sector – both the burden of taxation and regulation:

(ii) tax morality, i.e. the innate willingness of individuals to evade paying their taxes;

(iii) the incentives created by unemployment;
(iv) the level of economic development.

Measurement of some of these determinants creates difficulties. The tax burden is relatively easy to measure and is proxied by the share of direct and indirect taxes in GDP.[30] However, the burden of regulation is rather less easy to approximate and Frey and Weck-Hanneman suggest that it can be measured by the share of public-sector jobs in total employment. This is obviously less than ideal. Not all public-sector jobs necessarily entail regulation (and not all regulation necessarily involves public-sector employment, e.g. recent decisions to establish a self-regulatory body governing Stock Exchange dealings in the UK).

The measurement of tax morality presents even greater problems for Frey and Weck-Hanneman. Even they admit (Frey and Weck-Hanneman, 1984, p. 37, note 11) that 'the data on tax morality are of doubtful quality'. They begin by ranking the seventeen OECD countries in descending order of tax morality, i.e. the most moral (Switzerland) at the top down to the least moral (Italy). This ranking is based upon 'the limited literature presenting internationally comparable data' plus ignorance! Where no 'data' exist countries are 'attributed a median rank, lying between the Scandinavian countries . . . and the German-speaking countries' (ibid, p. 37). Then, using rather scanty evidence from the USA which purports to show that tax morality in that country has steadily declined since 1960, the ranking is converted into an index covering the years 1960–78. (As Frey and Weck-Hanneman assume that tax morality has declined uniformly throughout the OECD region the relative ranking of the countries remains the same in each year.) The level of economic development is measured by per capita real disposable income.

Frey and Weck-Hanneman predict that an increase in the burden of taxation and regulation will encourage the development of the black economy as will a decline in tax morality. The effect of an increase in unemployment is thought to be ambiguous, because whilst it increases the incentive to work in the black economy it simultaneously reduces the demand for such services. Likewise, Frey and Weck-Hanneman feel that the impact of economic development upon the black economy cannot be predicted unambiguously.

Three indicators of the size of the black economy are used by Frey and Weck-Hanneman. These are:

(i) the growth rate of measured real GDP;
(ii) the male labour-force participation-rate;
(iii) working hours.

They argue that an increase in the scale of the black economy will manifest itself in terms of falls in all three of these indicators.

The model connecting the exogenous determinants to the endogenous indicators and the unobserved measure of the black economy is estimated by a complicated statistical routine. The results suggest that the burdens of *direct* taxation and of regulation are important causes of irregular economic activity, as is tax morality. The other determinants – i.e. indirect taxes, unemployment, economic development, etc. – are not found to be significant.

Frey and Weck-Hanneman conclude that the relative size of the black economy can be found from the following equation:

$$H = 0.35T + 0.25P + 0.40M$$

where H is the size of the hidden economy,[31] T is the direct tax share, P is the share of public sector jobs in total employment and M is the index of tax morality.

Their ranking of the seventeen OECD countries for 1960 and 1978 is given in Table 4.2.

In order to be able to convert these relative sizes into an absolute measure of a country's black economy it is necessary to establish two points. The first acts as a base point and the second measures the distance between ranks (i.e. the scale). Frey and Weck-Hanneman utilise Klovland's estimates of the black economies for Sweden and Norway for this purpose (Klovland, 1980). This produces the estimates for 1978 which are reported (in brackets) in Table 4.2.

The value of this last exercise is somewhat reduced when one realises that Klovland has subsequently repudiated his estimates of Norway's black economy using the currency-demand approach (see Chapter 3). Also, a recent study of the black economies of Sweden, Norway and Denmark by Schneider and Lundager (1986), using the currency-demand approach suggests (i) that the gap between Sweden and Norway is only half as large as Frey and Weck-Hanneman assume, and (ii) that the rankings of Denmark's and Norway's black economies should be reversed. Again see Chapter 3.

Before we consider the shortcomings of this approach in more detail we briefly report other, earlier versions of it used by Frey and

Table 4.2   Frey and Weck-Hanneman's ranking of the black economies of OECD countries, 1960 and 1978

Country	1978	1960
1. (Largest)	Sweden (13.2)*	USA
2.	Belgium (12.1)	Netherlands
3.	Denmark (11.8)	Sweden
4.	Italy (11.4)	Canada
5.	Netherlands (9.6)	France
6.	France (9.4)	Belgium
7.	Norway (9.2)	UK
8.	Austria (8.9)	Austria
9.	Canada (8.7)	Norway
10.	West Germany (8.6)	Italy
11.	USA (8.3)	West Germany
12.	UK (8.0)	Denmark
13.	Finland (7.6)	Finland
14.	Ireland (7.2)	Spain
15.	Spain (6.5)	Japan
16.	Switzerland (4.3)	Ireland
17. (Smallest)	Japan (4.1)	Switzerland

* Figures in brackets are estimates of the size of the black economy as a percentage of GNP. How they have been derived is explained in the text.

Source: Frey and Weck-Hanneman (1984, p. 42)

Weck-Hanneman. The development of the ideas which led to the approach outlined above can be traced quite clearly through a series of papers such as Frey, Weck and Pommerehne (1982) and Frey and Weck (1983a, b). We will not examine these in detail but merely report the major points.

An early version of the approach is used by Frey, Weck and Pommerehne (1982) to chart the development of the black economy of West Germany from 1960 to 1978. The underlying ideas are as described above, i.e. that a black economy emerges as a response to high burdens of taxation and regulation, and also to declining tax morality. Other factors indicating an increasing black economy are argued to be:

(i) a fall in working hours;
(ii) a fall in male labour force participation;
(iii) an increase in the proportion of foreign workers in the economy.

It is assumed that the size of the black economy is a linear function of these six factors, measured in standardised Z-values, i.e:

$$B \text{ (the size of the black economy)} = \sum_{i=1}^{6} a_i Z_i$$

where Z_i is the standardised Z-value for the ith factor and a_i is the 'weight', i.e. importance of th ith factor in bringing about irregular economic activity.

Of course $\sum a_i = 1$

Frey *et al.* experiment with various weighting schemes (five in all). However, the precise choice of weighting scheme does not affect their overall conclusion that there was 'a steadily increasing shadow economy in Germany for the period 1960–78' (Frey *et al.*, 1982, p. 157)

A basically similar approach is adopted by Frey and Weck in order to 'isolate the factors tending to *increase* the pressure for the formation and growth of the hidden economy' (Frey and Weck, 1983b, p. 824) in seventeen OECD countries between 1960 and 1978.[32] Using the notation above Frey and Weck calculate:

$$\Delta B = \sum a_i \Delta Z_i$$

The factors used as determinants of the black economy are the burden of taxation, the burden of regulation, the labour-force-participation rate, the unemployment rate and working hours in manufacturing industry. Tax morality is excluded because 'the comparative development of tax morality between countries over time is not known' (ibid, p. 825).[33] Various weighting schemes (eight in all) were used to produce a relative ranking of the seventeen OECD countries in terms of the *increase* in their black economy between 1960 and 1978. Results show the strongest increases occurring in Sweden, Norway, Netherlands and Denmark and the smallest increases in Japan, France, Canada and the USA.

The soft-modelling approach has certain advantages. For example, it focuses upon a number of determinants and indicators of the extent of the black economy's development. However, how important each of these is, relative to one another, is a matter of some debate (hence the rather large number of alternative weighting schemes used in early applications of the technique). Weighting schemes will always appear arbitrary and, when some variables (e.g. deterrence factors) have been excluded, rather pointless. This has no doubt forced Frey and Weck-Hanneman to abandon such weighting schemes and to move into the statistical theory of estimating relationships containing unobserved variables. This is an area about which most economists know little and it is sometimes difficult to understand and hence believe the results which are thrown up by such methods of estimation. However, perhaps even more important is the quality of the data that are used to produce parameter estimates. Here is probably the weakest aspect of Frey and Weck-Hanneman's work. Even they are forced to admit that '(a)n important shortcoming of our study is the weakness of the data at our disposition. This applies especially to tax morality and regulation' (Frey and Weck-Hanneman, 1986, p. 47). One cannot have a great deal of confidence in a technique which relies on some highly questionable data and which uses an estimation technique that is difficult to comprehend.

4.4 CONCLUSIONS

This chapter has discussed at length upon three broad approaches to measuring the size of the black economy. These are:

(i) studies based upon the discrepancy between incomes and expenditure, either at the household or national level;
(ii) interviews with participants in the black economy, usually suppliers of labour services but also purchasers of 'black' goods/services;
(iii) the soft-modelling approach.

I have already commented in detail on each of these methods and so will not repeat all those arguments here.

The discrepancy approach, particularly at the household level, is potentially useful provided that two main problems can be overcome. These are to ensure that (i) non-participants in the survey are not those who are most likely to be involved in the black economy, and (ii) entirely legitimate reasons for spending in excess of one's income are correctly identified. These points may seem fairly trivial, but they are in fact important. It is not apparent that the FES, for example, can guarantee the former or that Dilnot and Morris have successfully solved the latter problem.

The discrepancy approach based upon comparing estimates of national income and expenditure would seem to be a blind alley. There are just too many other reasons why such a discrepancy might exist and why irregular activity may not be revealed in such a discrepancy in any case.

Interviews with random samples of the population may cast some light on the extent of irregular work and purchases. Again there must be doubts about the willingness of individuals to reveal accurate and truthful information about such activities. If anonymity can be guaranteed then useful information may be obtained. Cost is a major factor which may also limit the adoption of such a technique.

The soft-modelling approach of Frey and Weck-Hanneman is interesting, but I think no more than that. It suffers so many data problems that one must remain highly sceptical about the results it produces.

On the whole one cannot be too confident about the results obtained using these various methods. However, the development of these different approaches says much for the ingenuity of economists.

5 Participation in the Black Economy: Theory

Chapters 2–4 considered in detail the question 'How large is the black economy?' As we saw that is not an easy question to answer. Indeed, some people might argue quite legitimately that it is impossible to answer that question. This has not deterred some economists from trying to do so and they have developed a whole range of techniques aimed at revealing the extent of such concealed economic activity. These techniques, and some of the studies using them, were extensively reviewed in Chapters 2, 3 and 4. It is clear from that review that there are significant weaknesses with *all* the methods that have so far been devised. However, despite their imperfections these studies do constitute possibly the best evidence of the existence and growth of irregular economic activity. As Cowell (1985b) has claimed, 'there is sufficient evidence to suggest that tax evasion is quantitatively a non-neglible problem in advanced Western-style economies' (p. 163).

If we accept this conclusion, then it is logical to ask why do people become involved in tax evasion and irregular economic activity? In other words, what are the incentives which lead individuals to underdeclare their income to the tax authority, to supply labour to the black economy and/or to buy goods and services from that sector? These questions will be the subject matter of this and the next chapter. This chapter will examine how economists have modelled individuals' decisions about participation in the black economy. Chapter 6 will review some of the empirical testing of the theoretical results.

It is not hard to think of reasons why people may evade paying their taxes. The 'man in the street' would no doubt point to very high income-tax rates, little chance of getting caught and minimal penalties if one is unlucky enough to be caught. But can one be more precise than this, for after all the design of anti-evasion policy (the subject of Chapter 8) requires rather more precise and rigorously established results than these? It is to be hoped that this is where both economic analysis and econometrics can offer some helpful solutions.

In fact it is only recently that economists have begun to construct theoretical models of the tax-evasion decision. The first rigorous theoretical analysis of individual behaviour was made by Allingham and Sandmo (1972). The impetus for this work seems to have come from two related sources – first, the newly emerging work on the economics of crime (Becker, 1968) and second, the work on the economics of risk and uncertainty (Arrow, 1970).

Deliberate underreporting of income to the tax authority is inherently risky and also illegal. It seems natural, therefore, to apply the analytical tools developed in these other fields to answer the question 'How much of my income should I declare to the tax authority, given the possibility that I might be caught and punished?'

This was precisely the question to which Allingham and Sandmo addressed themselves. They were able to produce some interesting predictions about the effect upon undeclared income of changes in various policy parameters, e.g. tax rates, detection rates and penalties. Their model and some modifications of it are considered in section 5.1.

However, the theoretical literature has been considerably developed since then. Most importantly, later contributors have relaxed Allingham and Sandmo's assumption that income is exogenously determined. Later contributions have argued that decisions about labour supply and tax evasion are made jointly. Unfortunately, once this is acknowledged the relatively clear predictions of Allingham and Sandmo's model disappear into a plethora of ambiguous comparative – static results. Several writers, e.g. Andersen (1977), Isachsen and Strøm (1980) and Cowell (1985a) have, with varying degrees of success, tried to salvage something of the clarity of Allingham and Sandmo's results. However, as Cowell (1985a) has shown, this rescue act requires us to make fairly strong assumptions about the nature of individuals' utility functions. We examine these developments in section 5.2.

As we will see, the bulk of economists' research effort has been concentrated upon *income*-tax evasion. Of course, there is no reason why the tools developed in this literature should not be applied to decisions by firms to avoid corporation tax or to questions of evasion of indirect taxes and so on. However, this chapter will concentrate upon the analysis of income-tax evasion. For most governments the income tax is the principal source of tax revenue, which provides an additional incentive for this concentration of effort.

We should emphasise that in virtually the whole of this literature individuals are assumed to be rational, amoral, risk-averse, expected-utility-maximisers, who observe the von Neumann–Morgenstern axioms of behaviour in situations of risk. Their utility is assumed to be a function either of income (consumption) alone or of income (consumption) and leisure. In other words, they do not directly derive pleasure from beating the tax man, neither do they suffer pangs of remorse from either working in the hidden economy or cheating on their tax return. In principle there is no reason why at least some of these factors should not be built into the individual's utility function. Something similar has been attempted by Block and Heineke (1975) in the analysis of criminal choice (see Pyle, 1984, ch. 2). Section 5.3 considers how the stigma of being caught for evasion might influence the behaviour of potential evaders.

All the models considered below analyse an individual's decision in a one-period framework. This is patently unrealistic. Decisions about evasion made in one period might be expected to influence opportunities and decisions in later periods. An erratic time-stream of declared income is likely to arouse suspicion, for example. Similarly detection and punishment in one period is not only likely to influence future choices but also detection for previous periods of evasion. Unfortunately, the mathematics of the multi-period (or dynamic) case is inordinately complex and so this particular generalisation will be left on one side.[1]

5.1   PORTFOLIO MODELS OF INCOME TAX EVASION

This sub-section examines Allingham and Sandmo's static model in which an individual decides in each time period whether and to what extent to evade payment of income tax. Underreporting is assumed to require relatively little effort and is considered not to affect decisions about labour supply. This is why models of this type are often described as 'portfolio models'. In each time-period the individual is assumed to be putting a proportion of his/her income at risk.

Each individual is assumed to attempt to maximise his/her expected utility, where utility is a function solely of income.[2] Actual income in each time period (W) is determined exogenously. A constant tax rate (θ) is applied to declared income (X). The probability of being investigated by the tax authority is p, which in the simplest version of the model is assumed to be constant.[3] If individuals are found guilty of evading tax then they have to pay tax on their undeclared income ($W - X$) at a penal rate $\pi(> \theta)$. This last assumption turns out to be crucial in determining the effect upon declared income of, for example, an increase in the rate of income tax. If the penalty is levied on evaded *tax* (i.e. $\theta[W - X]$) rather than income, Allingham and Sandmo's results are changed quite significantly (see below).

The taxpayer is assumed to choose the value of X that will maximise his/her expected utility (EU). More formally this can be written as

$$\underset{X}{\text{maximise}}\ EU = (1 - p)\,U(W - \theta X) + p\,U[W - \theta X - \pi(W - X)]$$

It is fairly easy to show that an individual will underreport his income if the expected penalty ($p\pi$) paid on each unit of undeclared income is less than the standard income-tax rate (θ).

The condition for 'entry' into tax evasion is simply that:

$$\left.\frac{dEU}{dX}\right|_{X = W} < 0 \tag{5.1}$$

i.e. when all income is declared to the tax authority the individual could increase his/her expected utility by reducing the amount (s)he declares. Differentiating expected utility (EU) with respect to declared income (X) we obtain:

$$\frac{dEU}{dX} = -\theta(1 - p)\,U^{1}[W - \theta X] - (\theta - \pi)p\,U^{1}[W - \theta X - \pi(W - X)]$$

If we evaluate this derivative at $X = W$ we have:

$$\left.\frac{dEU}{dX}\right|_{X = W} = -\theta(1 - p)\,U^{1}[W - \theta W] - (\theta - \pi)p\,U^{1}[W - \theta W]$$

It is then fairly easy to see that the entry condition (5.1 above) can be written as:

$$-\theta(1 - p) - (\theta - \pi)p < 0$$

or

$$p\pi < \theta \qquad\qquad (5.1')$$

i.e. the expected penalty must be less than the standard rate of income tax.

If for simplicity we assume an interior optimum i.e. $W > X > 0$, the first order condition for an optimum is then:

$$\frac{dEU}{dX} = -\theta(1 - p)U^1(Y) - (\theta - \pi)pU^1(Z) = 0 \qquad (5.2)$$

where $Y = W - \theta X$
and $Z = W - \theta X - \pi(W - X)$

The second order condition is:

$$\frac{d^2EU}{dX^2} = D = \theta^2(1 - p)U^{11}(Y) + (\theta - \pi)^2 pU^{11}(Z) < 0$$

which is automatically satisfied by the assumption that individuals are risk-averse (risk-aversion implies $U^{11} < 0$).

In principle it is possible to solve equation (5.2) to find the optimal value of X, the amount of income declared to the tax authority, although in practice we would need more specific information about the form of the utility function before this could be done, except in the most general sense, i.e.:

$$X = F(W, \theta, \pi, p)$$

However, it is still possible to derive qualitative predictions about the effect of changes in income (W), the tax rate (θ), the penalty rate (π) and the probability detection (p) upon the optimal income declaration (X). This can be done by differentiating equation (5.2) with respect to W, θ, π and p in turn and solving for $\frac{\partial X}{\partial W}$, $\frac{\partial X}{\partial \theta}$, $\frac{\partial X}{\partial \pi}$ and $\frac{\partial X}{\partial p}$.

We briefly summarise Allingham and Sandmo's results without going into the proofs which are quite long. The results make use of the Arrow–Pratt measures of absolute and relative risk-aversion. Allingham and Sandmo assumed decreasing absolute risk-aversion, but were undecided about relative risk-aversion. The results were as follows:

$$\frac{\partial X}{\partial W} = \frac{-1}{D}\,\theta(1-p)\,U^1(Y)\,[R_A(Y) - (1-\pi)R_A(Z)] \qquad (5.3)$$

where $R_A(Y) = -\dfrac{U^{11}(Y)}{U^1(Y)}$ and $R_A(Z) = -\dfrac{U^{11}(Z)}{U^1(Z)}$ are the Arrow–Pratt measures of absolute risk-aversion.

$$\frac{\partial X}{\partial \theta} = \frac{1}{D}\,X\,\theta(1-p)\,U^1(Y)\,[R_A(Y) - R_A(Z)] \qquad (5.4)$$

$$+ \frac{1}{D}\,[(1-p)\,U^1(Y) + p\,U^1(Z)]$$

$$\frac{\partial X}{\partial \pi} = \frac{-1}{D}\,(W-X)(\theta-\pi)p\,U^{11}(Z) - \frac{1}{D}\,p\;U^1(Z) \qquad (5.5)$$

$$\frac{\partial X}{\partial p} = \frac{1}{D}\,[-\theta\,U^1(Y) + (\theta-\pi)\,U^1(Z)] \qquad (5.6)$$

From (5.3) it can be seen that if $\pi > 1$ then $\partial X/\partial W > 0$, i.e. as actual income is increased individuals declare more income for tax purposes. This is perhaps not an unreasonable conclusion with a penal tax rate in excess of 100 per cent. However, if $\pi < 1$ then the sign of $\partial X/\partial W$ cannot be determined.

Allingham and Sandmo further investigated what would happen to the *proportion* of income declared for tax (X/W) as income increases. This is found by evaluating

$$\frac{\partial(X/W)}{\partial W} = \frac{-1}{W^2}\,\frac{1}{D}\,\theta(1-p)\,U^1(Y)\,[R_R(Y) - R_R(Z)] \qquad (5.7)$$

where $R_R(Y) = -\dfrac{U^{11}(Y)}{U^1(Y)}\,Y$ and $R_R(Z) = -\dfrac{U^{11}(Z)}{U^1(Z)}\,Z$ are the Arrow–Pratt measures of relative risk-aversion.

The sign of (5.7) depends upon whether individuals display increasing or decreasing relative risk-aversion and so cannot be decided unambiguously.

The sign of the derivative (5.4) is also ambiguous if we accept, as did Allingham and Sandmo, that individuals show decreasing absolute risk-aversion. It would seem that rigorous theoretical analysis can provide little support for the common assertion that evasion is encouraged by increasing tax rates.[4] Only recourse to empirical work could either confirm or reject that hypothesis (see Chapter 6).

However, Yitzhaki's modification of the Allingham and Sandmo model casts doubt upon this result (see below).

It is, however, possible to obtain unambiguous results concerning the two law-enforcement variables, π and p. From (5.5) it is clear that $\frac{\partial X}{\partial \pi} > 0$, whilst (5.6) shows that $\frac{\partial X}{\partial p}$ is also unambiguously positive. This means that increases in either the penal rate of tax or the probability of investigation result in more income being declared. This led Allingham and Sandmo to conclude that π and p could be treated as substitutes in a policy aimed at reducing evasion.[5] This can be seen if we imagine the tax authority setting the probability of detection just high enough to deter anyone from cheating. If we examine the 'entry' condition (5.1') this means that p should be set such that $p\pi \geq \theta$ or $p \geq \theta/\pi$. Policy issues and problems are discussed more fully in Chapter 8.

At about the same time a similar model was being developed independently by Srinivasan (1973). However, there were slight differences of approach. For example, Srinivasan assumed that individuals attempted to maximise expected income rather than utility (i.e. they are risk-neutral) and he made rather less restrictive assumptions about the form of the tax function and the penalty rate. In contrast with Allingham and Sandmo, he assumed that individuals would choose the *proportion* of true income not to declare in order to maximise expected income after taxes and penalties. However, these changes did not significantly alter the main comparative static predictions of his model. For example, an increase in the detection rate still unambiguously deterred evasion just as it had in the Allingham–Sandmo model. However, the effect of a change in exogenously determined income upon the optimal underdeclaration depended upon the progressivity of the tax system and the relationship between the probability of detection and true income. With a progressive tax function and a probability of detection which is independent of true income, an increase in income will be associated with declaring a smaller proportion of all income. However, with a constant marginal tax rate and a probability of detection which is an increasing function of true income, then an increasing proportion of income will be declared for tax purposes as income rises.

Both these results have a certain intuitive appeal. In the first case the progressive income-tax system acts as an incentive to under-declare income provided that there is no offsetting increase in the probability of punishment. In the second case it is the increased probability of investigation that acts as an incentive to declare more of one's income, provided there is no counteracting disincentive effect created by higher marginal tax rates.[6]

An important modification of Allingham and Sandmo's model has been made by Yitzhaki (1974). He has tried to remove some of the ambiguities from Allingham and Sandmo's results concerning the effect upon X (declared income) of changes in the tax rate (θ) and exogenous income (W). This is accomplished by one relatively minor modification to the penalty function. In Allingham and Sandmo the penalty (fine?) is imposed upon undeclared income ($W - X$). Yit-zhaki argues that under both American and Israeli (and indeed many other countries') tax-laws fines are in fact imposed upon the evaded *tax*, i.e. $\theta(W - X)$. This apparently minor amendment to the for-mulation of the problem is sufficient to establish that:

$$\frac{\partial X}{\partial \theta} > 0 \text{ and } \frac{\partial X}{\partial W} < 1$$

provided that individuals reveal decreasing absolute risk-aversion.

The first of these results seems to undermine further the claim that higher tax rates encourage evasion. In fact it points to raising tax rates as a means of discouraging evasion, which looks distinctly odd. It comes about because, under Yitzhaki's formulation of the penalty, the penalty rate ($F\theta$) and the tax rate (θ) are proportional to one another, so that there is no substitution effect. A rise in the tax rate is a pure income effect which reduces income and given decreasing absolute risk-aversion the taxpayer switches into safer activity, i.e. declares more of his or her income to the tax authority. The second result shows that declared income changes more slowly than true income.

Christiansen (1980) has modified the Allingham and Sandmo model by incorporating a link between the probability of detection (p) and the penalty rate (π). Depending upon the precise nature of this relationship he has shown that *in some cases* an increase in the penalty might actually encourage evasion.[7]

Witte and Woodbury (1985) have extended the basic Allingham–Sandmo model so as to incorporate additional sanctions variables. Rather than simply allowing for detection or not, they have widened the net to include the possibilities of audit, a civil penalty and finally a criminal penalty. This means that the individual is faced by four rather than merely two possible states of the world. Further, the costs (i.e. penalties) borne by the individual increase as the extent of agency action increases. Finally, Witte and Woodbury incorporate a progressive tax schedule. In all other respects their model is identical with that of Allingham and Sandmo.

The comparative static properties of this model are briefly as follows. First, an increase in the probability of agency action encourages reporting. An increase in the probability of being audited has a bigger effect than an increase in the probability of a civil penalty, which in turn outweighs the effect of an increase in the probability of a criminal penalty. This is a well-established result from the literature on the economics of crime (see Pyle, 1983, ch. 4). Second, an increase in lump-sum taxes (which are, of course, independent of income) will encourage declarations. This is because this sort of tax increase generates only an income effect. It serves to lower income and if we assume decreasing absolute risk-aversion agents will reduce risky activity i.e. they will reduce their tax evasion. However, it is impossible to sign the effect of a tax change which proportionately lowers tax payments at all levels of income. Finally, the effect of an increase in pre-tax income upon declarations cannot be signed. (Compare this result with Srinivasan's result discussed earlier and also see note 6.)

Cross and Shaw (1981, 1982) have attempted to model joint evasion-avoidance decisions using a framework similar to that adopted by Allingham and Sandmo for analysing tax evasion alone. Tax avoidance (the entirely legal use of tax loopholes in order to reduce tax payments) has not been discussed in any of the papers reviewed so far. Cross and Shaw claim that evasion and avoidance might be both substitute and complementary activities. For example, an increase in tax rates might lead tax-evaders to switch to tax avoidance. Complementarity can occur when, for example, a justifiable claim for expense allowances (avoidance) facilitates an inflated statement of such expenses (evasion).

They set up a simple expected utility maximising model with exogenously determined income in order to determine the optimum level of each of the activities. They then examine the comparative static effects upon evasion and avoidance of changes in tax rates, penalty rates and the detection probability. This is done along lines similar to those outlined above. For simplicity we concentrate on the effects of parameter changes upon the amount of tax-*evaded* income. First, the effect of a change in the tax rate upon the amount of evaded income is indeterminate (partly because the rise in the tax rate encourages avoidance, which in turn produces 'indirect' income and substitution effects). Second, an increase in the penalty rate reduces the amount of evaded income, except when income taxes are progressive. Indeed, with progressive taxes evasion might actually increase, because an increase in the penalty rate encourages a switch from evasion to avoidance, which lowers the effective tax rate which in turn engenders indirect income and substitution effects encouraging evasion! An increase in the probability of detection reduces tax-evaded income, except where there is a progressive income-tax rate. The reasons for this counter-intuitive result have been outlined in analysing the effect of an increase in the penalty rate.

5.2 MODELS OF TAX EVASION WITH ENDOGENOUS INCOME

It can be argued that the usefulness of the models discussed in the previous section is limited, because they fail to take into account possible interactions between the labour-supply decision and the decision to evade tax. This interaction may be especially important when the tax being evaded is one on earned income. Successful evasion raises the worker's net wage rate and so could have an effect upon his/her labour supply. In these circumstances both true and declared income become endogenous variables.

Recently there have been a number of contributions to the literature on this very point. For example, the papers by Andersen (1977), Baldry (1979), Cowell (1985a), Isachen and Strøm (1980), Pencavel (1979), Sandmo (1981) and Weiss (1976) all offer somewhat different analyses of this situation.

A simplified version of this kind of model would be as follows. Each taxpayer is assumed to have a von Neumann–Morgenstern utility function defined over total income or consumption (W) and hours of leisure (L) i.e. $U = U(W, L)$ with the usual assumptions that $U_w > 0$; $U_{ww} < 0$; $U_L > 0$; $U_{LL} < 0$ and $U_{WL} > 0$.[8] As before assume a constant proportional tax rate (θ) and a penalty rate of π per unit of evaded tax (following Yitzhaki).[9] The probability of being investigated and hence detected for tax evasion is assumed to be constant and is denoted by p. The wage rate in employment is w and total hours available for work (H) are equal to $T - L$, where T is fixed (say 24 hours per day). The amount of income declared to the tax authority is given by X.

The individual's disposable income will be given by *either* $w.H - \theta.X$, with probability $1 - p$ *or* $w.H - \theta.X - \pi\theta[wH - X]$, with probability p. The taxpayer's expected utility is then defined as

$$EU = (1 - p)\, U\,[wH - \theta X, T - H] + \\ p\, U\,[wH - \theta X - \pi\theta(wH - X), T - H] \qquad (5.8)$$

The taxpayer must now choose H and X so as to maximise expected utility. Again, for simplicity, assume an interior optimum and write:

$$Y = wH - \theta X$$

and

$$Z = wH - \theta X - \pi\theta(wH - X)$$

The first order conditions for a maximum are given by:

$$-\theta\,(1 - p)\, U_1^Y - p\theta U_1^Z\,(1 - \pi) = 0 \qquad (5.9)$$

and

$$(1 - p)\, U_1^Y w + p\, U_1^Z w\,(1 - \pi\theta) - U_L^Y - p U_L^Z = 0 \qquad (5.10)$$

where U_1^Y and U_1^Z are the first order partial derivatives of the utility function with respect to income evaluated at Y and Z respectively and U_L^Y *and* U_L^Z are the first order derivatives with respect to leisure evaluated at Y and Z respectively.

It is fairly straightforward, although rather time-consuming, to investigate the effects upon H and X of changes in some of the parameters of this model. In particular we are interested in the effect of changes in π, p, θ and w. This can be done by differentiating (5.9) and (5.10) with respect to each of these parameters in turn and the solving for $\dfrac{\partial H}{\partial K}$ and $\dfrac{\partial X}{\partial K}$, for $K = \theta$, π, p and w.

However, in general it is *not* possible to sign these derivatives. As Baldry (1979) has observed, using a model similar to the one described above, this happens because there are now three effects present – (i) a portfolio effect, (ii) an income effect and (iii) a leisure effect – and it is only possible to sign the portfolio effect ambiguously. A simple explanation for these results can be found if we consider the usual analysis of the labour-supply decision in the absence of risk. In that case when hours of work are perfectly variable it is impossible to sign the effect of, for example, a wage- or tax-rate change upon labour supply. The reason is that the tax change, for example, produces both income- and substitution-effects and these work in opposite directions. Consider the case of an increase in the rate of income tax. This reduces the net wage and so, by the substitution effect, encourages workers to take *more* leisure (the opportunity cost of an extra hour of leisure has fallen). However, the income effect works in the opposite direction, *if* leisure is a normal good, and so encourages the worker to supply more labour. Overall, one cannot say whether the increase in the tax rate reduces or increases the amount of labour supplied. That result depends upon the relative sizes of these two contradictory effects, which can not be decided *a priori*.

In the case of tax evasion and labour supply the situation is slightly more complicated. The tax change, for example, will still produce income- and substitution-effects, the net effect of which cannot be determined. In addition the tax-change influences the choice between risky and non-risky activity, i.e. tax-evaded income and non-evaded income. (Whilst the tax increase will tend to encourage declaration this itself will generate indirect income and substitution effects upon labour supply.) Not surprisingly it is impossible to reach an unambiguous conclusion concerning the overall effect upon labour supply.

This result has been brought home forcefully by Pencavel (1979). Using a model similar to the one described above, he analyses the effect upon reported (i.e. declared) income of various parameter changes, first when hours worked are held constant and second when they are variable. The contrast in the comparative static properties of these two variants of the model is startling. With fixed hours of work only one of some eighteen derivatives cannot be determined unambiguously.[10] With hours of work endogenous he concludes that 'it is evident that the predominance of unambiguous sign implications . . . is converted into a predominance of ambiguities' (Pencavel, 1979, pp. 120–1).[11]

In situations like this economists would normally be quite content to accept ambiguous theoretical predictions and seek salvation in the results of empirical analysis. For example, they are quite willing to accept that in some situations demand curves might slope upwards or labour-supply curves could be backward-bending. However, they have been most unwilling to accept such a theoretical no man's land in the tax-evasion literature. The reason for this must have a great deal to do with the inherent difficulty of empirical testing in this area. Satisfactory data are very difficult to find (see Chapter 6). As empirical analysis cannot be relied upon to furnish definitive conclusions, economists have tried instead to modify their theoretical models in an attempt to obtain unambiguous predictions. This has been achieved either by imposing some form of separability on the utility function or by making regular and black-economy work non-substitutable activities.

Here we focus on models incorporating restrictions on the utility function. Andersen (1977) proceeded by assuming that the utility function was additively separable in income and leisure (or hours of work), i.e.

$$U\ (W,\ H)\ =\ U_1\ (W)\ +\ U_2\ (H)$$

where W is income and H is hours of work. This is tantamount to assuming that the marginal utility of income is independent of leisure, i.e. $U_{WH} = 0$. All the other features of Andersen's model are as given on p. 95 above, except (i) for the inclusion of some 'unearned' income which was assumed to be exogenously determined, and (ii) the penalty being based upon evaded income rather than evaded tax payments.

Unfortunately the assumption of additive separability is sufficient to enable the signing of only some of the important derivatives. Andersen's results are summarised in Table 5.1. It should be observed that some of these derivatives are substitution effects only. When income effects are included the total effect once again becomes ambiguous. It would appear that Andersen's attempts at both generalising the model formulation and preserving its predictive clarity are not particularly successful.[12]

The model described above is in some senses still an unrealistic description of the choices facing some individuals. In it the individual decides how much labour to supply and how much of the income that this generates to declare to the tax authority. More realistically 'rather than concealing a portion of a uniform lump of income that is undistinguished as to its source, the person cheats the government by

Table 5.1 Comparative static results in Andersen's model

As a result of a change in	Effect upon	
	labour supply (H)	unreported income (X)
'unearned' income	< 0	> 0[a]
tax rate[1]	< 0[b]	?[c]
penalty rate[1]	< 0	< 0
probability of detection	?[d]	< 0
wage rate[1]	> 0	> 0

[1] substitution effects only; total effects are ambiguous.
[a] assumes decreasing absolute risk aversion.
[b] for $\pi < 1$ this requires non-decreasing relative risk-aversion.
[c] for $\pi < 1$ the substitution effect is positive, but indeterminate for $\pi > 1$.
[d] depends upon relative risk aversion.

taking one or more *different* jobs . . . the income from which is administratively difficult to tax' (Cowell, 1985a, p. 19). That is, in trying to evade taxes individuals must switch their labour supply from the 'official' economy to the black economy.

A formal attempt to model this process has been made by Isachsen and Strøm (1980). They present both a general model and a particular example. The special case assumes:

(i) a particular form for the utility function;
(ii) complete confiscation of all black economy income if caught.

Each individual is assumed to divide his or her time (T hours) between leisure, work in the regular economy (H_R hours) and work in the irregular or black economy (H_B hours). Wage rates in the two sectors, W_R and W_B respectively, are assumed to be fixed exogenously, i.e. each individual is a pricetaker in the market for his or her labour. The probability of detection (p), the tax rate on earnings in the regular economy (θ) and the penalty on undisclosed income (π) are also assumed fixed.

In those circumstances an individual's expected utility is given by

$$EU = (1 - p) \, U \, [W_R H_R \, (1 - \theta) + W_B H_B, \, T - H_B - H_R] + pU \, [W_R H_R \, (1 - \theta) + W_B H_B \, (1 - \pi), \, T - H_B - H_R]$$

Note that individuals declare *none* of their black-economy earnings, but declare *all* their earnings from working in the official economy.

Each invididual is assumed to chose H_B and H_R so as to maximise expected utility. In general the solution to this problem will be two labour-supply functions of the form

$$H_R = f(W_R, W_B, p, \theta, \pi)$$

and

$$H_B = g(W_R, W_B, p, \theta, \pi)$$

There are two easily interpretable 'entry' conditions for an interior optimum. These are that

$$W_R(1 - \theta) < W_B(1 - p\pi) \tag{i}$$

and

$$W_R(1 - \theta) > W_B(1 - \pi) \tag{ii}$$

The first of these conditions requires that the expected net wage in the black economy must exceed the net of tax wage in the regular economy. Otherwise no one would bother to take the risk of working in the black economy. The second condition requires that the net of tax wage in the regular economy exceed the wage rate in the black economy when punishment is certain. If this did not hold no one would bother to work in the regular economy. They would do better by working in the black economy and paying their fines.

Isachsen and Strøm present a special case of this problem for in-depth treatment. In this case (i) $U = \log W + \log L$, where W is income and L is hours of leisure and (ii) $\pi = 1$, i.e. all black-economy income is confiscated. When the utility function takes this form total working time is fixed [at $\frac{T}{2}$] and the model simply divides this available time between H_R and H_B. 'Entry' into the irregular sector requires that $(1 - p) W_B > W_R(1 - \theta)$, i.e. the expected black-economy wage rate exceeds the net of tax wage rate in the official economy. Apart from that several comparative static predictions follow. These are that

(i) an increase in the wage rate in the irregular sector encourages a switch from the regular to the irregular market;

(ii) an increase in the wage in the regular sector, *ceteris paribus*, reduces hours allocated to the irregular sector;
(iii) an increase in the probability of detection deters irregular economic activity;
(iv) increasing tax rates pushes labour out of the regular sector into the irregular labour market.

This last result is totally at variance with that suggested by Yitzhaki.

Of course, the model used by Isachsen and Strøm is very specific, particularly in its choice of utility function. In fact, with this particular utility function the total hours of labour supply ($H = H_R + H_B$) are fixed and the model simply explains how those hours are allocated between the two labour markets. In this respect this model is similar to that of Allingham and Sandmo, with $W_B H_B$ playing the role of undeclared income and $W_R H_R$ being declared income. The models would be almost exactly the same if $W_B = W_R$. In a more general formulation, in which total labour supply were to be variable, then unambiguous predictions would be difficult to obtain.

Cowell (1985a, b) has argued that it may still be possible to produce unambiguous theoretical predictions in a rather more general model if one is prepared to assume some form of separability between the decisions about (i) leisure versus work, and (ii) work in the official sector versus work in the irregular sector. He has shown that when the utility function is written as

$$U(W, L) = f[g(W)L + h(L)]$$

where f, g and h are all increasing functions and W and L are income and hours of leisure respectively,[13] then the labour-supply functions can be written as

$$H_B = \emptyset[W_R(1-\theta), B, H(W_R(1-\theta), B), \pi, W_B, p] \qquad (5.11)$$

and

$$H_R = H[W_R(1-\theta), B] - \emptyset(\cdot) \qquad (5.12)$$

All variables are as defined previously except for B, which can be regarded as a lump-sum grant from the government to the taxpayer (Cowell incorporates B in order to introduce an element of progressivity into a linear tax schedule).

If we accept Cowell's formulation of the problem then the comparative static properties of his model can be found quite simply from equations (5.11) and (5.12) above. The ones that are of particular interest to us are the effects of tax and penalty changes, alterations in wage rates and a change in the probability of detection. These results are summarised in Table 5.2.

Table 5.2   Comparative static results in Cowell's model

Of a change in	Effect upon labour supplied to the black economy	
	(a) No hours restriction	*(b)* With an hours restriction
Tax rate (θ)	$> 0^1$	$> 0^3$
Penalty rate (π)	< 0	?[4]
Wage rate in the official economy (W_R)	$< 0^1$	$< 0^3$
Wage rate in the black economy (W_B)	$> 0^2$	?
Probability of detection (p)	< 0	?[4]

[1] requires decreasing absolute risk-aversion, increasing relative risk-aversion and a backward-bending or vertical labour-supply curve.

[2] requires decreasing absolute risk-aversion and increasing relative risk-aversion.

[3] requires leisure to be a superior good.

[4] < 0 if labour supply is upward-sloping, but > 0 if labour supply is backward-bending.

The difference between the columns headed *(a)* and *(b)* in Table 5.2 is that the results in *(a)* are derived from a model in which individuals are free to choose both H_R and H_B without restraint. In column *(b)* the results are for a model in which the hours worked in the official economy (H_R) are fixed (a special case of which is complete specialisation in the black economy, i.e. $H_R = 0$). Of course, in the latter model there is no need for separability of the utility function as there is only one work/leisure margin around which decisions can be made.

It is clear, therefore, that separability in Cowell's sense is quite useful in helping to sign derivatives. However, even then, signing requires further strong assumptions (for example about relative risk-aversion) and considerable empirical knowledge (is the labour-supply curve backward-bending?).

5.3   SOME CRITICISMS AND DEVELOPMENTS OF THE ECONOMIC MODEL

The models presented in sections 5.1 and 5.2 have a number of important common features that are worth exploring in rather more detail. First, individuals are assumed to be basically amoral utility maximisers. If an opportunity for successful evasion opens up they will leap at the chance to underdeclare their income or do a bit of moonlighting on the side. Casual observation suggests that not all individuals behave in quite this fashion. Indeed, Skinner and Slemrod (1985) argue that whilst the odds are heavily stacked in favour of evaders getting away with it the vast majority of taxpayers behave honestly. Skinner and Slemrod claim that this requires us to believe either that taxpayers exhibit a remarkable degree of risk-aversion or that they attach a considerable disutility to dishonest behaviour. They claim that the former is unrealistic and the latter does not fit into the subjective expected utility approach. However, this section shows that by incorporating psychic costs (or stigmas) directly into the utility function we can explain the case of the honest taxpayer perfectly well by the expected utility model. This approach is based upon an earlier insight into criminal behaviour made by Block and Heineke (1975) and has been developed by authors such as Benjamini and Maital (1985) and Gordon (1987).

Second, the models discussed so far assume that individuals have perfect knowledge about all the factors influencing their decision. In particular they are assumed to be perfectly informed about the tax rate, the probability of being caught and the penalty if found guilty. This seems most unlikely. For example, the results of a questionnaire issued to North American students by Benjamini and Maital (1985) shows that individuals tend to *under*estimate both the probability of being audited by the Internal Revenue Service and the marginal income-tax rate. We consider below an attempt to incorporate imperfections in knowledge into a formal model of individual taxpayer behaviour.

Finally, existing models treat individuals as 'pricetakers' whose decisions, taken in isolation from one another, have no impact upon the chances of their being caught, the punishment if caught, and so on. Obviously this too is 'being economical with the truth', to use a well-known phrase. Within limits, it may be a realistic description of the situation facing the individual taxpayer. However, one can envisage situations in which an individual's action – e.g. on how much income to declare to the tax authority – could significantly influence the tax authority's decision to instigate an audit. I do not investigate models of taxpayer–tax-authority interaction in this chapter, but will do so in Chapter 8, where the policy implications of income-tax evasion are considered. However I will examine the interaction between taxpayers themselves. As will become apparent in Chapter 6, there is some evidence that individuals are more likely to evade paying their taxes if they know that other people are also evading. The models of taxpayer behaviour discussed above assume that each taxpayer makes his/her decision about how much income to declare in total isolation from other taxpayers. Work by Benjamini and Maital (1985), Schlicht (1985) and Gordon (1987) has recently produced models in which taxpayers' decisions are interdependent and these models are briefly examined next.

(a)   Tax evasion and social stigma

The first question to answer is why do some individuals declare all their income to the tax authority even though the expected monetary rewards from underdeclaration may be considerable. In the notation of Allingham and Sandmo's model the expected penalty ($p\pi$) can be less than the standard rate of income tax (θ) and still individuals choose to declare all their income, i.e. $W = X$.

Recently, Benjamini and Maital (1985) have offered one solution to this conundrum. They suggest that underreporting of income may entail a considerable cost for the taxpayer – the social stigma that (s)he would suffer from behaving dishonestly. The 'stigma cost' (or psychic cost) is incorporated into the utility function by assuming that the utility function is additively separable,[14] i.e.

$$U = U(Y) - V(X)$$

where Y is net income (e.g. $W - \theta X$ if not caught) and X is income declared to the tax authority. If $X=W$ then $V(X) = 0$, otherwise $V(X) = \bar{V}$, i.e. stigma costs are fixed and accordingly independent of the extent of evasion. Only when all income is declared will stigma costs be avoided.

As stigma costs are fixed in this model the first- and second-order conditions for an interior optimum are, of course, unaffected. However, the 'entry' condition becomes tighter. It is not sufficient that the net financial gain be positive, i.e. $\theta - p\pi > 0$. It must now be large enough to offset the stigma cost of becoming a tax-evader. It is an implicit assumption of Benjamini and Maital that there is a substantial number of individuals for whom this is precisely the case.[15] As a result they get 'stuck' at a corner and refuse to evade. The importance of corner solutions like this is that they are relatively sticky. It may take significant changes in tax and other policy parameters to induce a change in the behaviour of individuals who are located at such points.

Consider, for example, an increase in the tax rate. Suppose that $p\pi < \theta$. In an Allingham–Sandmo world in which taxpayers have no social conscience and in which penalties are levied on evaded *tax* (following Yitzhaki) then a rise in the income-tax rate will encourage individuals to declare more of their income to the tax authority (the explanation of this rather odd result has been given in section 5.1). However, in a Benjamini–Maital world inhabited by both honest taxpayers and dishonest ones the result is quite different. Certainly for those who are evading anyway the 'Yitzhaki result' still holds, but it does not do so for the non-evaders. A marginal rise in the tax rate may at first do little. However, if the rise is sufficient to drive the expected net financial gain from evasion above the stigma cost of becoming an evader then some honest taxpayers will have been driven to become tax-evaders. If this group is sufficiently large the aggregate effect will be an increase in tax evasion. This result accords much more with common sense and empirical evidence (see Chapter 6) than the now widely accepted Yitzhaki result. It has been recently reaffirmed by Gordon (1987) in a model with variable (but constant unit) stigma costs, which themselves vary across individuals.[16] So far, stigma costs have been incorporated only into models in which income is exogenously determined. This suggests an avenue for further development of the idea.

(b) Tax evasion with information uncertainty

Sproule (1985) has examined the effect on taxpayers' decisions about evasion when the available information about the parameters of the tax system is imperfect. In order to do this he utilises Isachsen and Strøm's model (in its more general form) in which both labour supply and declared income are endogenous variables. He has shown that when the tax rate is treated as a stochastic variable, then Isachsen and Strøm's entry conditions (see above) no longer hold. 'In general *the I–S condition for an interior solution is affected by the amount of information about the parameters of the tax system which is available to the decision-maker.* Therefore . . . the availability of information can be viewed as a factor which affects the decision to work in the hidden economy' (Sproule, 1985, p. 445).

He has also shown that the effects of a mean-preserving decrease in uncertainty concerning the tax rate will be different from the effects of mean-preserving reduction in uncertainty surrounding either the probability of detection or the penalty tax rate. His results here rest on two assumptions. These are that:

(i) regardless of the type of work – i.e. whether in the black economy or in the regular economy – work is an inferior good, i.e.

$$\frac{dH_k}{dY} \bigg| \quad < 0 \; k = R, B;$$

$$Y = E(Y)$$

(ii) the (expected) utility function exhibits

constant risk-aversion to concentration, i.e.:

$$\frac{dUYY}{dY} \bigg|_{dU = 0} = 0$$

Sproule argues that if these two assumptions hold then 'a Sandmo-type decrease in the uncertainty of the tax rate increases the optimal amount of time devoted to work in the visible economy [and] decreases the optimal amount of time devoted to work in the hidden economy' (ibid, p. 449). However, a similar decrease in uncertainty concerning either the detection rate or the penal tax rate 'increases the optimal amount of time devoted to the hidden economy [and] decreases the optimal amount of time devoted to the visible economy' (ibid, p. 450).

It would seem then that the effects of uncertainty, and particularly changes in the degree of uncertainty have quite different effects upon optimal tax-evasion behaviour depending upon which parameter of the tax system has been affected by changes in information. As yet there has been no further development along these lines.

(c) Interaction amongst tax-evaders

The models of sections 5.1 and 5.2 treat individuals as isolated decision-makers. However, it seems reasonable to expect that an individual's decision whether or not to evade paying taxes will be influenced by the extent of other people's evasion. If evasion is widespread (s)he might feel that it is only fair that (s)he evades too, whereas if few evade (s)he might feel the need to toe the line and declare all his/her earnings. In Chapter 6 I show that there is some evidence to support the hypothesis that an individual is more likely to engage in evasion if (s)he knows (or feels that others are also evading.

Benjamini and Maital (1985), Schlicht (1985) and Gordon (1987) have all recently tried to model this interaction betwen taxpayers. Benjamini and Maital suggest a utility function of the form,

$$U = (-B + AN) X + CN$$

where B is the stigma or psychic cost associated with evasion;

A is the decline in stigma for each *other* person who evades;

N is the number of other people who evade;

X takes the value of 0 if the individual does not evade, but 1 if (s)he does, and

C is the utility or disutility the individual obtains from each other person who evades. (Benjamini and Maital assume that $C > 0$ i.e. the individual derives a benefit from others' evasion!)

If the individual decides not to evade then utility is

$$U_0 = CN$$

On the other hand, if (s)he decides to evade utility will be

$$U_1 = -B + (A + C) N$$

Suppose that all individuals have identical utility functions (see Figure 5.1). If the norm is to declare one's income honestly then the model will have a stable solution with $X = 0$ and $N = 0$. Given the expectation that no one else will cheat I cannot improve my welfare by cheating. In fact I suffer a utility loss of B (stigma). However, suppose there is a change in expectations and some people start to

Figure 5.1   Utility functions with taxpayer interdependence

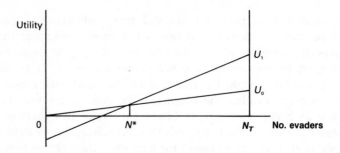

cheat. So long as this number is less than N^* the equilibrium will eventually be returned to $N = 0$, because for any number of evaders $0 < N < N^*$ the utility is higher for everyone if they do not cheat. If, however, the number of evaders goes above N^* then everyone will be better off if they cheat and the model generates another stable outcome in which $N = N_T$ (the whole taxpayer population). The equilibrium at $N = N^*$ is clearly unstable.

As Benjamini and Maital conclude, '(t)his model suggests that "incremental" anti-evasion policies may be ineffectual, if an "everyone evades" norm has been established. On the other hand, success is reducing evasion to less than N^* makes further anti-evasion efforts unnecessary' (Benjamini and Maital, 1985, p. 254). We examine policy implications in more detail in Chapter 8.

An alternative formulation by Schlicht (1985) suggests that a stable outcome between zero and N_T evaders is possible. Suppose that we can measure an individual's adherence to the tax laws by a parameter a_i which lies in the range zero to one. Zero denotes total dishonesty, and one, total honesty (honesty could be measured by the proportion of total income declared to the tax authority). Each individual chooses his/her optimal a_i along the lines suggested in section 5.1, except that psychic costs are now taken into account.

Schlicht suggests that:

$$a_i = f^i\,(a, e) \text{ with } f^i_a > 0 \; f^i_e > 0$$

where a is the average degree of tax evasion in the economy as a
        whole
and e is an externally fixed economic incentive (e.g. tax rate, penalty
        rate etc)

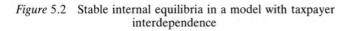

Figure 5.2   Stable internal equilibria in a model with taxpayer
interdependence

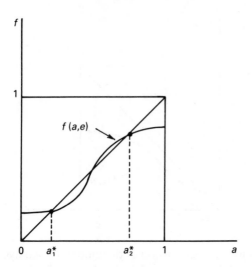

Averaging over all individuals we obtain:[17]

$$\bar{a} = f(a, e)$$

Schlicht argues that a plausible shape of the function $f(a,e)$ is that given in Figure 5.2. If we assume some kind of error-adjustment mechanism,[18] then it is clear that two stable internal equilibria (a_1 and a_2) are depicted in Figure 5.2.

However, suppose that there is initially a high degree of morality, so that the actual equilibrium is a_2^*. Suddenly there is a change in incentives (e.g. a tax increase) which causes some individuals to transgress. The whole function $f(a,e)$ shifts downwards. If it shifts far enough the equilibrium could move all the way to a_1^* (see Figure 5.3).

Gordon (1987) has tried to marry the approach of Benjamini and Maital with that of Schlicht. This model produces a number of different outcomes – e.g. polar equilibria, internal stable and unstable equilibria, etc. Which situation will prevail depends largely upon the relative sizes of stigma- and reputation-costs relative to the pecuniary rewards from tax evasion. The model also generates some interesting predictions about the effects of changes in tax rates, penalty rates and the probability of detection.

Figure 5.3   A unique internal equilibrium in a model with interdependent
taxpayers

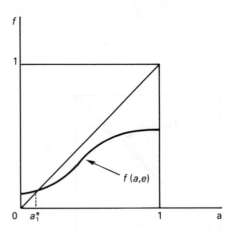

In some senses this discussion of the models of taxpayer interaction
is going beyond the concerns of this particular chapter and is straying
into issues of anti-evasion policy. However, these models clearly
show that the growth of the black economy weakens the rule of tax
law and generates a further spread of the 'disease'. Accordingly, it
may be dangerous to draw conclusions from models which treat the
individual taxpayer as someone whose decisions are taken entirely
independently of other taxpayers.

5.4   CONCLUSIONS

The theoretical models of tax evasion have been considerably developed over the last few years. At the same time some of the clarity of
the comparative static predictions arising from earlier models has
tended to evaporate. In some ways it is an example of 'the more we
understand the less we know'. No doubt further theoretical advances
will be made, but it is not clear that this is all that is required. As
Pencavel has so rightly argued 'this literature requires . . . a healthy
infusion of empirical work to confront these hypotheses with actual
behaviour and to resolve the ambiguities' (Pencavel, 1979, p. 124).
This is the task of Chapter 6. However, empirical work is not that
easy to perform.

6 Participation in the Black Economy: Evidence

Chapter 5 showed that on the whole economic theory cannot provide totally unambiguous predictions concerning the effects of many of the factors thought to influence involvement in the black economy. Even if it could do so, the design of policy towards tax evasion requires more than just qualitative predictions. It requires precise estimates of elasticities and these can only be obtained by rigorous empirical testing. However, whilst there is now a healthy and growing literature concerned with the theoretical modelling of tax evasion, the number of empirical studies aimed at testing these models is still few indeed.

This should not come as a surprise. The paucity of studies in this area is not at all symptomatic of a lack of interest in the subject. It merely reflects the absence of good data upon which tests can be performed. By its very nature tax evasion means (successfully) hiding taxable income from the tax authority. Therefore, it is fairly obvious that accurate statistics on the true extent of tax evasion simply do not exist. At best all that is available to work from are estimates based upon the approaches outlined in Chapters 2–4 and results of relatively small, possibly non-random examinations of taxpayers' affairs. In some respects the empirical analysis of tax evasion faces problems similar to those confronting econometric studies of crime. The difference is that the data problems facing researchers into evasion are even more daunting. At least there are only a finite number of reasons for failing to declare crime. There are *no* reasons for declaring tax evasion!

Faced by these difficulties, research into the determinants of evasion (and participation in the black economy) has followed three broad fronts. First, analysis of sample surveys of taxpayers' attitudes to taxation and involvement in tax evasion. Second, experimental tax games in which participants are given information on income, tax rates, conviction rates and penalties for evasion and are then asked to file a tax return. Third and finally, there has been a limited number of econometric analyses, mostly of samples of individual income-tax returns. We examine some of these studies below. (The dividing lines between what we have labelled as econometric analyses and surveys and experimental evidence is not a precise one.)

111

There have been few attempts to relate macro measures of the size of the black economy (obtained by the methods outlined in Chapters 2–4) to variables such as tax rates, sanctions measures, income and so on. One exception has been Matthews (1984) who regressed the initial residual difference between the income and expenditure measures of GDP on the average tax rate (this work has been discussed in Chapter 4). Another is Crane and Nourzad (1986) who use an aggregate measure of unreported income (the gap between the Bureau of Economic Analysis's and the Internal Revenue Service's estimates of adjusted gross income). This study is examined in section 6.3.

Estimates of the size of the black economy obtained by monetary methods cannot in general be used to test theories of participation in the black economy, for the simple reason that they are usually obtained on the assumption that the tax rate is positively related to the size of the black economy. Quite clearly the resulting estimates cannot then be used to test for the influence of the tax rate upon the extent of tax evasion.

6.1   SURVEYS OF TAXPAYERS' ATTITUDES

Studies of this kind are broadly similar. They usually take the form of a questionnaire issued to a relatively small and possibly non-random sample of the population. The questionnaire is an attempt to discover what individuals think about the tax system – e.g. whether they consider that tax rates are too high, whether they feel that they are paying more tax than others of similar income, whether they feel that small or large scale evasion by others is fair, and so on.

Of course, the responses to questionnaires of any kind should be treated with the utmost caution and questionnaires relating to possible tax evasion are probably more suspect than most. For example, would tax-evaders bother to respond? If they did, would they answer truthfully? Are respondents consistent? Can the results of a questionnaire issued to a very small and possibly biased sample of the population tell us anything about the population at large?

Obviouly there are good reasons for treating surveys of this kind with some caution. Despite this, they do provide some interesting and possibly useful information for other, more rigorous analyses. With this cautionary note very much in mind I will briefly examine several attitudinal surveys of this kind.

Song and Yarbrough conducted a sample survey of 640 households in North Carolina in 1975.[1] Only 287 questionnaires (i.e. 45 per cent) were successfully completed and returned. The questionnaire attempted to explore both attitudinal and behavioural aspects of tax ethics.

Respondents were asked to agree or disagree with a list of seven statements designed to 'measure their ethical predisposition toward tax obligations' (Song and Yarbrough, 1978, p. 444). Responses were marked on a range from zero to four. Typical statements were 'Since tax-dodging hurts no one but the government, it is not a serious offence' and 'In dealing with the Internal Revenue Service (IRS) the main thing is not to get caught' (ibid, p. 444).

Scores for the statements were then summed and converted to a percentage. Song and Yarbrough asserted that 'scores higher than 50 indicate(d) positive tax ethics and scores below 50 indicate(d) negative tax ethics' (ibid, p. 444) Using this somewhat arbitrary division the authors found that '(*a*) little over two-thirds of the respondents revealed positive tax ethics, one-fifth had negative tax ethics and the rest exhibited neutral tax ethics'[2] (ibid, p. 444) They conclude that 'American tax ethics receive a score, in our judgement, of "barely passing"' (ibid, p. 445).

Analysis of the responses to individual questions shows that whilst the vast majority of the sample (i.e. 88 per cent) regarded tax dodging as a crime, they did not feel that they had an obligation to report tax-cheaters to the authorities (only 30 per cent of respondents felt that they had such an obligation). Further, nearly one-half of respondents (i.e. 48 per cent) felt that they were under no obligation to volunteer information to the tax authority when their own affairs were being audited.

It appears that, whilst most people feel that the tax laws should be obeyed, they do not regard violations as serious crime meriting a severe punishment. As Song and Yarbrough state 'the typical tax-payer apparently considers tax evasion only slightly more serious than stealing a bicycle' (ibid, p. 445).[3]

Song and Yarbrough avoided asking respondents whether they had violated tax laws, but instead asked them to guess what proportion (most, some, a few, etc.) of others committed acts such as not reporting some income, padding expenses and so on. Whilst the vast majority (90 per cent) of respondents felt that few individuals would be foolish enough not to make a tax return, nearly three-quarters felt that some or most people inflate their expenses and 64 per cent felt that some or most people did not report all of their income. Interestingly those who were inclined to believe that others were capable of cheating tended to have low scores for tax ethics, although the correlation was not particularly strong ($R = -0.27$).

Simple correlations between scores for tax ethics and various socio-economic, demographic and other variables were also undertaken. These showed that individuals with high levels of income and education exhibited a high level of tax ethics. However, people who generally distrusted others, felt alienated, or felt that local politicians/officials would not listen to them generally had low scores on tax ethics. An interesting relationship between age and tax ethics was found. Those under 40 and over 65 years of age had low scores, whereas those aged 40 to 65 had high scores. Finally, whites had higher scores than blacks and married people outscored others.

Respondents were generally satisfied that the tax system was fair. Three-quarters thought that taxation should be based upon ability to pay and only one in five thought they paid more tax than others in similar circumstances.[4] Despite this there was considerable disenchantment with the federal income tax, largely it seems because the burden was felt to be borne by the middle class!

There must be some doubt about the value of this research, particularly that relating to attitudes to tax ethics. The scoring of responses seems somewhat subjective, to say the least and the division between 'positive' and 'negative' attitudes highly dubious. Nevertheless, some of the responses are illuminating.

Lewis (1979) conducted a similar survey amongst 200 male taxpayers in Bath (UK) in 1977. Again, the sample was somewhat unrepresentative of the population at large containing more old people, fewer manual workers and more Conservative voters.

The questionnaire consisted of sixteen 'Likert' attitude statements with responses measured on a five-point scale.[5] The statements (grouped into eight pairs) concerned both tax avoidance and evasion. We concentrate upon the responses to statements concerning evasion. In addition there were statements about the fairness of progressive taxation, the function of the tax system and about amounts paid in tax.[6]

Respondents generally disapproved of *large-scale* tax evasion and thought that tax evaders should be treated harshly by the law (85+%). However, responses concerning small-scale evasion were less clear-cut. High-income earners, the middle class and the old generally felt that small-scale evasion should be treated fairly leniently. On the whole respondents believed that a reduction in taxation would have little effect upon the extent of evasion.[7]

It seems that people in the sample did *not* regard income taxation as an imposition, but as a necessary means of paying for essential services.[8] Nevertheless, the majority felt that their own contribution was unreasonably large (53.5 per cent of respondents felt this). This was particularly noticeable amongst higher income groups who felt that progressive income taxation was unfair.

Lewis claimed that the survey supported the view that attitudes to income taxation depend quite critically upon income. He observed that 'people with higher incomes . . . have less favourable attitudes towards income taxation yet are happy to go along with it provided there are adequate avenues for tax avoidance and evasion' (Lewis, 1979, p. 253) Further, he argued that 'the "exchange" model of tax mentality is not a central part of respondents' cognitive field . . . To say that tax mentality is based mainly on self-interest is perhaps too strong, yet it is something akin to this . . . (M)ost people consider their individual contributions too large, a feeling most apparent among higher income earners' (ibid, p. 254–5). This feeling to some extent echoes one found by Song and Yarbrough amongst taxpayers in Carolina.

Finally, this section analyses the results of a questionnaire completed by 424 adults in Fife (Scotland) in 1977 (Dean, Keenan and Kenney, 1980). Respondents to this survey were all attending adult education classes which makes them distinctly unrepresentative (e.g. a heavy overrepresentation of middle-aged and middle class). The response rate was 76 per cent, which may be partly because of the kind of people approached, but perhaps also because the researchers refrained from asking questions about income and political affinities.

The vast majority of respondents (93 per cent) thought that 'income tax in this country is (much/a little) too high' whilst a substantial proportion (i.e. 62 per cent) did not think that 'the Government spends taxpayers' money wisely'. On this latter point many thought there was evidence of considerable waste and inefficiency in the public sector, which combined with what they regarded as incorrect spending priorities, caused dissatisfaction. In addition, many respondents felt that they were paying too much in income tax compared with other people, even when compared with those on similar incomes. This opinion was most strongly held by the older members of the group.

This feeling of unequal treatment is strange in view of the way that the British tax system is reputed to treat like individuals in a like manner. Dean *et al.* speculated that this might have been because respondents 'were . . . conscious of other people's tax evasions' (Dean *et al.*, 1980, p. 36).

The survey also included questions concerning perceptions of opportunities for evasion and it is interesting that more than a quarter of respondents thought that all or most taxpayers could get away with failing to declare a small part of their income to the tax authority. Another quarter thought that about one-half of taxpayers had such opportunities. However, few thought that taxpayers could get away with large-scale evasion (only 3.6 per cent thought that all or most taxpayers could get away with failing to declare a very large part of their income).[9]

Respondents took a relatively dim view of the morality of their fellow-people. Two-thirds thought that all or most taxpayers would exploit an opportunity for small-scale evasion if they thought that they could get away with it. Likewise, nearly a quarter of respondents thought that all or most taxpayers would attempt large-scale evasion if they felt that it would go undetected. This 'lack of faith' in others was most noticeable amongst the young and the lower occupational groups.

However, rather like the groups surveyed in Carolina and Bath, this group did not appear to exhibit strong moral objections to evaders who practise small-scale evasion. Less than 37 per cent of respondents felt that failing to declare a small part of income was either 'quite bad' or 'very bad'. Unfortunately, Dean *et al.* failed to examine whether members of their sample held stronger views about large-scale evasion. Presumably they did.

Unlike previous surveys Dean *et al.* did ask respondents to offer reasons why 'people decide to evade tax'. The most popular single reason (given by more than 25 per cent of the respondents) was that the general level of taxation was considered too high. A further 10 per cent of the sample thought that the tax system was generally unfair. Significant numbers (about one-third) suggested economic motives such as 'greed', 'poverty or financial hardship' or 'other financial pressures'.

The researchers concluded that 'there is a pent-up demand for safe evasions . . . and . . . moral considerations do not always weigh heavily as an inhibiting force, particularly where small amounts of tax are involved' (Dean *et al.*, 1980, p. 44).

So far relatively little has emerged about the factors leading people to engage in acts of evasion. More importantly none of the specific hypotheses developed in Chapter 5 have been rigorously tested. Several studies which also used sample survey methods to obtain information about evasion, but which have gone one stage further than those already encountered will now be considered. These have tried to establish the reasons for 'admitted' tax evasion by relating statistically measures of evasion to measures of certainty and severity of punishment, socio-economic and demographic characteristics and so on.

One such study was undertaken by Spicer and Lundstedt (1976) in Central Ohio. It was aimed at isolating factors which affected individual's decisions to evade tax. Their sample consisted of 130 upper- and middle-income heads of households taken from two suburbs in large metropolitan areas. In an attempt to ensure that responses were as truthful as possible they did not inform participants that the study was concerned with tax evasion. Further, like all previous surveys they guaranteed anonymity to all respondents.

Spicer and Lundstedt were concerned to test a number of specific hypotheses about evasion. First, did certainty and severity of punishment deter potential evaders? Second, did taxpayers' (dis)satisfaction with the bundle of government services and taxes influence their decision to evade? Finally, were individuals persuaded to engage in evasion by knowing someone who had got away with tax evasion?

They began by using a questionnaire aimed at measuring individuals' propensity to evade taxes and collecting other socio-economic and demographic information relevant to the study. They then constructed two indices – first, a measure of tax resistance, and second, an index of tax evasion.[10] The scores of the individuals for each of these two indices were then regressed against a number of socio-economic variables such as age, education, whether or not the respondent was self-employed, severity of punishment, taxpayer satisfaction with government services and acquaintance with tax-evaders.[11]

Unfortunately, the regression results were rather mixed. Both equations had poor fits (at least when measured by R^2) and t-statistics were often insignificant, especially for the deterrence variables. Of these only the probability of punishment was significant in the tax-resistance regression equation. On the other hand, the variables measuring taxpayer satisfaction with government services and acquiantance with evaders were found to be significant. Older people were found to be less resistant to tax, as were those with higher incomes. However, this latter result may simply reflect the possibility that the rich had more opportunities to *avoid* tax. Individuals who had had some experience with tax audits tended to be both more resistant to income tax and more likely to engage in evasion.

Mason and Calvin (1984) report the results of a survey of some 800 taxpayers in Oregon, undertaken originally in 1975 and repeated in 1980. They found that between the two interview dates there had been a slight increase in the proportion of respondents who admitted to some form of evasion[12] At the same time the proportion of the sample who said that they thought that the tax system was fair dropped from 71 per cent to 56 per cent. In addition, by 1980 respondents thought that the chances of being caught for evasion were less than they had been in 1975. Finally, the proportion of respondents who felt that people cheated on their taxes because taxes are too high rose from 48 per cent to 64 per cent between sample years.

Mason and Calvin used logit analysis on a pooled sample of approximately 1400 observations to test the effects more vigorously. They found that fear of apprehension exerted a statistically significant deterrent effect and that those with larger incomes were less likely to engage in evasion. However, views about the fairness of the tax system seemed to have no effect upon whether an individual evaded or not. Clearly fear of being caught was keeping the majority of taxpayers in line. However, it was noticeable that a vastly increased proportion of the dissatisfied but honest taxpayers blamed too high taxes for others' transgressions. Their group could eventually become tax-dodgers if 'compliance norms are negated and sanction fear weakened' (Mason and Calvin, 1984, p. 494).

Yet a substantial majority of the sample were honest and a small majority thought the tax system was fair. This was sufficient for Mason and Calvin to advocate the use of positive rather than negative incentives for upholding the law – e.g. appeals to conscience.

Geeroms and Wilmots (1985) have attempted to remove some of the ambiguities of the theoretical literature (see Chapter 5) by means of a questionnaire answered by some 300 people in Belgium. A rather (unnecessarily?) complicated simultaneous equation model is suggested which links individuals' attitudes to evasion (and avoidance) to various socio-psychological and economic determinants. The former set of explanatory variables includes factors such as belief in the law and the attitude of the individual's reference group towards tax evasion. The latter set includes things such as the perceived certainty and severity of punishment, attitude towards risk, the individual's marginal tax rate and knowledge of tax law.[13]

Regression results indicate that whilst the probability of detection exerts a significant negative (deterrent?) effect upon attitude towards tax evasion, the size of the fine does not. Also, Geeroms and Wilmots could find no evidence to support the hypothesis that higher tax rates led to more evasion. Indeed, the sign of the regression coefficient was negative. However, one cannot place too much emphasis upon the findings of Geeroms and Wilmots. There is first of all much *ad hoc* theorising (the 'model' has no fewer than eleven endogeous variables). Second, few of the variables have been precisely defined and little is said about how exactly they have been measured.

Finally, Isachsen, Klovland and Strøm (1982) have used survey data to estimate labour 'supply' functions for the black economy. Data on hours worked in the black economy, marginal tax rates, penalty rates, probability of detection and wage rates in both the regular and black economies were collected in a survey of some 877 people in Norway in 1980. In addition, various socio-economic and demographic variables were included in the regression equations. Unfortunately, results were poor. For example, '(i)n the case of females no coefficients are different from zero at acceptable levels' (Isachsen *et al.*, 1982, p. 218). And in the case of males 'only the coefficient associated with the [subjective] probability of detection is significant' (ibid, p. 218). This coefficient suggests that a 1 per cent increase in the probability of detection reduces hours worked in the black economy by about 2 per cent.

6.2 EXPERIMENTAL TAX GAMES

This section discusses three tax 'games' played under experimental conditions by relatively small numbers of individuals. The first carried out by Friedland, Maital and Rutenberg (1978) examined the effect upon evasion of factors such as the tax rate and the certainty and severity of punishment. The second reported by Spicer and Becker (1980) examined the relationship between tax evasion and perceived inequities in the tax system. Finally, a third game reported by Spicer and Hero (1985) examined the link between levels of evasion and perceptions of evasion by others.

The rules of the games were basically similar. Participants were asked to supply certain personal information – e.g. age, sex, occupation, etc. They were then told about the game they were about to play. The game lasted a specific number of rounds. In each round every participant was told what his/her income was during that time-period. S/he was also given information about (i) tax rates, (ii) the probability of being audited in any time period, (iii) the punishment if s/he was caught for evading tax and so on. So that participants took the experiment seriously small money prizes were paid to those who achieved the highest net income at the end of the game.

Friedland *et al*'s sample consisted of fifteen Israeli psychology students with an average age of 25 years. They each played the game for four rounds of 10 'months' per round. At the end of each round researchers calculated for each individual:

(i) the number of times (out of 10) that income was under-declared;
(ii) the average fraction of income not reported for months in which underdeclarations occurred;
(iii) the overall fraction of income declared.

They found that when the tax rate was increased from 25 per cent to 50 per cent the probability of underreporting rose dramatically from about 0.5 to about 0.8. When the fine was increased from three times to fifteen times the amount of tax evaded the probability of an underdeclaration fell, but only marginally.[14] Similar results were found for the overall fraction of income declared. An increase in the tax rate (from 25 per cent to 50 per cent) caused overall declarations to fall from 87.4 per cent (79.6 per cent) to 66.4 per cent (56.5 per cent).[15]

Friedland *et al*. regressed these measures of the probability and extent of underreporting upon the tax rate, the size of fine and various socio-economic/demographic variables.[16] The single most important factor influencing evasion was the tax rate. Age and sex tended to influence the extent of underdeclarations (younger participants and women declared less). Also, married people were less likely to underdeclare and when they did behave in this way, they underdeclared less. However, few other variables proved to be significant and the equations explained only a small part of the variation in the dependent variable (R^2 was approximately 0.4).

An almost identical approach was used by Spicer and Becker (1980) to examine the link between tax evasion and perceived inequity in tax treatment. They recruited fifty-seven students from the University of Colorado to play the Friedland–Maital–Rutenberg tax game over a period of 10 'months'. The difference between Spicer and Becker's game and Friedland *et al*'s game was that participants in the later game were fed erroneous information on the tax rates being levied upon other individuals playing the game. All individuals were told that they would pay tax at a rate of 40 per cent. However, one-third were told that the average tax rate was 65 per cent and another third were told that the average tax rate was 15 per cent. The remaining one third were told the truth.

The effect upon declarations was quite noticeable. Those who thought that they were paying more tax than others evaded nearly 33 per cent of taxes payable, whilst those who thought they were paying less evaded only about 12 per cent. Those who knew the truth evaded approximately 25 per cent of tax.[17]

Regression analysis using the percentage of taxes evaded as the dependent variable did not reveal any other influences, except that men were more likely than women to underdeclare. Of course, variables such as age and income would be unlikely to show much variation across this particular sample and so negative results in this case should not be given too much importance.

Spicer and Hero (1985) report a similar game played by thirty-six University of Colorado psychology undergraduates. The object was to examine the link between levels of evasion and (i) perceptions of other people's evasion, and (ii) previous experience of being audited. The game was played along identical lines to those previously examined, except that individuals were now given (incorrect) information about levels of evasion in previous plays of the game. Twelve participants were told that in a previous playing of the game participants had revealed only 10 per cent of taxes due, twelve were told that previous participants had paid 50 per cent of taxes due and the remaining twelve were told that previous players had paid 90 per cent of taxes.

Statistical analysis revealed that this information did not significantly affect the students' evasion decisions. However, Spicer and Hero found that men tended to evade more taxes than women. They also found that the amount of taxes evaded in the last round of the game was strongly and positively correlated with the level of evasion in the first round of the game and that the number of (random) audits had a significant, negative effect upon tax evasion in the last round.

6.3   ECONOMETRIC STUDIES

The studies discussed so far have not examined the amounts of income that individuals actually declare for tax purposes. The surveys discussed in section 6.1 were concerned with eliciting either information about individuals' willingness to evade tax, or confessions of previous acts of evasion. The danger with the experimental approach examined in section 6.2 is that individuals might act quite differently in a game from the way they would in real life. After all, it is one thing to act illegally when the punishment is a 'paper fine', but quite another when the punishment is a real one. In addition, the audit probabilities and fines may be quite different in experimental situations from what they would be in reality.

For various reasons then it is preferable to examine how individuals really behave. In other words we would like to analyse a sample of income-tax returns. In the past few years a small number of econometric studies of individuals' income-tax returns have been published and these studies will be examined. In addition, there have emerged several econometric analyses of aggregate tax returns and these will be discussed too.

For example, Mork (1975) examined the relationship between underdeclarations and 'true' income in Norway in 1970. For this he used two data sources. First, interview data from the Norwegian Occupational Life History Study in which respondents were asked, among other things, to state their income. Mork assumed that this was an acceptable measure of each individual's true income. Second, for each individual in the above survey income data was also obtained from their income-tax declaration. Mork found that for 'true' incomes in excess of 8000 Norwegian krone per year the proportion of income declared for tax declined as 'true' income increased. He attributed this finding to the existence of a progressive income-tax rate. Unfortunately, Mork did not attempt to estimate this relationship and so no formal statistical results are available.

A rather more rigorous statistical analysis has been undertaken by Clotfelter (1983), who examined the relationship between marginal tax rates and income-tax declarations using the actual returns of individuals. This data set came from the IRS's Taxpayer Compliance Measurement Programme (TCMP) survey for 1969 and includes tax returns on about 47 000 individuals.

Clotfelter measured underdeclared income as the difference between the amount of income which the IRS auditors determined was due and the amount actually reported by each individual. Of course, this difference might also contain some 'honest", i.e. mistaken, underdeclarations as well as deliberate evasion.[18] However, Clotfelter shows that if mistakes of under- and overdeclaration of income are randomly distributed across the population, then the vast majority of underreporting would appear to be deliberate (see Table 6.1).

Table 6.1   Reporting errors by audit class, USA, 1969

	Percentage of tax returns for which adjusted gross income (AGI) was	
	TOO LOW	*TOO HIGH*
AGI < $10 000		
Non-business	25.6	9.0
Non-farm business	67.4	7.5
Farm	66.0	11.3
AGI $10 000–$50 000		
Non-business	26.6	8.6
AGI $10 000–$30 000		
Non-farm business	58.0	9.5
Farm	63.5	12.4
AGI > $50 000		
Non-business	39.7	8.6
AGI > $30 000		
Non-farm business	63.4	7.6
Farm	56.5	10.6

Source   Clotfelter (1983)

The dependent variable used in Clotfelter's analysis is the logarithm of underdeclared income. However, because for many individuals underreported income is zero, the equations were estimated using the Tobit maximum likelihood procedure.[19] Explanatory variables included:

(i)   the logarithm of after-tax income;
(ii)   the individual's marginal tax rate;
(iii)   wages as a proportion of true gross income;
(iv)   interest and dividends as a proportion of true gross income;
(v)   dummy variables for marital status, age, region and those having to return four or more tax forms.

Separate analyses were performed by type of return and audit class (i.e. by type and level of income, etc.).

Notable omissions from Clotfelter's list of explanatory variables are any measures of the probability of detection and severity of punishment. He argued that it was inappropriate to include such measures because of possible simultaneity bias.[20] However, if there *is* a simultaneous relationship between evasion and sanctions variables, it is totally inappropriate simply to exclude the sanctions variables from the estimating equation. This merely introduces specification error. The correct approach is to build a simultaneous equation model, ensuring that the various equations are identified. At one point he seems to suggest that the proportions of income obtained from (i) wages and salaries, and (ii) interest and dividends, are measures of the detection rate. This is presumably because withholding is quite common for these sources of income. However, this seems to reflect opportunities for evasion rather than the effect of sanctions.[21]

Clotfelter's main findings were that underreporting increased with both the after-tax income, and the marginal tax rate. The elasticity of underreporting with respect to income varied from 0.29 to 0.66 depending upon the type of tax return, whilst the elasticity with respect to the marginal tax rate ranged from 0.52 to 0.84. This latter finding led him to conclude that 'higher tax rates tend to stimulate tax evasion' (Clotfelter, 1983, p. 368).

Subsidiary findings were that where wages, interest and dividends formed a larger proportion of income then underreporting was less common. Greater complexity in returns (measured by more than four forms) is associated with lower reporting of non-business income, but not of business income. The performance of the age and marital status variables is mixed, significance varying across types of income and return. The regional variables are not discussed here.

Witte and Woodbury (1983, 1985) have attempted explicitly to test for the effects of sanctions variables on tax compliance. In order to do this they have used a data set provided by the Internal Revenue Service (IRS) which relates to 1969 tax returns filed in 1970. Unlike Clotfelter's data, however, these data are aggregated to the three-digit zip-code level.

The dependent variable in this study is an IRS measure of voluntary compliance, calculated following a series of audits of a stratified random sample of taxpayers for the 1969 TCMP. It is measured by the ratio of total taxes paid to the sum of total taxes paid and the absolute value of both tax overpayments and underpayments.[22]

A large selection of independent variables was used, including before-tax income, measures of the probability and severity of punishment,[23] a measure of return complexity, proxies for knowledge of tax laws, awareness of the IRS and attitude to government, various demographic variables such as age, education, race, ethnic origin, mobility, marital status and indices of unemployment, poverty, drop-outs and urbanisation.[24]

Separate regression equations were estimated by Zellner's seemingly unrelated regression (SUR) technique for each of seven audit classes (i.e. largely by income group in order to proxy the effects of different marginal tax rates and the gains from underreporting).[25] The equations were originally estimated separately and for *all* audit classes together by ordinary least squares (OLS) and a modified Chow test was used to test homogeneity of coefficients across equations. Homogeneity was strongly rejected. Tests of the covariance matrix of the equation residuals rejected the use of OLS and so the equations were then re-estimated using the SUR technique.

In the words of Witte and Woodbury, 'results are strong but differ markedly by audit class' (Witte and Woodbury, 1983, p. 16). The principal results are as follows. First, higher overall probabilities of audit are associated with higher compliance rates, except for low-income non-business taxpayers.[26] However, the effects of increased probability of civil and criminal sanctions are not as expected. Where these variables are significant (which is not often) they are generally associated with lower compliance rates.[27] It is possible that these variables have been poorly specified or more likely that there is some simultaneous equation bias present (see the above discussion of this in relation to Clotfelter's work). If the latter is true then the regression equation is picking up the effect of evasion activity upon sanctions variables rather than the reverse effect, which is the one that is being sought. In other words, groups with low compliance rates are being subjected to increased likelihood of punishment.

Second, increased average severity of prison sentences for criminal fraud generally increased compliance, although in only three cases is its coefficient significant. Third, *fear* of detection (measured by the proportion of taxpayers receiving warning notices) usually increased compliance, with its coefficient being significant for five of the seven audit classes. Fourth, the effect of income is complicated. Compliance rates are found to increase with income up to incomes of approximately $30 000 per year, but beyond that compliance rates begin to go down. This is true for all audit classes. Fifth, taxpayers with higher proportions of labour income in their total income are more likely to comply with tax regulations than those with higher proportions of non-labour income. This once again confirms that withholding increases compliance. Finally, the old are more likely to comply whilst the better educated, the poor and the unemployed are less likely to do so.[28]

Dubin, Graetz and Wilde (1987) have criticised Witte and Woodbury's estimates on a number of grounds. Their first criticism relates to Witte and Woodbury's inclusion of audit rates for 1969, 1968 and 1967 (both within audit class and for all other audit classes) in each regression equation. In their 1985 paper Witte and Woodbury report audit-rate elasticities which seem to have been obtained by summing across all six audit-rate coefficients. Dubin *et al.* argue that this may be partly responsible for some of the odd results reported by Witte and Woodbury. Dubin and Wilde further claim that some of the agency variables, e.g. audit rates, are 'likely to be endogenous so that their model is mis-specified' (Dubin *et al.*, 1987, p. 242). Certainly, the signs of some of the reported coefficients suggest the presence of simultaneous equations bias, as we suggested earlier.

Slemrod (1985) argues that the tax function is in reality made up of a series of steps rather than a continuously differentiable function and that in 1977 in the USA the step length was only $50 wide in terms of income (this seems amazingly narrow). He claims that as a result of this, tax-evaders will declare incomes which are bunched near the top of the $50 steps, but that non-evaders will have no such tendency.[29] He then uses the position of taxable income within the $50 bracket to construct an index of the presence of evasion. An individual's score on the index will range, therefore, from one (totally honest) to fifty (totally dishonest) with honesty diminishing (if such a thing is possible) as the score on the index increases.

The data used by Slemrod came from a 1977 stratified random sample of tax returns collected by the IRS. In all Slemrod uses data on some 23 111 individuals. He reports the results of a regression of his tax-evasion index on

  (i)   the individual's marginal tax rate;
 (ii)   adjusted gross income;
(iii)   various dummy variables for age, marital status and type of income.

These must constitute some of the worst regression results ever reported. Not a single variable is statistically significant and R^2 is approximately 0.8×10^{-3}. He concludes that Clotfelter's finding 'that marginal tax rates and evasion are positively correlated . . . cannot be confirmed' (Slemrod, 1985, p. 232).

However, even if we accept Slemrod's argument that an individual's position in the tax band indicates the presence of tax evasion, his method does not tell us anything about the extent of evasion by that individual. In that case his statistical results are of rather limited value.

At various points in this section we have queried the assumption that has been made by many investigators that enforcement activity undertaken by the tax authority (e.g. audit rates) can be treated as an exogenous variable. If it cannot, then empirical work based on the assumption that it is exogenous, must be seriously flawed. Dubin, Graetz and Wilde (1987) have used state-level data for the USA to estimate a simultaneous equation model of compliance and tax enforcement. The data comes from the *Annual Reports* of the Commissioner of Internal Revenue for 1977 to 1985.

The measure of 'evasion' used by Dubin *et al.* is the percentage return per audit for individual returns, i.e. the additional tax and penalties resulting from audits as a percentage of total tax collections. This measure is regressed on the lagged value of the audit rate (lagged one year) and a whole host of socio-economic and demographic variables, such as per capita income, the unemployment rate and the percentage of the audit population with high-school education.[30] A separate equation models the determination of the audit rate.[31]

Dubin *et al.*'s estimates suggest that '(1) the audit rate *is* an endogenous (variable) . . . (2) there *is* a deterrent effect associated with increases in the audit rate . . . and (3) compliance increases with per capita income, but at a decreasing rate, peaking below the maximum income. In addition, there is a significant negative time trend in the audit rate and in compliance' (Dubin *et al.*, 1987, pp. 243–4, my emphases).

Finally, this section reports two studies which have used aggregate measures of tax evasion. The first by Poterba (1987) examines the link between compliance and tax rates for capital gains in the USA between 1965 and 1982. The second by Crane and Nourzad (1986) tests for the effect of inflation upon aggregate tax evasion, measured by the gap between the Bureau of Economic Analysis's estimate of adjusted gross income and that reported by the IRS.

Poterba's work needs only a brief mention, as his results are based on only six observations. He uses an IRS estimate of the fraction of realised capital gains that are reported on tax returns to measure voluntary compliance. This is then regressed on a measure of the marginal tax rate on capital-gains income and a time trend. The estimates indicate a statistically significant negative effect of the tax rate upon compliance. However, given that many other factors have been ignored and that only six observations are available not too much can be read into this result.

Crane and Nourzad (1986) also report a significant impact of tax rates upon the extent of evasion, using a macro measure of the extent of unreported income. The tax rate is measured by a weighted average of marginal tax rates in each year's tax schedule, the weights being given by the percentage of total income in each tax bracket. Other explanatory variables are the audit rate, the fine rate, true income, the inflation rate, the share of wages and salaries in national income and a time trend.[32]

Two equations are estimated. The dependent variable in the first equation is the absolute amount of underreported income and in the second the proportion of income that is underreported. All coefficients are statistically significant, except for the audit rate in the second equation. The sanctions variables exert their expected deterrent effects, whilst both the tax rates and the inflation rate are positively related to evasion.[33] Again, a larger share of wages and salaries in income is associated with reduced evasion. The absolute amount of evasion increases with income, but the proportion of income not reported falls as income rises. Finally, the time trend is positive for absolute evasion but negative for relative evasion.

6.4   CONCLUSIONS

What can be reasonably concluded about the determinants of tax evasion? Of course, it is difficult to make sweeping generalisations because the amount of solid evidence is quite small and much empirical work yet needs to be done. Also, some of the studies examined above are based upon relatively small and/or possibly biased samples. Furthermore, they sometimes offer conflicting evidence.

Survey evidence would indicate that whilst the majority of taxpayers regard evasion as a crime, they do not feel that small-scale evasion should be treated harshly. In addition, there is a substantial number of taxpayers who are now somewhat disenchanted with the income-tax system. This is particularly true of middle-income groups, who seem to feel that a disproportionate share of the tax burden falls upon them.

It is difficult to generalise, but from what we have seen it would appear that at least some taxpayers see evasion as a 'legitimate' means of reducing what they consider to be the excessive demands of taxation. Evasion helps to offset some of the costs of a progressive tax system and in a world in which others are seen to be evading it offers a means of preserving both vertical and horizontal equity.

Certainly there is some econometric evidence to support the view that those on higher incomes and those paying higher marginal rates of income tax are less likely to comply with the tax laws than others.

Evidence of the impact of certainty and severity of punishment upon the extent of evasion is rather less clear-cut. Whilst the majority of evidence points to a significant deterrent effect of increases in the probability of detection/auditing, there is less evidence that more severe penalties act in the same way. This may be explained in some cases by misspecification of relationships and in others by possible measurement error. Finally, there is strong evidence that tax withholding has a substantial impact upon the extent of tax evasion.

The policy implications of these findings are examined in Chapter 8, but before then it is necessary to consider precisely what are the consequences of tax evasion. Only then can it be decided whether it is a socially undesirable activity which should be reduced or even eliminated. It is not immediately obvious that tax evasion is an economic and social catastrophe.

7 The Consequences of Tax Evasion and the Black Economy

So far two major issues have been examined. First, how large is the black economy? and second, what leads people to become involved in the black economy? It should be clear that economists have invested a great deal of effort to answering these questions. This chapter looks at the consequences of such illicit activity. So far, this is an area of the subject that has received much less attention, but there are signs that this may be changing.

One 'obvious' consequence of the existence and growth of the black economy is the loss of tax revenues for the government. The existence of this loss – and indeed whether there is one at all – is discussed in section 7.1. It turns out that it is not at all obvious how much the government's revenue is reduced by the existence of moderate evasion. If the 'extra' income of evaders is spent on buying goods and services produced by non-evaders then there may be little or no tax-revenue loss.

But, *why* should we worry about a loss of tax revenue? To some extent it depends upon what the revenue would have been used for and what effect taxing previously tax-evaded goods and services will have upon their supply. These issues are discussed in section 7.2.

It has been claimed by Feige (1979), for example, that the existence of widespread black-economy activity makes it much more difficult for the government to control the economy and even to recognise what is happening to the economy. The argument here is that because so much economic activity is not recorded, then statistics of, for example, gross domestic product, unemployment, growth and inflation are no longer reliable indicators of what is really happening. Feige even believes that the stagflation which occurred in the advanced industrial economies from the mid-1970s is, in fact, no more than a statistical illusion, which arises from relying upon a misleading set of economic statistics. The implications of the black economy for macroeconomic management are also examined in section 7.2.

Evasion has effects too upon the allocation of resources and these issues are considered in section 7.3. For example, the coexistence of a taxed and an untaxed sector means that initially at least net returns to factors will be greater in the untaxed sector. This will encourage a flow of resources from the taxed to the untaxed sector until net expected returns are equalised (except for risk premia required by factors working in the black economy). However, the gross return will be lower in the black economy and it is the gross return which reflects the (social) productivity of the factor (unless externalities arise). The upshot of this is that some resources are diverted into less efficient uses. In addition, the existence of tax evasion means that governments feel obliged to devote resources to tax-law enforcement and this in turn uses scarce resources and imposes costs upon the rest of society.

Finally, section 7.3 briefly considers the distributional consequences of both the existence of a black economy and government attempts to eliminate (or at least reduce) it. Obviously evasion could influence the distribution of post-tax incomes and could possibly thwart attempts by governments to achieve a desired distribution of income. This might well lead to injustices. However, we will also argue that the choice of anti-evasion policy might itself lead to distributional problems. This point is discussed in more detail in Chapter 8.

7.1 TAX-REVENUE LOSSES

The first and most obvious consequence of the existence of a black economy is that some income goes untaxed and also that certain indirect taxes, e.g. VAT, excise duties, etc., are also evaded.[1] It seems natural to conclude from this observation that tax revenues are lower than if everyone had paid their taxes. The standard approach to assessing the extent of tax losses (see, for example, Feige, 1981) has been as follows. First, an estimate of the size of the black economy has been obtained either by pure guesswork or by one of the methods outlined in Chapters 2–4. Second, tax-revenue losses have been estimated by assuming that a standard tax rate would have been paid upon this income had it been declared to the tax authority. For example, the Inland Revenue in evidence to the Keith Committee (1983) calculated the size of the UK's black economy in 1982 as approximately £15 billion per year. Assuming a constant income tax rate of, say, 30p in the £ this gives a tax loss of about £4–5 billion per annum.

Of course, it is possible that the Inland Revenue's estimate of the size of the black economy may be wildly inaccurate, so that this estimate of tax-revenue loss may be somewhat uncertain. For example, other estimates of tax-revenue losses in the UK range between £0.2 billion and £11 billion per year (see Pyle, 1987, p. 25). However, that is irrelevant to our present discussion. It is the *method* of calculating tax losses that is the issue here, rather than the particular estimate of their extent.

The assumptions of a constant effective tax rate could also be criticised. This gross simplification has usually been adopted simply because estimates of the size of the black economy do not generally distinguish between different sources of income and their distribution between different classes of income recipient. Obviously this introduces a further source of error, but it is not thought to be large in comparison with the uncertainty over the sheer size of the black economy.

Indirect taxes, such as VAT and excise duties, can be evaded too, but it is probably the case that income-tax evasion is of rather greater importance. For example, estimates by the UK Customs and Excise suggest VAT 'losses' of between £250m and £500m per year due to evasion, and the Driver and Vehicle Licensing Centre (DVLC) believes that motor-vehicle-tax evasion may be about £170m each year. These sums are dwarfed by the Inland Revenue's estimate of annual income-tax evasion of nearly £4000m.

However, most importantly, Peacock and Shaw (1982a, b, c) and Peacock (1983) argue that the method of calculating income-tax evasion described above has three major defects. First, it ignores the possibility that some goods and services are only produced in the black economy *because* they are not taxed. If they were, the amount of these goods would be less, because there would either be reduced demand or reduced supply or both.[2] Second, the method does not allow for the proceeds of the tax-evaded income being spent upon goods that are taxed or produced by people who pay their income tax. This gain in tax revenue will at least in part offset the losses associated with the original evasion. Third, the expenditures of tax evaders generate, via a multiplier effect, increased incomes for other people (non-evaders). These incomes, when taxed, will generate a further offsetting sum of tax revenue.

Peacock and Shaw (1982a) have shown, using a simple income-expenditure model, that in the case of a closed economy where the marginal propensity to consume out a disposable income is 1, there will be no loss of tax revenue. This can be seen as follows. In a closed economy, equilibrium requires that

$$Y = C + A$$

where Y is national income, C is planned consumption and A is planned autonomous spending (investment and government expenditure). Further, assume that

$$C = bY^d$$

where Y^d is disposable income and is given by

$$Y^d = [1-t(1-e)]Y$$

where e is the proportion of income upon which tax is evaded. Solving for Y gives

$$Y = \frac{A}{1-b[1-t(1-e)]}$$

In the absence of evasion (i.e. $e = 0$) the tax yield will be

$$T_1 = tY = \frac{tA}{1-b(1-t)}$$

However, if $1 > e > 0$ then

$$T_2 = t(1-e)Y = \frac{t(1-e)A}{1-b[1-t(1-e)]}$$

The tax revenue loss due to evasion is then given by

$$T_1 - T_2 = \frac{tA\,e\,(1-b)}{[1-b(1-t)][1-b\,[1-t(1-e)]]}$$

Clearly if $b = 1$ then $T_1 - T_2 = 0$ and evasion will not involve any loss of income tax revenue.[3] The reason for this slightly odd result is that whilst the effective tax rate is reduced by evasion, this is offset by the fact that output is larger, stimulated by the extra consumption expenditures of evaders.

Obviously, this model is something of an over-simplification, but it serves as a salutory reminder that the measurement of tax revenue losses due to evasion is rather trickier than it might at first appear.[4] Peacock and Shaw argue that '(t)he study of the effects of evasion on revenue yields can only be carried out within the framework of a fully articulated macroeconomic model which pays close attention to the model's microeconomic foundations' (Peacock and Shaw, 1982a, p. 277).

Ricketts (1984) has extended Peacock and Shaw's model from a simple one-sector income–expenditure framework by building on a monetary sector. A crucial assumption of this approach is that the demand for money depends upon disposable income. In this case an increase in evasion by increasing disposable income increases the demand for money. With a fixed supply of money equilibrium can only be restored by a rise in interest rates, which will tend to counteract the expansionary effects of evasion upon revenue yields listed by Peacock and Shaw.

The articles discussed above concentrate on the demand side and say nothing about the supply of output. The full effects upon tax revenue can only be estimated from a full-blown economic model incorporating production sectors (for each kind of output, i.e. black output and official output) and influences upon the supplies of factors of production to each sector and the economy as a whole. Feige and McGee (1983) attempt such an approach, but it is limited in a number of important respects. First, they implicitly assume that production functions in each of the sectors are the same. Second, factor supplies to the black economy are not affected by deterrence factors. Third, they adopt a particularly restrictive form of utility function which assumes a zero cross-price elasticity of demand between the outputs of the regular and black economies.

It is clear, therefore, that calculations of the loss of tax revenues arising from evasion is not as straightforward as it might appear at first sight. In order to estimate this loss at all accurately a fairly complex two-sector model of the economy is needed, which takes into account, for example, law enforcement variables. So far, the construction of such a model does not seem to have taken place. However, it would be a useful vehicle not just for measuring the extent of revenue losses, but also for focusing attention upon a number of perhaps rather more important macroeconomic issues which are a result of evasion – for example, what happens to prices, inflation, real output, employment and so on if evasion is tolerated, (or at least not eliminated) compared with a situation in which there is no evasion.

Measurement of the extent of tax-revenue losses has not attracted a great deal of attention from economists. In a way this is not surprising. The loss of revenue is in a sense almost a secondary issue. At least it is secondary to the issues raised in the last paragraph. Even if an accurate measure of the amount of lost tax revenue could be obtained it would be entirely incorrect to regard this as a measure of the 'cost' of tax evasion. After all, evaders gain from underdeclaring and as long as they are regarded as members of society, then the lost revenue will overstate the extent of the social loss. One might argue that the unpaid tax is really just a transfer payment from the honest taxpayer to the dishonest evader. The extent of the cost to society will depend upon how the government would have used the extra revenue and society's valuation of these uses compared with the social value of the extra consumption of evaders. This is clearly a thorny issue which involves considerations such as the externalities generated by feelings of injustice and jealousy on the part of the honest taxpayers.

I will not attempt to answer such questions, but merely trace through some of the possible macroeconomic and microeconomic consequences arising as a result of tax evasion. Decisions about whether evasion is on balance a good or bad thing will have to await a much more detailed study.

7.2 MACROECONOMIC ISSUES

The previous section has already begun to consider some of the macroeconomic consequences of tax evasion. It focused upon the loss of tax revenue as a consequence of evasion, but also briefly discussed the effect that tax evasion might have upon the levels of output and employment.

It should be clear from earlier discussions that the true extent of evasion remains something of a mystery. Unfortunately, this makes precise measurement of the direct and indirect consequences of evasion virtually impossible. All that is possible is to analyse some of the consequences and leave the reader to decide how important these are. This is obviously an area which requires some painstaking attention to detail. Really what is needed is a fully articulated econometric model of the economy which takes account of evasion.

Should we worry about tax evasion or does it serve a useful social function, for example, in providing employment that would otherwise not exist? According to some observers evasion does have potentially harmful consequences, whilst others feel that it has some beneficial ones.

(a)   Information bias

One – perhaps unusual – consequence of evasion is its effect upon indicators of economic activity. Evasion occurs when some individuals fail to disclose either employment or income or both to the tax authorities. As a result some economic activity goes unrecorded in the official statistics. If evasion becomes widespread then these indicators may cease to be useful guides to economic performance. Statistics of GDP and unemployment, for example, may indicate a depressed economy operating considerably below its full employment potential, when in fact the 'true' level of GDP is much larger and the level of unemployment much lower.[5] The real problem this causes is *if*, as a consequence of this misinformation, the government decides to use expansionary monetary and fiscal policies to restore 'full' employment. The economy may already be working at or very close to its full potential and the impact of these unfortunately inappropriate macroeconomic policies is to raise not output and employment but prices.

Of course information about prices, inflation and growth rates too may be distorted if the black economy is taking an increasing share of total economic activity. Feige (1981) believes that this is the principal reason for the breakdown of macroeconomic theories in the 1970s. He claims that the existence and growth of the unobserved sector has distorted the information system to such a degree that the inflation and recession of the 1970s is really a statistical illusion![6]

This view lends rather unusual support to the monetarist doctrine that governments should refrain from using demand management policies for stabilising the level of economic activity. The arguments against supply-side policies are rather less strong, however. Reductions in taxes, deregulation of labour markets and so on should encourage the movement of resources away from the black to the official economy (but see Chapter 5 for a discussion of the effects of taxes on the allocation of resources between the black economy and the official economy). Of course, the argument about the reliability of the GDP and other indicators still applies. The growth in recorded

GDP which could arise from such policies *may* largely reflect a reallocation of resources away from the black economy and towards the official economy, rather than a real growth in 'true' GDP. Nevertheless, supply-side policies will be less harmful and might actually generate some net increase in 'true' GDP.[7]

The next subsection will examine in more detail the relative efficiency/effectiveness of different kinds of macroeconomic policies. However, it is necessary first to consider in slightly more detail the extent of the bias that the existence of a black economy imparts to macroeconomic statistics.

Feige, for example, has claimed that 'if the irregular economy is growing faster than the official economy . . . then clearly the official statistics on income will *grossly* understate the true growth rate of the overall economy' (Feige, 1979, p. 11, my emphasis). He further claims that 'official unemployment statistics are almost certain to overestimate the true situation' (ibid, p. 11) and that 'the official inflation statistics are themselves likely to be *substantial* overestimates' (ibid, p. 12, my emphasis).

The extent of any bias upon the growth rate of real GNP, can be illustrated, for example, by adapting a model suggested by Cassel (1984). Define real (actual) GNP as

$$Y = Y^O + Y^B$$

where Y^O is real output produced in the official economy (i.e. measured GNP)

Y^B is real output produced in the black economy.

Differentiate with respect to time and divide both sides by Y thus obtaining

$$\frac{1}{Y}\frac{dY}{dt} = \frac{1}{Y}\frac{dY^O}{dt} + \frac{1}{Y}\frac{dY^B}{dt} \tag{7.1}$$

Let $b = \dfrac{Y^B}{Y^O}$

i.e. b is the ratio of black economy output to measured GNP.[8]
Rewrite (7.1) as

$$g - g^o = \frac{b}{b+1}(g^B - g^o) \tag{7.2}$$

where g is the growth rate of real (actual) GNP
g^O is the growth rate of real official (measured) GNP
and g^B is the growth rate of real output in the black economy.

The left-hand side of equation (7.2), i.e. $g - g^O$, is an indicator of the error in measuring real, actual GNP growth arising from the existence of the black economy. This bias is seen to depend upon two things – (i) the size of the black economy relative to the official economy, given by b, and (ii) the discrepancy in growth rates between the black economy and the official economy, given by $g^B - g^O$. The larger are b and $g^B - g^O$ then the greater the misinformation which is imparted by looking solely at g^O. There are two clear cases where information bias will not be present. These are when *either* $b = o$, i.e. there is no black economy or $g^B - g^O = o$, i.e. both sectors are growing at exactly the same rate.

It is also fairly clear that bias will increase with both b and $g^B - g^O$. This can be seen more clearly in Table 7.1. What is also clear from Table 7.1 is that for most 'reasonable' values of b, the discrepancy between growth rates has to be quite substantial before reliance upon the growth of measured GNP causes any substantial information bias.[9]

Table 7.1 Information bias and the black economy

b	± 1.0	$g^O - g^B$ ± 2.0	± 4.0	± 8.0
0.05	± 0.05	± 0.1	± 0.2	± 0.4
0.10	± 0.09	± 0.18	± 0.36	± 0.72
0.20	± 0.17	± 0.33	± 0.67	± 1.34
0.40	± 0.28	± 0.57	± 1.14	± 2.28
0.80	± 0.44	± 0.89	± 1.78	± 3.56
1.0	± 0.5	± 1.0	± 2.0	± 4.0
2.0	± 0.67	± 1.33	± 2.67	± 5.33

In the light of this simulation it seems unlikely that the degree of informational bias imparted to measurement of the growth rate, by the existence of the black economy, could have played much of a role in distorting macroeconomic policies. In most countries governments simply do not fine-tune their macroeconomic policies to the degree required for informational bias to play a significant part in policy selection. For example, it is common practice in many countries –

e.g. UK and West Germany – to set target ranges for money supply growth which are quite wide (6–10 per cent or 4–7 per cent per annum, etc.). In the words of Cassell this indicates 'a quantitative vagueness in comparison to which diagnostic errors related to the shadow economy are of minor importance' (Cassell, 1984, p. 224).

A similar analysis could be made of the distortion imparted to the level of prices and the rate of inflation (see Cassell, 1984). However, the conclusions would be broadly similar. The extent of the bias will depend upon the size of the black economy relative to the official economy and the extent to which prices are higher or lower (rising faster or slower) in the black economy than they are elsewhere. There is much anecdotal evidence to the effect that the prices of black economy services are lower than their 'official' counterparts (see, for example, Feige, 1979, p. 12).[10] However, there is remarkably little hard evidence which would allow us to say precisely how much lower (or higher) black-economy prices are, or indeed how much more rapidly (or slowly) they are in fact rising. From the previous analysis all that we can say is that the differential in price changes would have to be fairly large for it to have any major impact upon the reliability of the measured inflation rate. It would seem, then, that contrary to popular opinion the measured inflation rate is probably not seriously impaired by the existence of a black economy. If that is the case then the inflation rate does not present biased information to policy-makers and could not, therefore, be expected to have adversely affected the formulation of economic policy.

Quite obviously, however, the official unemployment rate will overstate the true extent of unemployment, if people working in the black economy are in fact registered as unemployed. The extent of this overstatement is once again a matter for speculation. Most of the estimates of the size of the black economy reported in Chapters 2–4 are given as either a percentage of GNP/GDP or in monetary values. The conversion of these statistics into numbers of jobs requires information about labour–output ratios. In order to calculate the effect upon the true level of unemployment it is necessary to know how many of those estimated to be working in the black economy were actually registered as unemployed (as Chapter 4 shows, some of those working in the black economy may have full-time jobs in the official economy and may simply be moonlighting).

Gutmann (1977) has estimated that the USA's black economy in 1976 of some $176 billion corresponded to some 8.2 million jobs (using the labour–output ratio of the official economy). He argues that 'if 20 per cent comes from the officially unemployed, total employment is more than 1.6 million greater' (Gutmann, 1977, p. 34) and so unemployment should be 1.6 million less than is officially recorded. He later calculated that 'the official August 1979 unemployment rate of 6.0 per cent is, in reality, only 4.5 per cent' (Gutmann, 1979, p. 17).

As Chapter 4 shows, Contini (1982) has suggested that some 4 million people were working in Italy's black economy in 1977. Of these Contini estimates that about 1.5 million were also employed full-time in the legitimate economy. However, it cannot be inferred that *all* the remaining 2.5 million should be deducted from the unemployment register. Many may not have been recorded as unemployed in the first place. Indeed the number of people registered as unemployed in Italy in 1977 was only about 1.5 million (*Eurostat Review*, 1976–85, p. 138, Table 3.4.36).

Finally, Matthews (1983) has estimated that some 1.3 million workers claiming to be unemployed in the UK in 1983 were actually engaged in the black economy. If this were true it would have a dramatic impact on the UK's unemployment rate, reducing it by nearly 50 per cent. However, it has already been argued that Matthews's approach to measuring the size of the black economy should be treated with a great deal of circumspection. Consequently his calculation of the impact on unemployment needs to be regarded in a similar fashion.

Denison (1982) has argued that recent US official statistics on employment, GNP and growth of GNP have *not* been seriously impaired by the existence and growth of the black economy. His claim rests upon his finding that the employment–population ratio since 1973 (the year in which productivity growth began to slow down) has not fallen below (and, indeed, by 1978–80 had risen above) its pre-1973 level. It is difficult to know what to make of this finding, particularly if, as seems likely in the USA, most people engaged in black-economy work also work in the legitimate economy. In those circumstances a steady or rising employment–population ratio could be entirely consistent with an increasing black economy.

Further estimates are not needed. It should be abundantly clear that estimates of the number of people who are registered as unemployed, but are also working in the black economy, are subject to a considerable margin of error and guesswork. The question remains whether, because recorded unemployment overstates the extent of true unemployment, this should or does have any influence upon macroeconomic policy. This, of course, depends upon whether the government decides to adopt Keynesian demand management policies in response to the artificially high level of unemployment. These policies may *in some circumstances* prove to be inappropriate, although it is clear from the somewhat casual evidence cited above that the recorded unemployment rate is not always drastically overstated by the existence of a black economy. To the extent that governments do not respond to high recorded levels of unemployment in this way (and there is little evidence in recent years that they have) then no harm is done.

Cassell argues, however, that '(s)tabilisation policy should still focus on the officially recorded unemployment rate as long as immigration into the shadow economy is a by-product of unemployment in the official sector' (Cassell, 1984, p. 225). He claims that it is unemployment that drives workers to the black economy, not the black economy that leads them to register as unemployed. This may well be true, but some might argue (see Chapter 4, for example) that it is high levels of taxation and government controls that have forced people to leave the official economy. Further increases in government spending (financed by higher taxes?) may well exacerbate the situation in addition to the inflationary pressures they would impart.

(b) Effects upon output, employment and prices

The last subsection examined how the existence of the black economy distorts *information* about *measured* output, (un)employment, growth and inflation. The focus of this subsection will be slightly different. It asks whether the existence of the black economy means that, for example, *actual* output and employment are higher than they would have been in the absence of the black economy. An alternative way of looking at this is to ask whether the existence of a black economy means that more goods are produced in the economy *as a whole*.

One way of trying to answer such a question is to ask what would happen to the level of overall economic activity if those activities which at the moment successfully evade the tax net were actually to be brought within it.

For the time being let us ignore any supply-side effects. That is, let us assume that taxation of black economy activity will not discourage people from supplying their services to the black sector. This would seem to be a very important assumption and it will need to be relaxed eventually.

For the purposes of illustration, let us consider the UK situation and further assume that the Inland Revenue are correct in guessing that the revenue lost through income tax evasion is roughly £4bn per year. If all of this could be successfully recouped what effects could this reasonably be expected to have upon output, unemployment and inflation? To some extent the answer depends upon how the extra revenue is used – to finance increased public spending, tax cuts or reductions in the public sector borrowing requirement.

Take first the case where the extra revenue is used to increase government expenditure by £4bn per year. In effect this is no more than a balanced budget expansion of £4bn, because whilst government spending has increased by that amount so too has taxation. The expansionary effects on real GNP of such a change are likely to be small if not non-existent![11] The short-run effect upon real GDP (after one year) might be an increase of between $1bn and $3bn per year or rather less than 1 per cent. In the long run (say beyond three years) GDP might actually fall by perhaps £2bn per annum. However, these calculations are based upon the assumption that evaders and non-evaders have identical marginal propensities to consume (mpcs). If, as seems likely, evaders have higher mpcs then the multiplier effects will be even smaller. The effect upon unemployment of such changes will be quite small, perhaps reducing unemployment even in the short-term by less than 100 000. This in turn would generate a slightly higher inflation rate. Overall, however, the macroeconomic effects of spending the extra revenue would be very small indeed.

Suppose, instead, that the extra revenue was used to reduce income taxes. Then the overall effect would depend upon which group had the larger mpc – evaders or non-evaders. If, as we have argued, evaders on the whole have higher mpcs, then the overall effect would be deflationary, although the probable net effect upon aggregate demand would be so small as to be negligible. In that case no significant impact upon real GDP and unemployment could be expected. Neither could such a policy be expected to have much effect upon the rate of inflation, unless somewhat lower rates of income tax help to moderate wage demands. The extra £4bn of revenue would be sufficient to reduce the standard rate of income tax by perhaps 3*p* in the £.[12]

Of course, if the £4bn was used to reduce indirect taxes it might have a more substantial effect upon prices and inflation. However, the net expansionary or contractionary effects upon GDP would probably be small too.

So far at least the macroeconomic effects of evasion seem small, so that bringing the black economy within the tax net does not appear to produce any substantial net benefits. Indeed, if supply-side effects are considered taxation might actually appear harmful. By reducing the incentive to supply labour and goods, 'true' GDP could actually be reduced.

The one possibility that has not so far been considered here is that the extra tax revenue could be used to reduce the public sector borrowing requirement (PSBR). In the UK this would have a substantial effect upon the PSBR (more than halving the deficit for 1985–6). But what benefit would this produce? Some economists have argued that the size of the PSBR is closely related to either the growth of the money supply (which in turn is a major cause of inflation) or to the level of interest rates.[13] However, both these views are the subject of considerable disagreement. Certainly, Kaldor (1982) could find no evidence to support either view. Likewise, Nevile (1984) has been unable to find evidence of a link between bond sales and interest rates in Australia in the recent past.

If this view is correct then it seems unlikely that a cut in the PSBR can be expected to bring about any large-scale reduction in interest rates. Accordingly any induced increase in real GDP would be small. Against this must be set the possibly substantial contractionary effect of a £4bn increase in income taxes. For example, Lewis and Ormerod's (1979) simulations with the treasury's econometric model suggest an income-tax multiplier of approximately 1.4 after six years (although it builds up fairly slowly, being only 0.4 after one year and 0.6 after two years). Such a tax 'increase' would, therefore, cut real GDP by about 2 per cent after six years and thereby increase unemployment.

This, of course, assumes that the extra revenue generated would be as much as £4bn per annum and this figure is far from being universally accepted. Even so, except in the case where the extra tax receipts are used entirely to reduce the PSBR, the macroeconomic effects seem to be relatively insignificant.

However, evasion may have a major qualitative impact upon macroeconomic policy if it lessens the ability of the government to regulate the economy by fiscal means. If changes in tax rates cause output to be diverted from one sector to the other – i.e. the official to the hidden economy or vice versa – then the government may be misled about the effectiveness or otherwise of its fiscal policies. In this case the effect is to overstate the size of the income-tax multiplier, so that governments would tend to change taxes by smaller amounts than would really be justified. Of course, there are some economists who would see this as a positive advantage!

On the other hand, the government-expenditure multiplier will appear to be smaller in an economy which includes a hidden sector than in one which does not have such a sector. This is because some of the increased demand is diverted to the black economy, thus lessening the expansionary effect upon the official economy. If, in formulating its expenditure plans, a government were to ignore this spill-over effect then it would tend to increase government spending by more than would be necessary to achieve a particular increase in total economic activity. An extreme version of this would occur when the official sector of the economy was characterised by classical unemployment, i.e. there is excess demand for goods in this sector. If the government then follows a misguided Keynesian demand-management expansion, output in the official economy will not rise, but the black economy might expand if there is a sufficiently large excess supply of goods and/or labour there (Adam and Ginsburgh, 1985). In that case the official-economy multiplier is zero, although the 'true' multiplier is positive.

Adam and Ginsburgh show that one need not adopt such an extreme view of the world in order for the multiplier to be an inaccurate predictor of the effect upon *total* output of a fiscal expansion. Using data for Belgium they have shown that even if the official economy is operating with excess capacity (i.e. Keynesian unemployment) 'the regular sector multipliers are reduced by 5 to 12 per cent . . . when they are compared to the multipliers prevailing in an all-regular economy' (Adam and Ginsburgh, 1985, pp. 27–8).[14]

Errors of that magnitude are probably not that crucial, however. It would seem much more important to diagnose correctly the kind of regime in which the official economy finds itself. On the whole, then, the black economy has probably not reached such proportions as either to make macroeconomic information totally meaningless or render macroeconomic policy totally impotent. Certainly no more impotent than some macroeconomists would claim it already is!

7.3 MICROECONOMIC ISSUES

The last section showed that tax evasion may have an effect upon the overall level of economic activity and the ability of the government both to interpret macroeconomic statistics and to formulate appropriate macroeconomic policies. The effects of tax evasion may not stop there. Indeed it was argued that it is easy to overstate the macroeconomic effects of tax evasion. Much more damaging may be the effect which tax evasion has upon the allocation of resources and the distribution of income. This is because taxes also play major roles as distributive and allocative devices. First, then, this section briefly considers the impact which tax evasion has upon income distribution and then examines resource-allocation issues in slightly more detail.

(a) Income distribution

If the structure of income-tax rates has been set so as to achieve some desired distribution of post-tax incomes, then income-tax evasion may very well cause the actual distribution of post-tax incomes to diverge from that which was desired. The precise extent to which this will happen obviously depends upon how widespread evasion is and how the propensity to evade is distributed throughout the population. Only guesstimates can be made of these things. Nevertheless, it would seem most unlikely that the actual distribution of post-tax incomes will be exactly like the desired distribution. Evasion, therefore, will undoubtedly disturb accepted notions of both vertical and horizontal equity. If, for example, the self-employed have much better opportunities for engaging in successful acts of evasion then they will gain in comparison with employees who have income tax deducted at source.

The real problem with this is that evasion redistributes income in an almost entirely arbitrary way, in part because the opportunities to evade and get away with it are not evenly distributed across society.[15] The danger is that if a significant number of taxpayers begin to feel aggrieved about others' evasion activities, then they too might decide to evade taxation (recall the evidence about this point in Chapter 6). This will further erode the tax base and force the tax authorities to incur further expense on enforcement. Eventually the whole tax-collection system may break down, although on the basis of the evidence quoted in Chapters 2–4 and the earlier part of this chapter that may still be a long way off.

Peacock (1983) has argued that '(e)vasion may itself be a result of inequities in the tax system and not only a cause'. He uses the example of a worker choosing whether to work overtime as an employee or on his own account. If (s)he chooses the latter the individual incurs much heavier compliance costs e.g. having to keep detailed accounts, file separate returns, etc. How much easier simply not to declare this income at all.

It is difficult to reach an overall conclusion as to whether evasion leads to greater inequality or equality. To the extent that typical tax-evaders are window-cleaners, chars and part-time gardeners then it might actually make for less inequality. If, however, evasion is generally practised by the moderately wealthy self-employed business person it would have the opposite effect.

Persson and Wissen (1984) have provided a formal analysis of the effect of income-tax evasion on the distribution of income using a model based upon the work of Allingham and Sandmo (see Chapter 5). In this model they show that the effect of evasion upon the distribution of *reported* incomes (compared with *actual* incomes) depends in a rather subtle way upon the interaction of individuals' attitudes to risk and the parameters of both the tax and penalty systems. In general, however, the distribution of actual incomes (including black-economy earnings) is more unequal than the distribution of reported incomes. (The inequality measures used are (i) the ratio of incomes and (ii) the difference between incomes. In Persson and Wissen's model there are only two types of individuals. Wage rates between types are different but within types are the same.)

However, evasion will lead to a different distribution of income from that which would occur if everyone paid their taxes. Presumably this is the distribution which society acting through its elected government chose as its most preferred income distribution. (Unless, of course, one is prepared to argue that the government set the tax rates knowing that not everyone would declare their incomes honestly. That is an argument that few, if any, would find credible.)

(b) Resource allocation

As all taxes (other than lump-sum taxes) are distortionary, it might be thought that evasion would improve the efficiency with which resources are allocated within the economy. After all, some of the taxes which are distorting resource allocation and imposing welfare losses on society are no longer being paid. However, in a second- (or perhaps third-) best world, removal of one or more distortionary taxes does not necessarily lead to an overall gain in economic welfare. As Stiglitz has argued this is merely 'the fallacy of counting distortions' (Stiglitz, 1986, p. 388).

In fact it is much more likely that tax evasion, far from improving the allocation of resources, actually imposes welfare losses upon society. For example, Peacock has suggested that evasion may lead to inefficient uses of resources by encouraging 'individuals with particular aptitudes and acquired skills, more appropriately exercised as an employee in industry, to enter forms of employment (including self-employment) that are difficult to tax but in which they are less skilled and not so well trained' (Peacock, 1983, p. 14).[16]

The issue here is a fairly simple one. In deciding how to allocate their resources, factor owners are interested in the net of tax return. However, the 'social' productivity of the resource is indicated by its gross return provided factor payments are related to marginal products. The simultaneous existence of a taxed and an untaxed sector drives a wedge between the net returns in the two sectors and this causes resources to flow into the untaxed sector. In a perfectly competitive world with perfect factor mobility returns in the untaxed sector would eventually be driven into line with net of tax returns in the taxed sector (except for possible risk premia required by factors employed in the black economy). However, the gross return in the taxed sector would exceed the return in the black economy and so resources would move from more efficient to less efficient uses. The result is that there is an inefficient allocation of resources within society and this imposes a cost which in principle can be measured.

Theoretical analysis of the welfare losses caused by evasion has been reported by Bhagwati and Hansen (1973), Schweizer (1984) and Yitzhaki (1987).

Bhagwati and Hansen were actually concerned with smuggling, which of course is a form of tax evasion, i.e. evasion of import tariffs. They were able to show that in some circumstances evading tariffs might reduce welfare in comparison with a situation in which smuggling did not take place (provided legal trade was not completely eliminated by prohibitive tariffs. Of course with prohibitive tariffs smuggling must of necessity increase welfare.)

Schweizer has developed their approach but also within the context of excise taxes. Schweizer assumes that the government has a target for revenue which has to be raised from excise taxation. Whether evasion is desirable depends upon the cost structure of evaders. If

Figure 7.1   The excess burden of income tax evasion

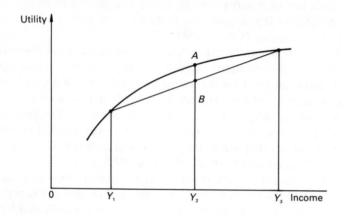

evaders and non-evaders have the same 'production' costs, but evaders incur additional costs in avoiding detection, then evasion imposes welfare costs upon society and it is desirable to eliminate it by imposing a sufficiently large penalty (Schweizer, however, ignores the resource costs of punishment; see chapter 8). However, if the marginal costs of evaders are less than those incurred by non-evaders, then evasion may serve a useful social function and an efficient allocation of resources would point to tolerating some evasion.

Yitzhaki shows that income-tax evasion will lead to a loss in utility over and above the loss that would be incurred if there was only lump-sum taxation. He calls this the excess burden of tax evasion. It arises because income-tax evasion leads to uncertainty which lowers utility. This can perhaps be seen rather more clearly with the aid of a diagram (Figure 7.1).

In the diagram Y_1 is the income which the individual would receive *if* (s)he tried to evade payment of income tax but was caught. However, if successful the individual's income would be Y_3. His/her expected income is given by Y_2 and the utility of that uncertain prospect is given by BY_2 [$= pU(Y_1) + (1 - p) U(Y_3)$, where p is the probability of being caught].

However, *if* the government guaranteed a tax payment that was equal to the tax and expected penalties on evaded income, then the individual could have an after-tax income of Y_2 with complete certainty by not evading income-tax. The utility of that income level is, of course, AY_2. The excess burden/deadweight loss of income-tax evasion is, therefore, given by AB. (This assumes that individuals are risk-averse.)

Yitzhaki attempts to measure the extent of the deadweight loss for a particular utility function in a model with endogenous labour supply (see Chapter 5). The utility function he uses is given by

$$U = 2Y - 2Y^2 + 0.5L$$

where Y is income and L is leisure.

Further, Yitzhaki normalises the wage rate (to 1), assumes a proportional income-tax rate of 0.4, a probability of detection of 0.7 and a penalty rate on evaded income of 100 per cent.

The maximum level of utility that can be achieved by selecting an optimal evasion strategy is $U_1 = 0.58333$. If individuals had not evaded, but instead paid the same taxes and penalties to the government utility would rise to $U_2 = 0.61395$. With lump-sum taxes utility would rise to $U_3 = 0.63344$. This seems to raise the question, though, of why individuals would willingly choose a suboptimal policy. The answer seems to be that, in the way Yitzhaki has formulated it, the government is offering somewhat lower taxes in return for an agreement not to evade tax.

So far, discussion of the welfare costs arising from tax evasion has been largely theoretical. There have as yet been few attempts to estimate the full extent of these costs. However, we shall now consider one such exercise.

Alm (1985) has attempted to estimate the welfare cost arising from the coexistence of an untaxed underground economy and a taxed legitimate sector using data for the USA. He has estimated that the underground economy may have imposed a welfare cost of between $100 bn and $217 bn in 1980 (i.e. between approximately 5 and 10 per cent of GNP).

The model used by Alm is an extension of one used earlier by Harberger (1962) to examine the incidence of corporation tax. The US economy is divided into three sectors – one producing legitimate (taxed) output; a second producing criminal goods and services; and a third, black sector, which produces substitutes for the goods produced in the legitimate sector. Alm assumes that total factor supplies are fixed, but that there is perfect factor mobility between sectors and perfect competition in each sector. Further, each sector is characterised by a linear homogeneous production function. The only taxes in Alm's model are taxes on labour and capital in the legitimate sector.

In order to generate estimates of welfare cost a number of rather more specific assumptions need also to be made. These include:

(i) the size of the underground economy;[17]
(ii) amounts of capital and labour in each sector and
(iii) elasticities of demand and of substitution.

Alm assumes that the USA's underground economy was 2.5 per cent of GNP in 1950 and that this grew at a constant rate to 5 per cent (or 10 per cent or 20 per cent) by 1980. He assumes that the two 'hidden' sectors use rather more labour-intensive methods of production (different simulations assume that the shares of labour are between 5 per cent and 20 per cent larger in the black and criminal sectors). He further assumes no substitution between criminal goods and black goods, and criminal goods and legitimate goods. The only possible substitution is between legitimate goods and black goods. In order to generate estimates of welfare loss it is necessary to assume a value for the own-price elasticity of demand for taxed output. Alm assumes that this is either −0.5 or −1. Given the assumption of zero substitution with criminal goods and the adding-up conditions, this then determines the cross-price elasticities.

Finally, the elasticity of substitution in the legitimate sector is assumed to be either −0.5 or −1. Separate simulations of welfare cost are attempted for each of these elasticities and for elasticities of substitution in the other two sectors of 0, −0.5 and −1. The welfare cost is fairly unresponsive to changes in assumptions here.

Alm uses this information to generate estimates of welfare cost in 1980 dollars. This cost is argued to be between $25.5 bn and $51.4 bn in 1950, assuming that the underground economy amounted to 2.5 per cent of GNP in 1950.[18] If the undergound economy grew to only 5 per cent of GNP by 1980 the welfare cost soars to between $107.5 bn and $216.2 bn (4.7 per cent to 9.5 per cent of GNP).[19] Strangely, if underground output rises to 20 per cent of GNP this has little effect upon the estimate of welfare costs which now lie between $109.8 bn and $218.2 bn.

These measures may underestimate the true extent of welfare costs, because they ignore:

(i) resource costs of tax-law enforcement;
(ii) private expenditures on tax minimisation;
(iii) expenditures incurred in trying to avoid detection.[20]

In addition, the procedure adopted is only legitimate for infinitesim-ally small taxes, because it ignores income effects. However, Alm claims that these income effects may themselves be quite small, adding perhaps only 3–10 per cent to the welfare costs reported above.

On the other hand, Alm's calculations ignore any welfare gains which underground employment provides, e.g. job creation, avoid-ance of inefficient regulations, etc.

Finally, Alm's estimates are for the welfare costs of the under-ground economy as a whole and not just the black economy. How-ever, given his assumption of zero substitution between the criminal sector and the other two sectors, it would seem that his estimate could be regarded as a measure of the welfare loss arising from the existence of a black economy alone.[21]

In view of these limitations it cannot be unambiguously stated that tax evasion reduces economic welfare. However, there seem to be good grounds, both theoretical and empirical, for believing that it does, so that a reduction in evasion would increase welfare generally. However, reducing evasion may involve quite substantial resource costs. In that case it may not be optimal to eliminate tax evasion completely. This policy problem is discussed more fully in Chapter 8.

7.4 CONCLUSION

This chapter has considered the economic consequences of tax eva-sion. The discussion has examined separately (i) macroeconomic effects – e.g. upon output, employment and growth and information bias, and (ii) microeconomic effects upon resource allocation and income distribution.

From what we have seen it seems reasonable to conclude that the macroeconomic effects have been overstated by some commentators. It is unlikely that the informational bias imparted by having unre-corded output has much effect upon the choice of macroeconomic policies and cannot be blamed for the serious deterioration in econ-omic peformance in the advanced industrialised economies after 1973. The reason for that is quite clearly the oil-price shock, the consequences of which were exacerbated by inept government policies.

The aggregate demand effects generated by the existence of an untaxed sector do not appear large either (at least in the UK, and as Chapter 4 shows the size of the UK's black economy is fairly typical). The supply-side effects *may* be more substantial. Unfortunately it is not possible to be at all precise about how many jobs in the black economy exist simply because they are not taxed. The theoretical 'evidence' is ambiguous and in any case would only generate a qualitative prediction. Empirical evidence is, on the whole, of rather dubious quality. On balance one feels that the supply-side effects may be more substantial, but it is no more than a feeling.

On the whole, the macroeconomic effects may not be very significant. However, the effect upon the allocation of resources may very well be much more substantial. Evasion can be shown to generate inefficiencies in the allocation of resources and one recent estimate for the USA puts this welfare cost at nearly 10 per cent of GNP. If to that is added the undoubtedly adverse effect which evasion has upon the distribution of income and the harmful externality which this generates, then there may be a powerful case for reducing tax evasion.

The next chapter examines in detail some of the policy issues raised by tax evasion. In particular, it considers the design of an 'optimal' anti-evasion policy.

8 Policy Issues

The discussion in Chapter 7 provides a weak case for claiming that tax evasion is, on balance, probably a bad thing. Whilst there have been few detailed studies of the effects of tax evasion, there is some evidence that it imposes quite substantial welfare costs upon society.

The natural consequence of that finding is to consider what, if anything, should be done about evasion. This is obviously an issue of some importance and not necessarily an easy problem to solve. Reducing evasion by, for example, increasing the number of audits undertaken by the tax authority is a costly business. So complete elimination of evasion might prove to be more harmful than beneficial. Economists searching for 'optimal' anti-evasion policies would suggest spending on anti-evasion measures up to the point at which the marginal cost of such activity is just balanced by the marginal benefit it would produce. However, whilst such a policy is easy to suggest it is in practice rather more difficult to formulate and implement. It is made slightly more complicated because the authorities have a range of policy weapons with which to fight evasion – e.g. investigating officers, penalties, tax rates, etc. An 'optimal' policy requires a careful balancing of all of these instruments.

Section 8.1 examines a set of 'simple' policy rules. They are described as simple, because the tax authority is assumed to apply exactly the same weapons to everyone. For example, everyone has an equal probability of being audited. Likewise, if found to have been evading, every evader pays the same penalty. Despite the simplicity of the approach followed a number of interesting questions need to be answered – e.g. what is the optimal detection rate? what is the optimal penalty? what is the optimal level of evasion? One solution is to set very high penalties/fines with low audit rates, because fines are almost costless but investigation is costly. However, this raises issues of *ex-post* horizontal equity.

The tax authority may be able to operate a rather more sophisticated policy if it has some means of deciding whether a taxpayer is likely to be trying to evade payment of tax. For example, if it feels that someone is reporting a low income compared with other people working in the same occupation and/or living in the same area, then it may decide to audit that individual. In other words different audit probabilities are applied to different groups in society. Of course, the different audit rates could be applied purely randomly too. Likewise, persistent offenders could be subjected to different punishments from first-time offenders. Section 8.2 investigates such sophisticated policies. In general it can be shown that sophisticated policies are normally superior to simple policies in reducing evasion and/or raising revenue.

The policies considered in sections 8.1 and 8.2 are the rather traditional law-enforcement ones of certainty and severity of punishment. There are other weapons that could possibly be used to reduce tax evasion. One obvious one is a reduction (or increase?) in the income-tax rate. As Chapters 5 and 6 show it is not at all clear that a reduction in the rate of income tax would have a marked effect upon evasion. In addition it is not strictly a weapon that the tax authorities are free to choose. However, governments throughout the advanced, industrial world have been substantially lowering income-tax rates lately. One – admittedly minor – justification for this has been the claim that the highest rates of tax have rarely been paid. They have either been avoided or evaded. Section 8.3 briefly considers alternative anti-evasion policies and in particular considers the effect of a cut in income-tax rates.

In recent years the black economy and tax evasion have become topics of considerable public and political interest. One manifestation of this concern has been enquiries into the powers which tax authorities have to raise revenues. Section 8.4 briefly examines one such enquiry. This is the *Report of the Committee on Enforcement Powers of the Revenue Departments* (better known as the *Keith Report*, after its Chairman, Lord Keith of Kinkel) in the UK. This Report is used purely as a case study, in order to see how its proposals relate to the economists' approaches outlined in sections 8.1–8.4.

8.1   TAX-LAW ENFORCEMENT: SIMPLE RULES

Much of the literature on the economics of tax-law enforcement is predicated upon the assumption that evasion is basically undesirable and should therefore be reduced as far as possible, if not eliminated entirely (but see Cowell, 1987, for an alternative approach). In addition, analysis has focused upon the use of just two policy weapons – the probability of detection and the severity of the penalty. In this respect the literature on anti-evasion policy has many similarities with the literature on the economic approach to criminal law enforcement (see Pyle, 1983, ch. 5). The main difference is that in the crime literature economists, following Becker (1968), have been quite careful to spell out the social costs of crime and its control and to derive a social loss function. Work in the area of tax-law enforcement has generally not been quite so explicit.

The approach generally has been to find the optimal values of the probability of detection and the severity of punishment in order to eliminate evasion completely. This has been broadly the approach suggested by Singh (1973), McCaleb (1976), Fishburn (1979) and Christiansen (1980), although there are minor differences between them.[1]

This approach can be illustrated by drawing upon the model of Allingham and Sandmo, which was discussed in Chapter 5. There it was found that individuals would engage in tax evasion if $p\pi < \theta$, where p is the probability of detection, π is the penalty on undeclared income and θ is the standard rate of income tax. In other words, individuals would underdeclare their income if the expected penalty on each £ of undeclared income was less than the standard rate of income tax.

It is a simple matter for a tax authority wishing to eliminate evasion to set the values of p and π so that $p\pi > \theta$. If this were done no one would take the risk of underdeclaring their income and evasion would be completely eliminated.

Further, it seems that the tax authority can trade-off one policy weapon against the other. This can be shown fairly clearly by plotting the 'honesty set' (see Figure 8.1). This plots the curve $p\pi = \theta$ for a particular value of θ, i.e. $\bar{\theta}$. For points above the curve $p\pi > \bar{\theta}$ and no one will evade. The points above the curve are labelled H to indicate the set of values which will ensure complete honesty. Further, the optimal values of p and π will depend upon the size of θ. For values of θ larger than $\bar{\theta}$ the authority will need to set larger values for p or π or both in order to counteract the incentive to evade created by the higher tax rate.[2]

Of course, this particular optimal policy mix emerges from a specific model of tax evasion in which p, π and θ are fixed for the individual taxpayer, in which penalties are levied on undeclared income and in which taxpayers are risk-averse and assumed to maximise expected utility. However, remarkably similar policy rules can be derived for alternative specifications of the taxpayers' problem.[3]

Given that there is an infinite set of combinations of p and π that

Figure 8.1   The trade-off between certainty and severity of punishment

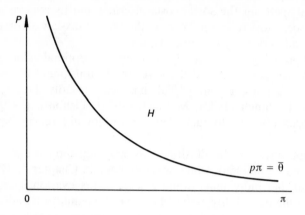

would satisfy the requirement that $p\pi > \theta$, which one should the government or tax authority choose? It might seem natural to conclude that as increasing p is costly (e.g. employing more tax inspectors), but that increasing π is relatively costless (fines are merely transfers), then an optimal policy would involve setting p at almost zero and π at an almost infinite level.

Given this result one must ask why it is that governments do not raise penalties indefinitely in order to eliminate evasion. In fact the penalties for tax evasion are, on the whole, quite minor (see Skinner and Slemrod, 1985; *Keith Report*, 1983).

There are at least two reasons for this. One is the need to make the punishment fit the 'crime' and the other relates to equity considerations. Presumably the first of these is the stronger reason for limitations on the size of penalties. No one would wish to see people either executed or sentenced to life imprisonment for minor acts of tax evasion. That would seem to be 'unfair'.

Economists working in the area of criminal law enforcement (Stigler, 1970) have pointed to the need to preserve an element of marginal deterrence in the structure of penalties. To use an extreme case, suppose that the penalty for both tax evasion and murder was death. Then quite clearly it would be in the interests of evaders to murder anyone who might know about their involvement in evasion. The penalty system would then be producing rather strange signals indeed. As Chapter 6 shows people do not regard evasion as a major crime (only slightly more serious than bicycle theft!), so it seems reasonable to assume that a relatively low upper limit would be imposed upon π.

Severe penalties applied very infrequently would also mean that detected and undetected evaders would be treated quite differently. This would introduce a further inequity into the distribution of income.[4] Whether this should be taken too seriously in deciding upon the size of penalties is a debatable point (but see below). However, perhaps it is the recognition that on occasions taxpayers can make genuine mistakes that has caused penalties to be held down in some cases of evasion. For example, in the UK legislation a clear distinction is drawn between minor offences (largely of a regulatory nature) and major offences of a fraudulent kind. Conviction for minor offences usually carries a fixed monetary penalty, whereas the penalty for major offences incorporates some element of tax-gearing, i.e. the maximum penalty is some proportion of the tax lost, perhaps up to 200 per cent, although cooperation with the authority can reduce this substantially.

Despite its apparent attractions it would appear that a policy of setting very high penalties for tax evasion has some major drawbacks. A policy aimed at eliminating evasion would have to accept limits to the value of π (the severity of punishment). Presumably these limits would be determined by wider considerations of criminal-justice policy, e.g. the need to relate the punishment to the offence in order to preserve an element of marginal deterrence.

However, if the tax authority cannot rely upon costless punishment to eliminate evasion, but has to use costly detection methods, then a policy of completely eliminating evasion may not be optimal.[5] It would need to balance the costs of deterring evasion against the gains that would result from more investigative effort. It has often been claimed that the return to investigative effort is substantial. For example, the Inland Revenue in evidence to the Public Accounts Committee (1981–2) claimed that in 1981 the yield (in extra tax revenue) from investigative work was about £92 000 per official, considerably in excess of the costs of employing an investigator. Likewise, Skinner and Slemrod quote estimates by the IRS Commissioner which indicate that 'every extra dollar of resources allocated to the IRS could be expected to bring in more than ten dollars in tax revenue' (Skinner and Slemrod, 1985, p. 350).

Cost–yield calculations like these could no doubt be used to justify a considerable expansion in resources for the tax authority. However, we must be careful here, for such a policy may not be socially optimal. Skinner and Slemrod have argued that 'the appropriate rule is to equate the marginal cost of additional enforcement to the marginal reduction in the total welfare cost of tax evasion (ibid, p. 350).[6] To increase investigative effort up to the point at which the marginal cost of enforcement is exactly balanced by the extra tax revenues it generates may produce an excessive (i.e. suboptimal) tax collection. This is because the extra revenue generated is merely a transfer from the private to the public sector. The 'gain' to society will be the difference between the social valuation of the extra public goods that can be provided as a result and the social valuation of the lost private consumption. It seems reasonable to assume that this sum will be less than the amount of the tax collected.[7] If that is the case, then it points to reducing investigative effort below the point at which its marginal cost just balances marginal tax receipts.

However, even this result is not universally accepted. Sandmo claims to have shown that:

> the marginal cost of catching an additional evader should at the optimum be equal to the marginal tax revenue, computed along the compensated supply curves, plus a term reflecting the curvature of the utility function or the degree of risk-aversion. In other words, marginal cost should be greater than marginal tax revenue; the presence of risk-aversion leads to an optimal probability of detection which is *higher* than a simple cost – revenue calculation would seem to indicate (Sandmo, 1981, p. 284).

Yet in the same article he argues that 'at an optimum there should be positive marginal revenue from raising . . . the probability of detection' (ibid, p. 278), i.e. marginal tax revenue should exceed marginal detection costs, except when evaders' utility carries a zero weight. In that rather special case detective effort is pushed to the point at which marginal costs and revenues are equated. This second result, at least, seems intuitively reasonable. When evaders' utilities do not count any revenue raised by bringing them into the tax net represents a social gain (reduced taxes, etc., for others). In that case the rule for deciding optimal investigative effort is the standard marginal one.

This apparent inconsistency in Sandmo's results is disturbing. Unfortunately the source of the discrepancy is not immediately apparent. It is difficult to find a simple explanation for his counterintuitive result, so it must for now remain something of a curiosity that requires more detailed investigation.

There may be other reasons for doubting the wisdom of a policy aimed at completely eliminating tax evasion. We have questioned the desirability of enforcing complete honesty on the grounds that to do so could be inordinately expensive. The government is forced to take a purely pragmatic approach to enforcement. It should do so as long as the benefits are not substantially outweighted by the costs. However, setting aside the question of costs, there may be a societal preference for less than total honesty. Various writers – e.g. Kolm (1973), Baldry (1984) and Cowell (1987) – have argued that if society's social welfare function is of the utilitarian kind then it can never be optimal to eliminate tax evasion. This argument can be illustrated as follows. Suppose that all households are identical and would, given the values of π, p and θ, prefer to engage in some evasion. Society's welfare function would be given by the expected utility of the representative household. In those circumstances it is quite clear that enforcing compliance would reduce each individual household's expected utility and hence would reduce social welfare.[8] A utilitarian social optimum would, therefore, tolerate a certain amount of evasion.

The problem with the utilitarian approach is that it is concerned with *ex ante* utility and not *ex post* utility. If one is more concerned to design a tax and penalty system that is equitable in an *ex post* sense then a number of considerations suggest themselves. Any system which detects only a small proportion of evaders and imposes penalties upon them will generate *ex post* horizontal and vertical inequities. If one has an aversion to *ex post* inequality then the optimal policy would shift in favour of a higher detection rate and lower penalties. Furthermore, how much weight should be given in the utility function to the welfare of known (i.e. detected) evaders? The more weight they receive then the more likely one is to opt for a policy of more lenient penalties (Cowell, 1987). Of course, if proven evaders receive very little weight in the soceital welfare function then full compliance might once again become a reasonable goal of the tax authority.

8.2 TAX-LAW ENFORCEMENT: MORE SOPHISTICATED STRATEGIES

So far it has been assumed that each taxpayer faces precisely the same probability of being audited, detected and punished. Recently, Landsberger and Meilijson (1982) and Greenberg (1984) have argued that a more efficient use of the tax authority's resources may require differential audit probabilities across individuals. It should be emphasised that both these approaches take a rather narrow view of society's objectives. They are concerned with raising tax revenues and minimising the number of evaders respectively. The wider issues of what is done with the raised revenue, or whether evasion should be discouraged, are not addressed.

If one is only concerned with raising a certain amount of revenue or eliminating evasion, then it is clear that a policy of discretionary auditing may very well be superior to one which applies the same audit probability to all taxpayers.

Landsberger and Meilijson suggest a state-dependent penalty system. Individuals are initially classified into different groups quite arbitrarily. These groups are then subjected to random audits with known, but different probabilities. Suppose there are two groups (which we label as G_1 and G_2) that are audited with probabilities p_1 and p_2 respectively, where $p_2 > p_1$. If an individual in G_1 is audited and found to have been cheating, his/her 'punishment' – in addition to the normal fine – is to be moved to G_2. An individual in G_2 who is audited and found to have declared all his/her income is 'rewarded' by being transferred to G_1, the group with the lower audit probability. If individuals are not audited they remain in their existing groups.

Landsberger and Meilijson show that such a policy will generally increase tax revenues collected by the authorities for fairly large ranges of p, compared with a system based upon a single audit probability. Unless, of course, p is so large that no one cheats anyway. The superiority of the state-dependent penalty system is most pronounced where evasion is already widespread.

Greenberg analyses essentially the same problem using a repeated game-theoretic approach in which both individuals and the tax authority have to pick optimal strategies. The tax authority faces a budget constraint which determines the maximum fraction of the population that it can audit in any time-period. The tax authority's goal is assumed to be to minimise the number of tax evaders, although it cannot ever get this down to nil. Greenberg derives an optimal strategy for the tax authority. This involves initially dividing the population into three groups, the relative sizes of which (in proportion to the entire population) are a, $1 - a$, and 0, where a is the 'acceptable' proportion of evaders from society's point of view.

The probabilities of being audited in each of these groups are $\frac{p}{2}$, $(a/1-a)$ $p/2$ and 1 respectively, where p is that probability of detection at which everyone decides to cheat.

Clearly anyone allocated to Group 1 (G_1) will decide to cheat. However, if they are audited they will be moved into Group 2 (G_2). Greenberg shows that the best response for anyone assigned to G_2 is to report truthfully. (If audited s/he will be returned to G_1 if found to have been honest, but moved to G_3 if found to have been lying.) Anyone assigned to Group 3 (G_3) will always report truthfully, because the probability of audit is 1 and there is no movement out of that group. However, as no one is assigned to that group initially and no one 'chooses' to enter it, it will remain empty.

Each time period $ap/2$ individuals will move from G_1 to G_2 and $ap/2$ will move in the opposite direction, so that the sizes of Groups G_1 and G_2 will remain the same and the number of evaders will stay at society's acceptable level (a).

Of course, if individuals collude and all decide to cheat, then eventually everyone will end up in G_3 and the authority would be unable to carry out its threat to audit everyone in that group. If this were to happen taxpayers on the whole would be better off. Given the massive numbers of taxpayers in most advanced economies it seems unlikely that such collusion will take place and so Greenberg's result will hold.

The use of game theory to derive optimal strategies for the tax authority has also been suggested by Reinganum and Wilde (1984) and Graetz, Reinganum and Wilde (1984). Reinganum and Wilde consider the sequential process by which the taxpayer and the tax authority achieve equilibrium detection and reporting strategies. The 'game' is characterised by assymetries in information. Each taxpayer knows his true income, but the tax authority can only find that out by undertaking an audit. The authority must decide on the basis of the individual's declared income whether or not to instigate an audit.[9] Reinganum and Wilde show that, in equilibrium, taxpayers with larger true incomes underreport *less* than those with smaller true incomes, and that investigative effort by the tax authority is reduced the larger is reported income. This analysis points to the tax authority using other information which is related to income, e.g. occupation, for classifying taxpayers into likely evaders. If this can be done the tax authority can devote more of its scarce resources to investigating these individuals.

Graetz, Reinganum and Wilde (1984) use a similar approach to analyse the optimal strategies of a budget-constrained tax authority that can only audit a fraction of all taxpayers. When the constraint is binding they find that high-income recipients will tend to underreport their income with a probability of 1. In these circumstances all that the tax authority can do is to audit as many taxpayers who report low incomes as it can. Recall Greenberg's conjecture about taxpayer collusion.

Reinganum and Wilde (1985) have also investigated the use of cut-off rules by the tax authority. A cut-off rule could be of the following form. If a taxpayer reports an income below a certain figure then his/her tax affairs are audited (with probability 1). However, if the taxpayer reports an income above the cut-off point no audit is carried out. The taxpayer is fully informed about the rule and its consequences. The advantages of this rule are:

(i) it provides an incentive for individuals to report their income accurately;
(ii) it is horizontally equitable in both *ex ante* and an *ex post* sense;
(iii) it raises at least as much revenue as a purely random audit policy of the kind described in section 8.1.

It should be emphasised, however, that Reinganum and Wilde's analysis is based upon the assumptions that all taxpayers are risk-neutral, that all taxes are of a lump-sum variety and that the tax authority's objective is to maximise net revenue – i.e. tax receipts less audit costs.[10] Their results may not hold for more general cases.

8.3   ALTERNATIVE POLICY OPTIONS

Sections 8.1 and 8.2 discussed how the tax authority might manipulate its auditing policy and how the government might set penalties so as to reduce the extent of income tax evasion. Those two sections followed a rather traditionalist discussion of law enforcement which led to the question whether a policy aimed at totally eliminating evasion was necessarily a good thing. It also briefly mentioned the possibility that a marginal relaxation of enforcement could enable a tax cut, although in practice the degree to which taxes could be reduced following an easing up on enforcement is likely to be minute. However, one option not so far considered is a rather larger reduction in income-tax rates. How effective would that be in reducing evasion?

Of course, tax-rate changes are not usually the preserve of the tax authority. The tax authority normally has to accept tax rates as given (by government ministers) and has the task of raising the revenue by using its enforcement powers. However, it would be a rather narrow approach to ignore the use of tax rates as a device in discouraging evasion. Indeed one (but maybe only a minor one) of the driving forces behind the recent reductions in marginal rates of tax in the industrialised economies has been the observation that higher tax rates are rarely actually paid. They are either avoided or evaded.

Income-tax rates are normally set with other considerations in mind – e.g. income redistribution, incentives on labour supply, saving, risk-taking and so on. This means that a full evaluation of their role in reducing evasion should not overlook these other issues. Unfortunately, space precludes such a discussion here. These arguments indicate that the discussion of optimal income taxes needs also to include an awareness of the effect that tax rates may have upon the degree of evasion and hence upon equity and efficiency issues (see Weiss, 1976, for an attempt to do this).

How effective would a cut in the rate of income tax be in reducing evasion? Unfortunately, the discussions of Chapters 5 and 6 could hardly be said to offer unequivocal support for such a policy. At best the theoretical prediction of the effect upon tax evasion of a tax cut could be described as ambiguous. At worst, when tax penalties are linked to the amount of unpaid tax (as in Yitzhaki, 1974) a tax cut would actually increase evasion. Recall that this happens because of the way that the penalty is designed. It eliminates the substitution effect leaving a pure income effect. With increased income, following the tax cut, and diminishing absolute risk aversion, individuals are willing to take on more risk and so declare less income.

Unfortunately many tax systems impose penalties on the amount of tax evaded.[11] The theoretical analysis suggests in that situation that tax evasion would be reduced by *raising* rather than lowering the tax rate. Of course this result comes from a model which assumes an exogenously fixed income and no stigma costs from engaging in evasion. As Chapter 5 shows once these assumptions are relaxed predictions are rather different. For example, in a model where stigma costs are included, raising the tax rate encourages some of those who are not already evading tax to do so. The net result may be an increase in the aggregate amount of evasion.

Nevertheless in designing an anti-evasion policy it might seem dangerous to have to rely upon the consciences of potential evaders.

In doing so one hopes that waverers will find that the benefits no longer compensate for their feelings of guilt and that the waverers outweigh the hardened evaders. Tax-cutting would be a much less risky policy if the tax authority took the trouble to redesign the penalty system. For example, authorities should move away from a system of penalties based upon the amount of tax evaded and towards one which relates them to undeclared income.

Support for such a view can also be found in the work of Koskela (1983), who uses an Allingham–Sandmo type model to investigate the effect of 'compensated' changes in the marginal tax rate. Here it is found that the effect of an increase in the tax rate, compensated by a corresponding change in lump-sum transfers so as to keep either expected tax revenues or expected utility constant, will depend upon how penalties are decided. If penalties are charged on undeclared income then evasion will increase. However, if they are charged on evaded tax evasion will decrease. The corollary of this is that a cut in the tax rate will reduce evasion *provided* that penalties are based upon undeclared income.

Cowell and Gordon (1986) have shown that an increase in the tax rate may encourage evasion *if public goods are underprovided*. This may seem an odd result. After all if public goods are underprovided would not consumers willingly pay to have more of them provided? However, improved provision of public goods (paid for by the higher tax rate) makes people feel better-off and with decreasing absolute risk-aversion they would be more willing to evade.[12]

On balance then there may be some theoretical support for a policy of tax cuts provided that penalties are correctly formulated. Unfortunately, in many countries at the moment it would seem that they are not.

Empirical support in favour of tax cuts is unfortunately difficult to find. The most directly relevant study is that of Clotfelter, which was reviewed in Chapter 6. Clotfelter used his results to simulate the effect of tax cuts upon tax compliance and concluded that 'tax cuts may result in sizeable reductions in unreported income (Clotfelter, 1983, p. 372). However, Clotfelter's analysis may be seriously flawed. It was suggested in Chapter 6 that his refusal to include deterrence variables may have introduced specification error and that he had not dealt adequately with the issues of simultaneity and identification. Furthermore, Graetz and Wilde (1985) have cast doubt upon the reliability of TCMP data as a means of estimating aggregate non-compliance.

Cox has questioned Clotfelter's interpretation of the strong direct relationship found between tax rates and undeclared income. He argues that this could simply reflect relationships between compliance and income levels, an hypothesis which he attempts to test by tabulating data on compliance rates for different income groups and income-tax rates. Admittedly this 'test' is a weak one and many variables affecting compliance have been ignored. However, he claims 'we find no evidence of an effect of marginal tax rates on compliance' (Cox, 1984, p. 287).

Casual evidence of another sort seems to undermine the idea that lower tax-rates might encourage compliance. Graetz and Wilde argue that underreporting of capital gains is a large share of all underreporting and yet rates of tax on capital gains are considerably below those on other forms of income. They conclude 'where there is an opportunity for underreporting of income people will understate such income even if the unreported income would be taxed at a low rate' and 'there is little reason . . . to believe that lower rates alone are likely to inhibit non-compliance' (Graetz and Wilde, 1985, p. 360).

Even if a tax reduction did encourage greater compliance the effect would not necessarily be to increase government revenues. Consider the following highly simplified characterisation. Government revenue is made up of tax receipts and penalties imposed upon detected evaders. Using the notation of Allingham and Sandmo then the expected revenue (R) obtained from the typical individual will be given by

$$R = \theta X + p\pi [W - X]$$

The effect of a change in the tax rate (θ) upon this revenue is given by

$$\frac{\partial R}{\partial \theta} = [\theta - p\pi] X_\theta + X$$

where X_θ is the first derivative of X (declared income) with respect to θ. Suppose that $X_\theta < 0$ i.e. an increase in the tax rate encourages people to declare less income. 'Entry' into evasion requires that $\theta > p\pi$ (Chapter 5) and so $\frac{\partial R}{\partial \theta}$ *cannot* be signed unambiguously. The reason for this is that whilst a tax cut encourages declarations and so increases tax receipts, it also means lower receipts from existing declarations. Obviously this analysis is highly simplified. It assumes a fixed income, a penalty based upon undeclared income, it does not consider detection costs and so on. Nevertheless, it is sufficient to show that even from a theoretical viewpoint the case for tax cuts as a means of encouraging compliance and therefore tax receipts needs careful scrutiny.

One possibility which seems much less contentious in its effect is the widening of witholding legislation. Empirical work shows quite clearly (see Chapter 6) that where incomes are subject to tax deduction at source compliance is significantly less of a problem. Likewise improvements in third-party reporting and the matching of third-party information with individual returns will encourage compliance. Unfortunately it is difficult to see how *all* sources of income could be subject to witholding – e.g. tips – but there seems little reason why some forms of employment – e.g. casual work on building sites – should not have tax deducted at least at the basic rate. Of course, this may increase costs of collection and employers too will bear some of that cost. Unfortunately, there is little detailed information about the exact size of those costs to help in deciding whether or not they represent 'value for money'.

8.4   THE KEITH REPORT: A CASE STUDY

Recently there has been a great deal of interest in and concern about the extent of tax evasion. For example, in the UK there has been much coverage of the activities of people working in the black economy and the various ways they evade their taxes. Also, the UK's Inland Revenue Department has devoted an increasing amount of resources to detecting these so-called moonlighters.

It is interesting therefore to examine some of this public debate and particularly how it relates to policy issues. In doing so we wish to see how suggestions for improving public policy on evasion compare with policies proposed by economists and outlined in sections 8.1–8.3. As a vehicle for this discussion this section will examine some of the recommendations of the *Keith Report*.

The Committee on Enforcement Powers of the Revenue Department was established under the chairmanship of Lord Keith of Kinkel in July 1980 by the UK government. Henceforth it will be referred to as the Keith Committee and its Report as the *Keith Report*. The *Keith Report*, which runs to four volumes and 1378 pages, began to appear in 1983 with the publication of the first two volumes covering direct taxes administered by the Inland Revenue and the value added tax (VAT). Two further volumes have since appeared covering topics such as petroleum taxation and development land tax. This section will concentrate upon the *Keith Report*'s treatment of income taxes and VAT, which are the subjects of volumes 1 and 2. Even so this is a substantial mass of material. Volumes 1 and 2 contain 804 pages and include 20 pages of recommendations covering some 158 separate items. Inevitably this review must be rather cursory.

The terms of reference of the Keith Committee were:

> To enquire into the tax enforcement powers of the Board of Inland Revenue and the Board of Customs and Excise, including: powers of investigation into the accuracy of returns including powers to call for information and documents; powers of entry and of search of premises and persons; powers relating to cases of fraud, wilful default or neglect and to cases of reckless action: but not including the ordinary processes of collecting outstanding tax and the charge of interest thereon. To consider whether these powers are suited to their purposes having regard both to the need to ensure compliance with the law and to avoid excessive burdens upon the taxpayers and to make recommendations.

At about the time the Committee was being established there was a great deal of public and official concern about the size and growth of the black economy. Certainly there was much discussion of the activities of casual workers, especially in Fleet Street and the construction industry, who were alleged to be involved in massive tax evasion (see Ilersic, 1979).

At the same time there was considerable disquiet, particularly from small traders, over what were claimed to be the Draconian and intolerable powers that had been granted to the Customs and Excise and Inland Revenue Departments by the *Finance Acts* of 1972 and 1976, respectively. Both Acts had conferred the power to search premises under warrant for evidence of an offence or fraud. These changes were so disliked that an adjournment debate was held in the House of Commons under the title 'Tax Inspectors (Powers of Entry)'. This came shortly after the Court of Appeal had likened the Inland Revenue's behaviour in the Rossminster case to 'a military style operation' (White, 1983).

In addition, the Conservative Party *Election Manifesto* of 1979 had pledged a future Conservative government to review the powers of the two Departments. It was, therefore, no surprise when in February 1980 the Minister of State at the Treasury announced his intention to set up a Committee 'to weigh the need to ensure compliance with the law against the need to avoid excessive burdens on taxpayers' (*Hansard*, 28 February 1980). This dual concern can be quite easily seen in the final sentence of the terms of reference of the Committee, although the taxpayer might be forgiven for thinking that the main concern of the Committee would be to ensure that his/her privacy was to be safeguarded from arbitrary invasion by officials.

The terms of reference did not allow the Committee to consider anything beyond enforcement powers and they focused particularly upon whether these were sufficient to ensure that evasion could be reduced to a bearable minimum. This is unfortunate, because it allowed the Committee to look at only a very small part of the problem. It should be clear from reading this book that there are a host of issues relating to evasion about which remarkably little is known as yet. The government missed an excellent opportunity to bring the discussion of these issues out into the open. The real problems are the extent of tax evasion; whether or not it is growing and if so, how rapidly; whether evasion is necessarily 'bad' and if so, what should be done about reducing it. The actual terms of reference of the Keith Committee took for granted that evasion should be reduced as far as possible, but even then only allowed the Committee to consider how the law should be enforced to achieve this aim.

The government and its advisers have failed to see the wood for the trees. In this case pressure to set up a Committee to investigate matters relating to evasion came from owners of small businesses who were concerned about what they saw as the Draconian powers of the Revenue Departments. It might be cynically argued that the Conservative Party, anxious to placate an important traditional source of their support before an election, sought to buy that support by offering to set up a committee to look at the Departments' enforcement powers. Whether they and their supporters are happy with the end result is another matter.

It is not entirely true to argue that the Committee did not consider the extent of tax evasion during the course of its deliberations. However, the only 'evidence' to which it refers is an 'estimate' by the Chairman of the Board of the Inland Revenue given to the Public Accounts Committee in 1980. Further, the only submission it published on this subject was a note on the black economy prepared by the Inland Revenue and Customs and Excise (*Keith Report* Note 41.).

The importance of this note is that it fails to offer an even-handed survey of existing evidence. Only two 'studies' are referred to i.e. those of Macafee (1980) and the Inland Revenue's own guesstimate (see Chapter 7). The considerable discrepancy between the results of these two studies is glossed over as 'not necessarily incompatible' (ibid, p. 772). No attempt is made to explain how the Inland Revenue's estimate of the size of the black economy (7½ per cent of GDP) has been obtained.[13] It is merely stated that 'we have seen no evidence which leads us to revise our view that 7½ per cent of GDP is a "not implausible" figure for the size of the black economy' (ibid, p. 773). It would have been interesting to see what the Committee would have made of the evidence had they been allowed to see it. The failure of the Inland Revenue to publish supporting evidence for its claim is particularly disturbing. Why were they so reluctant to publish this material? Is their estimate really nothing more than an informed hunch?[14] The fact that they have spurned the opportunity to lay evidence before the Committee should arouse feelings of concern and disquiet. Strangely, it seems that the Committee was quite content to accept this situation.

At various points in reading the *Keith Report* one is struck by how much the Committee had been influenced by the views of the Inland Revenue and the Customs and Excise. In this light the importance of Note 41 can be seen to be quite crucial. I will therefore, consider this Note in rather more detail.

The committee was told that the black economy now accounts for some 7½ of GDP. This figure is neither so high as perhaps to indicate that the Revenue Departments are incompetent nor so low as to suggest that there really is not anything to worry about. In other words the black economy is just large enough to cause concern and to indicate that with some increases in enforcement powers control can be maintained. Alternative policies, such as changes in the tax system, are gently dismissed. For example, there is a brief (one paragraph) discussion of the causes of the growth in evasion. The reasons are described as being 'to a considerable degree questions of opinion and judgement' (ibid, p. 773). At one point the level of tax rates is mentioned as a possible cause only to be dismissed in the next sentence by the judgement that 'history does not suggest that tax evasion is very closely related to this' (ibid, p. 772). Besides which changes in tax rates would probably have little effect because 'the habits of evasion, once acquired, may not be lost even where the advantages of evasion fall as a result of reduced tax rates' (ibid, p. 773).

Later, in Note 41, the Committee is told that 'if the black economy and tax evasion to which it gives rise are allowed to grow unchecked there must be serious implications for the integrity of the tax system and for the willingness of the ordinary taxpayer to comply with tax legislation' (ibid, p. 774).

Given its terms of reference, the limited evidence put before it and the Committee's willingness to accept that evidence so uncritically, it is not surprising to find the Report arguing that 'It is . . . necessary for the revenue gathering Departments to have an adequately equipped armoury of coercive powers to deal with the recalcitrant minority' (ibid, p. 3). How the Committee proposed to do this can be seen, for example, from its recommendations concerning the treatment of income-tax offences. To concentrate on the two more serious categories of offence – gross negligence and civil fraud: the committee proposed that the penalties for these should be tax-geared with the gearing ratio set at 100 per cent for fraud and 30 per cent for negligence. However, the Committee also recommended that 'the Inland Revenue should continue to have a general power to mitigate . . . penalties, but the use of the power should be restricted to *exceptional* cases' (ibid, p. 572, my emphasis). The Committee recommended that for civil fraud the penalty could be mitigated to 50 per cent of the tax lost. No mitigation was possible for negligence cases.

Currently those convicted of major offences can theoretically receive tax-geared penalties of as much as 200 per cent of the lost tax. On the face of it, it would seem that the Committee is proposing the adoption of considerably lighter penalties. In fact quite the opposite is true. In very many cases the Inland Revenue starts with a maximum penalty of 100 per cent (rather than 200 per cent) and then grants considerable reductions if the taxpayer makes a prompt and full disclosure of his/her irregularities. So much so, that for relatively minor offences (in terms of amounts defrauded) the penalty is reduced to zero.

The Committee, therefore, proposed quite substantial increases in penalties and much less discretion to the Inland Revenue in rewarding 'helpful' evaders. The second point is quite important because it reduces the incentive for the taxpayer to cooperate. It will probably make detection of evasion even more difficult for the Inland Revenue, because now the recalcitrant taxpayer has a greater incentive to cover up his wrongdoings. This will force the Revenue to use more of its scarce resources on detailed investigation work.

In addition, Chapter 7 has shown that adopting penalties that are related to the amount of tax evaded is potentially much more dangerous than relating them to the amount of undeclared income. With tax-geared penalties a cut in the tax rate (e.g. in the UK budget, 1988) will encourage evasion not reduce it. Quite clearly the Committee's deliberations on these issues and the influence of tax rates on evasion lacked any input from economists working in the area.

The failure of the *Keith Report* to consider resource questions is also disappointing. Debate about questions of policy cannot be divorced from the consideration of the resources required to carry them out. For example, at various points the *Keith Report* makes recommendations aimed at increasing the detection of evasion many of which, if implemented, would have considerable resource implications not just for the Inland Revenue, but also for the taxpayer.[15] Yet there is no serious attempt to rank these options in terms of some criterion of cost-effectiveness. Indeed sometimes where the Inland Revenue has attempted to reallocate resources so as to improve returns it comes in for criticism, being told that 'such a policy may be penny wise and pound foolish' (*Keith Report*, p. 8).[16]

Of course, the Report does make some useful suggestions. For example, the proposal that withholding should be introduced for various specialist trades, casual employees and agency workers. Withholding is a potentially important policy for reducing evasion. However, why the rate of withholding should be set at one-half of the basic rate of income tax must remain something of a mystery. Even here there is no discussion of the resource costs for society of adopting such a proposal.

The *Keith Report*, rather like the curate's egg, can be described as 'good in parts'. However, one cannot help feeling a great opportunity has been missed. Of course, that is not entirely the Committee's fault. Its hands were tied by its terms of reference. Interestingly, the Committee recommended that the power of search for evidence of fraud should be retained.[17] Yet, it was this very power which had caused taxpayers so much concern and had been influential in persuading the Conservative Party to propose establishing a Committee in the first place.

8.5 CONCLUSIONS

The design of policies to regulate the extent of tax evasion require careful elucidation and specification of society's objectives. It is not necessarily the case that evasion is altogether the evil that popular discussion of the problem would suggest. Also, except in the most likely situations, the detection and prevention of evasion require the use of scarce resources that have alternative uses. Inevitably then policy decisions must balance costs against benefits. The consequence is that it may in fact be desirable to allow some evasion to take place. Indeed, some authors suggest that an optimal tax system would provide incentives to cheat and that such a system is more efficient than one which fails to offer such an option (Weiss, 1976).

It is clear, too, that economists have devoted a great deal of effort to the design of optimal strategies for tax-enforcement bodies. Unfortunately, if the *Keith Report* is anything to go by, it is equally apparent that little, if any, of that material is known to the tax authorities.

9 Conclusions

There is an infamous quip that 'if all the economists in the world were laid end to end they still wouldn't reach a conclusion'. Whilst this is no doubt intended to be a humorous remark it does have a serious edge. Economists, as a group, seem to be naturally disputatious. No sooner does someone come up with a new theoretical result or some new evidence than it is immediately challenged. In recent years outsiders must have been puzzled to hear of some of the arguments between economists over macroeconomic policy, for example. Of course, the researches of economists into aspects of the black economy and tax evasion are much less in the public gaze. However, the disagreements are almost as widespread. Much more importantly, research into the economics of tax evasion is still in its infancy. There is much to be done, too many areas about which we know too little for us to produce unequivocal conclusions. To pretend otherwise would be a grave disservice to both the general public and the economics profession. I hope, therefore, that I can be forgiven for producing only a few rather inconclusive comments on the economics of tax evasion by way of a conclusion. It seems natural to arrange these remarks in the same way as the structure of the book.

I have examined four broad issues in this book. First, how large is the black economy (and, therefore, what is the extent of tax evasion)? This has naturally led to considering the alternative methods that have been used in order to measure the extent of such activity. Second, what are the 'incentives', broadly defined, that cause individuals to engage in tax evasion and to participate in the black economy? Third, what are the economic consequences of such activity, for example in terms of its effect upon macroeconomic variables, macroeconomic management, and resource allocation? Finally, what policies should be followed in order to achieve an 'optimal' level of evasion, whatever that might mean?

First, then, I considered the issue of size and measurement. Broadly speaking four ways of measuring the size of the black economy have been reported in the literature. These are:

(i) monetary approaches;
(ii) approaches based upon discrepancies between income and expenditure (either nationally or at the household level);

173

(iii) labour market surveys;
(iv) the soft-modelling (or black box!?) approach.

The rationale for the adoption of the various monetary approaches
is the argument that cash is the principal means of payment in the
black economy. This has led to the use of changes in currency levels
or ratios (to either bank deposits or the money supply) to measure
changes in the size of the black economy. There are, as we have seen,
many problems with this kind of approach. Cash is *not* the sole
medium for 'black' transactions and there are other causes of changes
in currency holdings. Even the more sophisticated use of currency
ratios suggested, for example, by Tanzi relies heavily upon the tax
rate being the primary factor driving transactions underground. In
addition there are further doubts about, for example, assumptions
concerning the income velocity of circulation in the black economy.

The alternative monetary approach, the transactions method,
which was suggested by Feige, has almost as many flaws. Additionally, it produces estimates of the size of the USA's black economy
which are difficult to believe e.g. a doubling of the black economy
between 1976 and 1978, so that by the later year it amounted to some
33 per cent of GNP.

On the whole it is difficult to believe that monetary approaches
offer a particularly satisfactory estimation technique. Yet they have
attained a remarkable degree of popularity. As Chapter 3 shows,
they have been used throughout the advanced, industrialised countries. In view of the inadequacies of the method it is hard to justify
why this has been so. One can only conclude that the alternative
estimation methods are even worse. More cynically one might conclude that the monetary approaches are rather easier to apply than
the other methods. Data on currency and other monetary instruments are readily and cheaply available. All that is needed is a
willingness to 'bash out' a few regression equations and as if by magic
we have an estimate of the size of the black economy.

Certainly estimation methods using household and labour-market
surveys are much more time-consuming and are rather expensive to
undertake. Additionally, it is tempting to conclude that those who
are heavily involved in the black economy would be most unlikely to
participate in such exercises. Measurement based upon either discrepancies between national income and expenditure or the 'soft
modelling' approach seems to be the most suspect of all.

Perhaps it is not so difficult after all to understand why the monetary, and especially cash, approaches have proved so popular. Of course, it may be that they have, quite accidentally, produced fairly accurate estimates of the size of the black economy. This is rather like the child who gets the correct answer to a maths test by entirely incorrect means. By pure chance the answer is correct. Unfortunately, unlike the child's examiner, we have no idea what the correct answer should be.

If we reject approaches based upon the use of monetary statistics, what can be done to estimate the size of the black economy? The honest answer to that is 'probably remarkably little'. The only truly reliable and believable source of information on undisclosed incomes comes from random audits of taxpayers. Even here there are problems. For example, auditors do not always uncover all sources of undeclared income and not many countries have random audits (the USA is an exception).

On balance then existing methods of estimation seem highly questionable. It would, therefore, appear foolish to place too much faith on the estimates reported in Chapters 2, 3 and 4. Further research along these lines would appear to be almost futile. Of course, it is very much easier to be negative than it is to offer constructive suggestions for future research. The only approach that does commend itself is one that has not been followed to any great extent. This is the detailed analysis of random samples of taxpayers in order to compare their declared income with the amount which they have been found to have earned.

Unwittingly, perhaps, the currency ratio has unearthed one rather interesting fact. This is that households, on average, hold unusually large amounts of cash – far more than they would seem to need in order to finance their daily transactions. If these holdings cannot be accounted for by the existence of the black economy, then what does explain this phenomenon? This is an interesting topic for further research.

The second major area of research by economists looking at the black economy has been the examination of the reasons why individuals participate in such activity and their response to both positive and negative 'incentives'. This has been approached by first constructing theoretical models of individual decision-making in situations of risk and uncertainty and second examining how individuals either claim to behave or actually behave.

The theoretical modelling of individuals' decisions to engage in tax evasion has basically followed the approach suggested by Becker

(1968) for analysing criminal behaviour. Whilst the degree of sophistication of these models has been considerably improved in the last few years this has brought its own problems. Also, there are still some major omissions. For example, as models have become more complicated, their comparative–static predictions have become much less clear. Economists are used to this. Most 'price' changes involve income and substitution effects which often work in opposite directions. As in demand theory, so in the theory of income-tax evasion. However, this does bring into question precisely what role further theorising should play in the study of evasion and what insights one can expect from further effort along existing lines. The second strand of criticisms about existing theoretical models is that they are deficient in certain important respects. For example, Skinner and Slemrod (1985) have shown that the odds are heavily stacked in favour of evaders getting away with it and yet, they claim, the vast majority of taxpayers play the game and declare all their income. The fact that they do so seems to require either belief in a remarkable degree of risk-aversion on taxpayers' parts or just that individuals attach a considerable disutility to dishonesty. The former seems unrealistic and the latter does not fit easily into the subjective expected utility approach.

However, on this last point there have been some interesting recent developments incorporating stigma costs into the utility function. Models of this type have been quite successful in explaining why some individuals will prefer not to become involved in the black economy. Further they have proved capable of explaining why an increase in tax rates would encourage such activity. Standard expected utility models have tended to produce at best inconclusive 'evidence' on this point and at worst rather odd predictions.

As yet models including stigma costs have been rather simplistic. For example, 'stigma' costs are incorporated by assuming an additively separable utility function. Further development of models of this type may prove worthwhile and should be encouraged. This would make the economic models more realistic and may even improve their predictive power. Further criticism of theoretical models focuses upon the failure to construct dynamic (i.e. lifetime) models and upon the treatment of enforcement policy as an exogenous factor influencing individuals' decisions. On this latter point it is interesting to note that Reinganum and Wilde (1983) claim that when a 'responsive' tax authority is incorporated into a general equilibrium model, then many of the comparative static properties of simpler, partial equilibrium models do not hold. This seems to bring us back full circle. More sophisticated models leave us rather perplexed about the effect upon tax evasion of changes in tax rates, penalties and detection rates.

The solution should lie in the results of econometric studies. Alas the current harvest of such studies is remarkably thin. The real obstacle to empirical work has been the absence of virtually any, let alone reliable, information on the extent of tax evasion at either the micro or macro level. The two studies (Clotfelter, 1983, and Witte and Woodbury, 1985) which have exploited perhaps the best data source must remain suspect, because of possible specification error and simultaneity bias. Others have turned to using questionnaires and game simulations. Whilst the results of this work are interesting one must remain sceptical about how far one can generalise from the results of such work. There is an overwhelming need for a careful, sophisticated econometric analysis of individual tax returns. Such a study, in whatever country it is undertaken, would obviously require the cooperation of the tax authority in providing the basic data. However, the authority would have much to gain from cooperating in such a venture.

It is only through careful econometric analysis that one can hope to uncover quantitative evidence on the extent to which income-tax evasion is influenced by changes in tax rates, detection rates, severity of punishment and so on. Whilst theoretical modelling can produce some interesting insights it tends to produce fairly inconclusive predictions. Even were this not the case and clear unambiguous predictions were to emerge this would be insufficient for policy formulation. Theoretical models produce qualitative predictions. Policy requires quantitative ones. The only way these can be obtained is through empirical research.

There is some disagreement about the exact economic consequences of tax evasion and consequently whether or not it is a socially harmful activity. On balance it was found that the macroeconomic effects, both in terms of evasion's effect upon macroeconomic information and upon aggregate economic variables, are probably not particularly large. However, the effects upon the efficiency of resource allocation and the distribution of income are potentially much more harmful. However, this is an area of the subject that has, as yet, received remarkably little attention from economists. One area of research definitely suggests itself: this is the construction of a macro-economic model incorporating a black-economy sector. Only when such a model exists can one hope to establish the extent of the macroeconomic effects of tax evasion. Unfortunately, the obstacles to the construction of such a model are considerable. As Chapters 2–4 have shown, there is no readily available information upon the amount of output produced in the black economy. Little is known about prices in that sector or of the amounts of capital and labour employed there. These data inadequacies prevent the development of such a model and the prospects for obtaining the essential data inputs look particularly bleak. A useful starting-point might be to build a simple general-equilibrium model incorporating a 'black' sector which can then be used to decide the critical data requirements.

By contrast there has been some considerable development on the policy front, although there is some implicit disagreement about precisely what the objectives of policy in this area should be. For example, there are those who simply regard evasion as bad and hence conclude that it should be eliminated or at least reduced as far as possible and those (utilitarians) who argue that some evasion should be tolerated – to remove it all would lower social welfare. In a way issues like that cannot be resolved by economists. It represents a fundamental disagreement over values. Once 'society' decides whether or not evasion is undesirable, then economists can suggest efficient policies to cope with it.

Research points to the dangers of imposing very high penalties as a means of deterring evasion. The need to retain a proper structure of penalties in order to maintain marginal deterrent effects and the dangers of *ex-post* horizontal inequality which severe penalties would create mitigate against their use. The seductive option of relatively costless, harsh penalties applied fairly infrequently does not, on closer examination, seem quite so appealing. However, once we acknowledge that realistically evasion can only be deterred by spending on increasing detection rates, we also have to acknowledge that a certain amount of evasion may have to be accepted. It is just too costly to eliminate it entirely: to do so would impose greater costs than could be justified.

There is now a growing literature examining what we have called sophisticated strategies for tax authorities. It is clearly the case that a more efficient use of the tax authority's resources requires differential audit probabilities across individuals. However, precisely how rules can be formulated is rather less obvious. Further research along these lines would obviously be quite informative.

The case for using tax rates to deter evasion is much less clear-cut. Indeed some people would argue that they are not a legitimate policy instrument at all. Setting that aside the theoretical and empirical analysis as yet hardly offers convincing proof that a reduction in income-tax rates would bring about an unequivocal increase in income declared to the tax authorities. At this point economics and 'common sense' seem to part company. Everyone 'knows' that evasion is a consequence of high tax rates. Of course, the failure of economists to confirm this view may itself be the fault of economists. The empirical work, for instance, has not been particularly distinguished in this respect and we have earlier recommended that a substantial research commitment should be undertaken in this particular area.

A rather overlooked implication of the theoretical literature is the apparent need to design penalties with greater care. It would seem that the effect of a tax change is quite sensitive to penalty formulation. If penalties are geared to the amount of tax evaded then a tax cut *may* produce a perverse response. Unfortunately that is precisely how penalties are designed in many countries.

One policy weapon which seems to be universally recognised as being an effective safeguard against tax evasion is the withholding of tax at source. Whilst such an option would be difficult to apply to the self-employed, there seems little to prevent its more rigorous application to employees, unless, of course, one is concerned about equity considerations. Further, the wider application of withholding might give employees an incentive to move into self-employment which is not necessarily a more efficient use of their time and skills. So even apparently non-controversial options such as withholding are not quite so obviously desirable when subjected to closer scrutiny.

The twin subjects of the black economy and tax evasion are fascinating topics. Over the past few years, a growing interest has been shown by economists in these areas. As this book has shown a great deal of interesting and imaginative research, both theoretical and empirical, has been undertaken during that time. Unfortunately, the subject presents peculiar difficulties for researchers and so whilst a great deal has been learned there is much that still needs to be done before economists can be confident in making policy proposals. Unfortunately research has been patchy. Much has been done on the 'easy' areas e.g. theoretical modelling of individual decisions, theoretical analysis of policy options, regression-bashing to estimate the size of the black economy. There are large gaps in the 'hard' areas.

Some of those gaps have been indicated in this book, but not doubt many more exist. Maybe we will never reach a conclusion but at least the journey should be fun.

Notes

1 Introduction

1. There is a sometimes confusing plethora of terms used to describe the black economy. The term 'underground economy' is a popular one, although in some cases it includes activities which we would not count as part of the black economy. For a definition of terms see section 1.1.
2. Many studies have, in fact, tried to explain the currency ratio rather than the level of currency itself. The currency ratio is defined as the ratio of currency either to demand deposits or to the money supply. See Chapters 2 and 3.

2 Measuring the size of the black economy: monetary approaches

1. The UK is not unusual in this regard. Indeed, figures quoted by the Bank of England (1982) show that cash holdings per head of population are even higher in other Western European and North American countries. For example, in the Netherlands and West Germany currency per head is nearly twice as much as in the UK, whilst in Sweden and Belgium it is three times the UK's level.
2. It is now widely acknowledged that the first person to suggest that variations in the ratio of cash to money supply could be attributable to tax evasion was Cagan (1958).
3. Isachsen, Klovland and Strøm (1982) found in a survey undertaken in Norway that some 79 per cent of black economy payments were made in cash. Likewise Miller (1979) found that slightly more that 70 per cent of all black economy services in the UK were paid for in cash. Whilst, these figures may seem high, it should be realised that they are not very different from those for the legitimate economy (see Smith, 1986, pp. 87–90).
4. Cagan assumes that currency and bank deposits have different income elasticities of demand: 'both deposits and currency are considered superior to other assets as a form of holding wealth, but not equally so, deposits being superior to currency. . . . the income elasticity of deposits is greater than that of currency' (Cagan, 1958, p. 306). However Garcia and Pak (1979) estimate that the long-run income elasticity of demand for currency is *greater* than that for demand deposits.
5. He argues that sales and other indirect taxes are difficult to evade.
6. The $M2$ definition includes currency in circulation with the public plus demand and time deposits of all commercial banks held by the non-bank public.
7. Tanzi (1980) claimed that this rate was 'likely to provide yearly rates that may be closer to some modal average tax rates experienced by the tax payers than would the (other) two alternatives' (p. 441). This justifica-

tion seems rather weak and one is led to conclude that Tanzi's choice has really been based upon the size of the *t*-statistic for this coefficient rather than sound *a priori* reasoning.

8. Note that again there is an implicit assumption that the income velocity of circulation in both the black and formal economies is the same.

9. The estimated equation for 1929–80 is:

$$\ln \frac{C}{M2} = -5.0262 + 0.2479 \ln T - 0.1554 \ln R$$
$$\qquad\quad (3.61) \qquad (5.81) \qquad\qquad (3.66)$$
$$+ 1.7303 \ln W - 0.2026 \ln Y$$
$$\quad (5.33) \qquad\qquad (1.90)$$
$$\bar{R}^2 = 0.95 \qquad\qquad D.W = 1.576$$

This should be compared with equation (2.1) on page 20.

10. Tanzi (1980) argues that one of the key assumptions of his approach was that 'underground economic activities are the direct consequence of high taxes' (p. 289). In a footnote to his paper (p. 289, footnote 6) he acknowledges that there might be other causes of black economy activity, but in this respect mentions only criminal activities that he claims should not be counted as part of GNP anyway. When challenged on this point by Acharya (1983), Tanzi (1983) claimed that the so-called Tanzi method 'had one and only one objective: to estimate . . . the magnitude of those underground economic activities that in the United States *have been generated by income taxes*' (p. 748), my emphasis). He further argues that 'much of the discussion of the underground economy in the United States has emphasised the importance of income taxes' (p. 748). These caveats surely diminish the power of Tanzi's results. As we shall see in the subsequent chapters, it is *not* clear that high taxes are even the main, let alone the sole, cause of black economy activity. To be told that he is only concerned with estimating a part of black economy activity is something of a disappoinment.

11. Total transactions include sales of intermediate and second-hand goods and so differ from GNP which covers only sales of final goods and services produced in the current year.

12. Apparently in 1957 the US Bureau of Engraving began to add a melamine-formaldehyde resin that doubled the durability of paper used to print currency.

13. Tanzi (1982) shows that the proportion of currency denominated in bills of $100 and over rose from about 22 per cent in 1970 to over 36 per cent in 1980. In the whole of the period between 1933 and 1970 the 'big bill proportion' had remained around the 20 per cent mark plus or minus 2 per cent.

14.

	1965	*1985*
Notes and coin in circulation with the public	£3 122m	£12 732m
Retail price index (1975 =100)	43.4	276.8

Source: *Economic Trends*, 1987, Annual Supplement

3   Monetary statistics and the black economy: some evidence

1. In an Appendix to their paper, Porter and Bayer re-estimate the size of the black economy using the ratio of currency to demand deposits. After 1975 this produces much larger estimates, so that by 1982 the estimated size of the black economy is $832 billion or 27 per cent of GNP.
2. The tax rate is measured as the ratio of personal income taxes to personal income net of transfers.
3. Notice that, unlike Tanzi, Mirus and Smith do *not* include the interest rate on time deposits as an explanatory variable. This is presumably because their dependent variable is the ratio of currency to *demand* deposits.
4. The M1 definition of the UK money supply includes notes and coin in circulation with the public and sight deposits.
5. The £M3 definition of UK money supply is M1 (see note 4) plus time deposits denominated in sterling.
6. This is tantamount to assuming a unit elasticity of demand for currency.
7. In any case the paper by Isachsen and Strøm (1985) merely reports an early version of Klovland's findings for Norway and does not offer any new results, except that they use a somewhat lower estimate of the income velocity of circulation. As a consequence Isachsen and Strøm estimate Norway's black economy to have been 6.3 per cent of GDP in 1978 compared with Klovland's estimate of 9.2 per cent (Klovland, 1980). However, as Klovland has since repudiated his earlier estimates of the cash-demand equation for Norway this is all rather academic. The paper by Schneider (1986) reports some results obtained by estimating a modified form of the equation used in the Schneider and Lundager (1986). This produces some slightly different estimates of the scale of black-economy activity, but these are not startlingly different from those reported in the text.
8. This reflects the difficulty of actually deciding what constitutes *the* marginal tax rate. The first measure includes income taxes only. The second measure includes both income and pay-roll taxes. The third and final measures include indirect taxes, in addition to income and pay-roll taxes.
9. This included employees' social security contributions.
10. For example, Schneider and Lundager (1986) conclude that 'the marginal influence of the tax rates on the demand [for] currency is quantitatively strongest for Norway' (p. 13). This should be contrasted with Klovland's comment that 'the tax variables did *not* directly contribute to explaining the demand for currency in Norway' (Klovland, 1984 p. 433, my emphasis).
11. The implicit assumption here is that the black economy did not exist in 1954 in any of the three countries.
12. Note that this is once again a reference to a pre-Hendrified estimate by Klovland that he has since rejected (Klovland, 1984).
13. Unfortunately Kirchgässner fails to include in his article the precise definitions of M1 and M2. (One presumes that the M1 and M2 measures

in West Germany are similar to the M1 and M2 measures of the money supply in USA.)

14. Kirchgässner experiments with two alternative specifications of the tax variable. These produce slightly different estimates of the size of the black economy; e.g. in 1980 they suggest that it could be either 8 per cent or 11.5 per cent of GNP.
15. No formal statistical tests of the relationship are reported by Boyle.
16. Boyle's formulation forces the price-level elasticity of currency demand to be indentical to the real consumers' expenditure elasticity. A less restrictive formulation would appear to be preferable. He has also ignored the influence of tax rates.
17. For example the average M1/GDP ratios for 1973–7 were:

Italy	0.52
USA	0.19
UK	0.16
France	0.27
West Germany	0.15

18. This estimate is presumably derived by assuming a constant money-income ratio and then multiplying the 'excess' money by an estimate of the income velocity of circulation.
19. It is statistically insignificant when the weighted average tax rate on interest income is used. It has the wrong sign when the tax rate is proxied by the ratio of total tax payments to income. See Porter and Bayer (1984, p. 188, note 18).

4 Non-monetary approaches to measuring the black economy

1. The income for self-employed households had to be scaled up, because information in the FES on the income of such households is some years out of date. Also, households 'with very "lumpy" expenditure patterns . .[were set]. . to the average for their type and group' (Dilnot and Morris, 1981 p. 64) i.e. households, for example, which had bought consumer durables during the period would have expenditures above their income. In order not to distort the estimates of black-economy earnings, the expenditure levels of these households were smoothed out along the lines indicated above. The danger is that households with 'black' earnings may very well buy consumer durables.
2. The cut-off point for the upper bound is slightly complicated. On page 66 Dilnot and Morris say 'we introduced an absolute minimum of £3 for the discrepancy' and 'we chose a 20 per cent cut-off as our principal criterion'. This presumably means that the upper cut-off point was an expenditure level greater than declared income by at least 20 per cent or £3, whichever is the larger.
3. There is no explanation of what they consider unusual expenditures to be. For example, would they include the purchase of a yacht or a second home in the Costa del Sol under this category? Note 1 has indicated that

households with 'lumpy' expenditure patterns had already had their expenditure adjusted to take account of this, so what is the second adjustment?

4. The terms 'upper' and 'lower' bound are slightly confusing here. By upper bound, Dilnot and Morris mean their estimate of the upper limit of the extent of the black economy. The lower bound is their lower-limit estimate of the extent of black-economy activity.

5. This compares with average household weekly income in 1977 of £93 per week.

6. Apart from employment status other household characteristics should be the same in order for this analysis to be valid – e.g. family size, type of housing tenure, ages of household members, etc., should all be the same.

7. This formulation of the consumption function allows both the slope and intercept of the employee and self-employed consumption functions to be different. An alternative form of equation (4.1) was also estimated. In this form the two types of household were constrained to have the same marginal propensity to consume, i.e. $b_3 = 0$.

8. If $b_3 = 0$, i.e. self-employed households have exactly the same marginal propensity to consume as employee households, then concealed income will be given by $\dfrac{b_1}{b_2}$.

9. The estimates of 'excess' expenditure and concealed income reported by Smith *et al.* are obtained from the revised version of equation (4.1) in which $b_3 = 0$ (see note 8).

10. Interestingly, the unconstrained estimates of the marginal propensity to consume (*mpc*) for white-collar self-employed households are usually larger than the constrained estimates. This suggests that self-employed households have a larger *mpc* than do employee households, which contradicts the underlying theory.

11. It is not hard to think why expenditure on certain pre-commitments, i.e. mortgage payments, may not reflect concealed income. In order to obtain a mortgage a self-employed household would have to declare its income to either a bank or building society. The lending institution would wish to see the accounts and/or tax returns of the household's business. These would show the income declared to the tax authority. Members of the household could hardly tell the bank that their income was actually higher than this because of some 'off-the-books' or undeclared earnings. Mortgage commitments will, therefore, be more closely related to declared income than to true income. However, it is difficult to see why expenditure on pre-commitments of 'blue-collar' households should be determined in a quite different manner.

12. It is clear also that Smith *et al.*'s results are quite sensitive to the specification of the consumption function (equation (4.1)). The size and significance of the coefficient of the self-employment dummy changes quite substantially between estimates based upon the equation (4.1) and its modified form.

13. This is why many economists argue that there are really only two ways of calculating GDP – the output/expenditure method and the income method.

Notes

14. This is why some other economists maintain that, in principle, there is only one *independent* method of calculating GDP.
15. As a consequence expenditure on tobacco and alcoholic drink used in estimating GDP is drawn from Customs and Excise information on duties paid rather than FES returns. By switching from surveys of household expenditure to surveys of sales by firms in order to measure certain expenditures, there is a risk that some black-economy expenditures will be overlooked. This will happen because government surveys of producers can only select firms supplying the regular market. It is difficult to know how important this is. Presumably most tobacco and alcoholic drink is bought from legitimate suppliers. In addition presumably expenditures on illegal goods, such as drugs, are not shown in the FES diary returns. As a result the expenditure measure of GDP fails to cover these items.
16. Of course, there will be other reasons why the income and expenditure methods could disagree. Macafee lists two – (1) timing errors, i.e. buyers and sellers recording the same transaction in different time periods; and (ii) sampling errors.
17. However, estimates by Smith (1986) of consumers' expenditure derived from the FES do *not* indicate that the CSO estimate of consumers' expenditure used in the national income accounts seriously understates expenditures. In fact the CSO estimate exceeded that based upon FES by about 14 per cent between 1979 and 1983 if expenditure on alcoholic drink and tobacco is included and by about 11 per cent if it is excluded.
18. For example, Matthews (1984) shows the IRD as a percentage of GDP: (i) as rising between 1972 and 1974 and (ii) falling in 1978. Matthews and Rastogi (1985) estimate that the black economy as a percentage of GDP (i) fell between 1972 and 1974 and (ii) rose in 1978:
19. The time-series estimates of the income/expenditure discrepancy reported by Blades for Sweden are:

Year	% of GDP
1970	3.8
1971	3.0
1972	3.2
1973	4.4
1974	3.9
1975	3.0
1976	3.7
1977	1.5
1978	2.9
1979	3.6

20. Blades (1982) reports that in six countries (Australia, New Zealand, Ireland, Sweden, UK and USA) estimates of the value of undeclared legal production are incorporated into GDP. For example, in Australia in 1976 this was 0.2 per cent of GDP, and in New Zealand it was 1.7 per cent of GDP in 1979. However, these estimates were *not* obtained by comparing the income and expenditure measures of GDP, but by com-

paring estimates of national income with income declared in tax returns (see text).

21. Frey and Pommerehne (1982) quote the following OECD statistics on labour force participation rates in 1975.

Country	Labour force as % of population
Italy	35.5
France	42.3
West Germany	42.7
USA	44.4
UK	46.4
Japan	48.0

22. The labour force (LF) consists of those in permanent employment in the official economy (E), those who are unemployed (U) and those working in the black economy (B), so that

$$B = LF - E - U$$

Contini estimates the labour force by multiplying population size by the estimated 'true' participation rate. The numbers working in the black economy are then obtained by substracting from this number the number of people in employment and those who are unemployed. These are found by multiplying population size by the measured participation rate.

23. Interestingly Contini says 'to my knowledge there has been as yet no attempt to estimate the size of hidden GNP in Italy using the monetary approach suggested by Peter Gutmann and Edgar Feige (Contini, 1982, p. 208). However, Del Boca and Forte report (Tanzi, 1982) an estimate by Saba which they claim uses monetary statistics. However, it is not at all clear from reading Del Boca and Forte what method Saba has used. Unfortunately, Saba's paper is only available in Italian. In view of this we have not reported this result in Chapter 3.

24. For example, we do not know how many people were interviewed, what the response rate was, how the sample was selected, whether it was representative and so on.

25. Women, as might be expected, tended to work more hours than men. The average was 179 hours per year for women compared with 88 hours for men. However, many more men (28 per cent) than women (9 per cent) admitted to working in the black economy. This result seems to fit in quite well with the view of 'off-the-books' work as being irregular and part-time, undertaken as a supplement to the primary source of income.

26. Early results from the 1983 survey, reported by Isachsen and Strøm (1985) show that the proportion of the sample admitting involvement in the black economy had fallen from 37.5 per cent to 33 per cent. Those willing to admit to working in the irregular sector has gone down from 18 per cent to 16 per cent.

27. The lower figure is based on income received from irregular labour supply, whilst the upper figure is derived using payment for such work.

28. In their earlier paper irregular activity is expressed as a proportion of GNP, whereas their later paper uses GDP as the denominator.
29. For example, De Grazia (1980) claims that '(e)ntire neighbourhoods of Naples have been transformed into secret workshops – specialising in shoe - and garment-making – which move on quickly or disappear the moment a visit by the labour force inspectors seems likely. In Milan there are only 5000 homeworkers listed on the city's commercial register, while fewer than 1000 homework enterprises carrying on business in the surrounding province are registered; the true members are estimated at about 100 000 and 50 000 respectively' (De Grazia, 1980, p. 550). Alas, De Grazia does not tell us who estimated the 'true' numbers and how. Martino (1980) provides another piece of anecdotal evidence. 'The Rome Post Office, which employs 1500 people to distribute the mail in the city, handles the same amount of correspondence handled by "Romana Recapiti", a private delivery agency, which employs 300. Needless to say, "Romana Recapiti" is faster and more reliable than the Post Office. But the interesting thing is that most of the 300 people working for "Romana Recapiti" are moonlighting employees of the Post Office. Not surprisingly, the rate of absenteeism at the Post Office is in the neighbourhood of 50 per cent' (Martino, 1980, p. 101).
30. This may measure the objective burden but it is not necessarily the burden perceived by taxpayers and it is the latter which is important in decision-making. Frey and Weck-Hanneman include the *increase* in the share of taxes as a proportion of GDP to measure the 'perceived' burden, presumably on the grounds that individuals are more likely to react to an increase in the level of taxation than to a high but stable level of taxation.
31. The resultant value of H is in terms of a standardised Z-value, which is used to rank the seventeen countries. Frey and Weck-Hanneman use the term 'hidden' rather than 'black' economy. Interestingly, the estimating equation reported by Frey and Weck-Hanneman is slightly different from the one reported by Frey and Pommerehne (1984) which is:

$$H = 0.36T + 0.28P + 0.36M$$

The result is that the sizes of the black economies reported in the two articles are slightly different, as indeed are the rankings for 1978!
32. Clearly, this is an early version of Frey and Weck-Hanneman (1984).
33. Obviously great advances were made on this issue in the following year!

5 Participation in the black economy: theory

1. Interestingly Allingham and Sandmo (1972) attempted an analysis of the dynamic case. However, this did not produce many easily interpretable results and seems to have been largely overlooked in the subsequent literature.
2. Allingham and Sandmo did briefly examine how non-pecuniary factors such as reputation might influence the decision to engage in tax evasion.

Results here were found to depend upon whether or not income and reputation were regarded as substitutes.

3. Investigation is assumed to lead without fail to detection and punishment.

4. However, if individuals are risk neutral then

$$\frac{\partial X}{\partial \theta} = \frac{1}{D} \ [(1 - p) \ U^1 \ (Y) + p \ U^1 \ (Z)]$$

which *is* unambiguously negative, i.e. an increase in the tax rate reduces the optimal declaration.

5. $\frac{\partial X}{\partial p} > 0$ even when p is assumed to depend upon X with $p^1 (X) < 0$. We discuss policies to reduce evasion in Chapter 8.

6. However, there must be some doubt about Srinivasan's signing of these two derivatives given his assumption about the penalty being an increasing, convex function of the level of true income.

7. This happens when the expected fine is held constant for given Y and both π and $(1 - p)$ take low values.

8. Concavity of $U(.)$ further requires that $U_{WW} \ U_{LL} - U_{WL} \ U_{LW} \geq 0$. U_W and U_L are partial derivatives of $U(.)$ with respect to W and L respectively. U_{WW}, U_{LL} and U_{WL} are second order partial derivatives of the function $U(.)$.

9. Pencavel (1979) has investigated the case of non-linear, including progressive, tax schedules.

10. This is the effect of an increase in gross income when there is a progressive tax rate.

11. Pencavel even assumed that 'the utility function is strongly separable in income and hours of work' (Pencavel, 1979, p. 116)

12. To be fair to Andersen he was primarily interested in generalising Allingham and Sandmo's model by integrating the labour-supply decision with the decision to evade income tax.

13. In the formulations used by Andersen (1977) and Isachsen and Strøm (1980) it is clear that $U_{WL} = 0$. This is not the case in the utility function used by Cowell, where $U_{WL} = f^1 \cdot g^1 > 0$. Instead Cowell's specification requires that $d^2 \left(\frac{U_L}{U_W} \right)/ dW^2 = 0$ which is a restriction on the rate of change of the marginal rate of substitution as income increases. This functional specification is due to Dreze and Modigliani (1972).

14. In fact separability of this form is not crucial to Benjamini and Maital's conclusion. See Block and Heineke (1975) for a treatment of the problem in the context of criminal choice where separability is not assumed. Separability is a great help in generating comparative static predictions, however.

15. One way of having both honest and dishonest tax-payers in the model would be by allowing V to vary across individuals. See Gordon (1987).

16. The utility function used by Gordon is also additively separable and is

$$U(Y) - V. E$$

where Y is net income and E is the amount of concealed income.
Unit stigma cost is given by V, so that total stigma costs are proportional to the amount of concealed income.

17. Schlicht further assumes that $f(0,e) > 0$ and $f(1,e) < 1$. These two conclusions help to generate internal (i.e. $0 < a < 1$) stable equilibria, but are not particularly convincing.

18. For example:

$$\dot{a} = \mu \left[f(a,e) - a \right]$$

with $1 \geqslant \mu \geqslant 0$

6 Participation in the black economy: evidence

1. A perhaps slightly odd feature of the sample was that nearly 65 per cent of respondents were Democrats.

2. There seems to be a mistake in Table 1 of Song and Yarbrough's paper, because the percentages and cumulative percentages do not correspond.

3. Respondents were asked to select the most serious crime from the following list: arson, embezzlement, bribery, tax evasion, stealing a bicycle. 7 per cent of respondents selected tax evasion compared with 4.4 per cent who picked bicycle theft.

4. Is this a consequence of the heavy representation of Democrats in the sample?

5. Strongly agree, agree, uncertain, disagree, strongly disagree.

6. Examples of statements are 'People who evade small (large) amounts of tax should be treated leniently (harshly) by the law', 'The amount of tax I pay is unreasonably high (about right)' and 'A similar number of people would still evade tax even if taxation was reduced.'

7. However, there was some inconsistency here. 80.5 per cent of respondents either agreed or strongly agreed with the statement 'A similar number of people would still evade tax even if taxation were reduced.' However, only 47 per cent either disagreed or strongly disagreed with the view 'If people had to pay less tax, fewer people would attempt to evade payment.'

8. Only 24.5 per cent either agreed or strongly agreed with the statement that 'taxation is an imposition' whereas 88.5 per cent agreed that 'taxation is a method of paying for essential services'.

9. Unfortunately, it is not clear what Dean *et al.* had in mind by the terms 'large' and 'small' in this context or for that matter what the respondents understood by these terms. It is quite probable that what one respondent considers to be a 'small' evasion would be classified as a 'large-scale' evasion by another participant.

10. Unfortunately, it is not possible to glean from reading Spicer and Lundstedt's article precisely how these indices were constructed.
11. The independent variable also included measures to reflect experience with tax audits, political party affiliation and the proportion of income derived from wages, salaries or pensions. Unfortunately, it is not clear how the perceived measures of certainty and severity of punishment were obtained.
12. From 24.2 per cent to 26.6 per cent which is not statistically significant. However, the proportion who admitted that they had failed to file a tax return went down from 6.8 per cent to 5.7 per cent. Of course, it is impossible to tell whether the increase in reported evasion reflects merely a greater willingness in 1980 to admit to acts of evasion or an increase in the number of people who evade.
13. It is not always clear precisely how Geeroms and Wilmots have actually measured some of these variables.
14. From 0.57 to 0.47 with a 25 per cent tax rate and from 0.81 to 0.78 with a 50 per cent tax rate.
15. Bracketed figures relate to a fine of three times the amount of tax evaded.
16. Notice that the probability of being audited was not included in the list of exaplanatory variables, although according to Friedland *et al.* it did vary from one time-period to another – 'either one out of fifteen or five out of fifteen' (Friedland *et al.*, 1978, p. 110).
17. Unfortunately, Spicer and Becker did not report any significance tests for these proportions.
18. Of course, the amount of income which the auditors decide should have been declared may itself be wrong. Individuals may appeal against the IRS judgement and have their taxable income reduced. Also, the auditors may not spot all hidden income. Clotfelter's data does not include people who fail to file a tax return.
19. Presumably Clotfelter (1983) has either ignored returns which overstate income or has set such overstatements to zero. He says on p. 367 that 'only understatements of income are examined'.
20. Clotfelter's argument here is that the probability of a person being audited will depend upon the extent of his/her under-declaration of income. Likewise, the greater the under-statement of income the more severe the penalty. If this is true then there is a simultaneous relationship between the amount of tax evasion and sanctions variables.
21. Indeed, by the faulty logic of Clotfelter's argument, if they did measure the probability of detection they should not be included anyway.
22. The inclusion of tax overpayments in the base will cause the compliance measure to understate true compliance. Similar criticisms can be made of Witte and Woodbury's measure as were made of Clotfelter's (see note 18).
23. Witte and Woodbury included several sanction variables – the probability of being audited (both within one's audit class and for other audit classes); the conditional probability of receiving a civil fraud penalty and the conditional probability of receiving a criminal fraud penalty and the average prison sentence imposed for criminal fraud. The deterrent effect

of these penalties is expected to diminish in size the further one moves into the criminal justice system. This is a well-known result from the economics of crime literature (see Pyle, 1983, chap. 4).

24. It would take too long to explain how each of these variables has been measured. Witte and Woodbury (1983, Table 4) give three pages of definitions.

25. The seven audit classes are similar to those used by Clotfelter (1983) and are roughly arrived at by having three broad income groups (high, medium and low) and two basic classes of return (non-business and business). There is in addition a rather mixed group including farm business. Witte and Woodbury did *not* include a measure of the marginal tax rate as a separate explanatory variable.

26. Witte and Woodbury found that audit rates worked with a lagged effect of one or two years. They also found that audits of taxpayers in the same class generally had more effect upon compliance than did audits in general. Somewhat strangely their regression equations included audit rates for 1969, 1968 and 1967 in the same equation.

27. A similar result is found for IRS criminal investigative effort i.e. increases in this variable are associated with reduced compliance.

28. Education is measured by the percentage of persons over 25 years of age with at least four completed years of high school. Old age is measured by the percentage of the population over 65 years of age. Poverty is measured by percentage of families below the official poverty line who are not receiving public assistance.

29. Slemrod's argument is complicated (mathematically), but boils down to saying that evaders will (i) try to get into the lowest tax bracket they can so as to reduce their tax burden, but (ii) within any tax band they prefer to be at the top with the aim of reducing the probability of detection.

30. Other explanatory variables are (i) the percentage of the population over 45 years of age, (ii) the percentage of the work-force employed in manufacturing, and (iii) a time trend.

31. The explanatory variables include all the exogenous variables in the other equation plus the tax authority's budget per return and the percentage of individual returns that are filed.

32. The audit rate is a moving average of the current, one-year and two-year lagged values of the percentage of total tax returns audited each year by the IRS. The fine rate is the ratio of additional taxes, penalties and interest assessed by the IRS to the amount of taxes evaded. The inflation rate is measured by the rate of change of the consumer price index.

33. The primary purpose of Crane and Nourzad's research had been to investigate the relationship between inflation and tax evasion. They argued that inflation could affect individuals' decisions to engage in tax evasion if tax thresholds were not revised in line with inflation. They found a positive and significant effect, although the elasticity is low – a 1 per cent increase in the inflation rate resulted in a 0.14 per cent increase in the *proportion* of income reported or nearly $600 million in absolute terms.

7 The consequences of tax evasion and the black economy

1. In earlier chapters we have focused exclusively on the issue of *income* tax evasion. However, in this chapter we will also consider the consequences arising as a result of evading other taxes in particular indirect taxes such as VAT, excise duties and so on.
2. If evasion opportunities are reduced then presumably returns to suppliers would be reduced and prices paid by buyers would rise. This would tend to discourage both supply and demand for these goods.
3. Peacock and Shaw also show that if the marginal propensity to consume (*mpc*) of evaders alone is 1, then tax revenues will be unaffected by evasion. They regard this as a more plausible case. Briefly, suppose that income can be divided into two parts – aY and $(1 - a)Y$, where a is a coefficient measuring evasion. Further, assume that the *mpc* of evaders is b_2 and of non-evaders is b_1. Then:

$$C = b_1 (1 - a) Y (1 - t) + b_2 aY$$

Using the national income equilibrium condition:

$$Y = C + A$$

then:

$$Y = \frac{A}{1 - b_1 (1 - a) (1 - t) - b_2 a}$$

With no evasion i.e. $a = 0$, the tax yield is given by

$$T_1 = tY = \frac{tA}{1 - b_1 (1 - t)}$$

However, if $1 > a > 0$ and $b_2 = 1$, the tax yield will be

$$T_2 = t (1 - a) Y = \frac{tA}{1 - b_1 (1 - t)}$$

and so $T_1 = T_2$
4. Even slight modifications to the model will change Peacock and Shaw's result. For example, consider an open economy model. If evaders spend some of their income on foreign goods this will reduce the multiplier effect of their income 'gain' and so tax revenues will be reduced.
5. Everyone could be working and total output (official + 'black') may be rising, but a smaller proportion of activity may be being recorded each year. This leads to the erroneous conclusion that the economy is entering a slump. Of course, if you are a new classical macroeconomist and so

believe that all unemployment is voluntary and that there is nothing the government can do in terms of macroeconomic policy (of a demand type) to raise output systematically above its 'potential' level, then the errors in recorded GDP and unemployment would not really concern you.

6. 'Stagflation is, in part, a statistical artifact resulting from systematic biases in our official statistics that arise from collecting and reporting data on a continually declining fraction of total economic activity' (Feige, 1979, p. 12).

7. For example, Petersen (1982, p. 206) has argued 'if public policy goes on using Keynesian measures for enhancing the growth of the formal economy this will require additional revenues (taxes or debt) which will strengthen the movement into the unobserved sector, thus reducing public tax revenues and increasing public deficits. Following the lines of supply-side economics would be less dangerous because reductions, particularly in marginal tax rates within the lower income brackets, etc. would diminish the incentive to shift into the unobserved sector'. The only reservation one would have about such a statement is that neither theoretical nor empirical analysis can give totally unequivocal support to the existence of a strong link between tax rates and tax evasion (see Chapters 5 and 6).

8. Quite clearly b can range between zero (no black economy) and infinity (no official economy). Larger values of b indicate a relatively larger black economy. The bias in using Y^o rather than Y as an indicator of the *level* of economic activity will be given by $\frac{Y}{Y^o} = 1 + b$.

9. Recall that the studies examined in Chapters 2–4 suggest sizes for the black economies of Western European and North American countries of around 10 per cent. This would put b at around 0.1 and certainly not more than 0.2. In those circumstances it would seem to require a differential growth rate of *at least* 4 per cent per annum before the official growth rate could be regarded as imparting inaccurate information.

10. In order, for example, to compensate for the risk involved in consuming such services. In addition, of course, these services are not subject to tax. However, as a counter, it could be argued that because such services are commonly very labour-intensive and not prone to technical change then their prices will rise *faster* than will the prices of other goods and services. In addition, price increases in the official sector are likely to spill-over into the black economy, either by encouraging the substitution of 'black' goods for official ones and thus raising demand for black goods or by black-economy suppliers basing their prices on official goods prices minus a 'markdown'. Eventually, of course, prices in the two sectors would be brought into line by the forces of competition. The only differences would be due to risk premia.

11. For example, Lewis and Ormerod (1979) in simulations with both the Treasury and NIESR econometric models found that balanced budget multipliers were invariably less than 1 and sometimes negative.

After x years		Multiplier
x	Treasury Model	NIESR Model
1	0.73	0.26
2	0.49	0.17
3	−0.06	−0.07
4	−0.37	−0.17
6	−0.60	−0.41

12. A 1p cut in the basic rate of income tax in the UK is estimated to 'cost' the Exchequer approximately £1.25bn in a full tax year (*Financial Statement and Budget Report*, 1987–8, p. 43).
13. The argument runs that if the government borrows from the banks this will cause the money supply to increase. If, on the other hand, it borrows from the public it can only do so at ever-increasing rates of interest.
14. Adam and Ginsburgh's model makes numerous specific assumptions. These include:

   (i) that Belgium's irregular sector is approximately 15 per cent of GNP;
   (ii) that the irregular sector is characterised by permanent excess supply of both goods and labour;
   (iii) that Belgium's regular sector was characterised by classical unemployment between 1953 and 1956, and between 1969 and 1974, and Keynesian unemployment in 1957–63, 1966–8 and 1975–80;
   (iv) that the production function in the regular sector is Cobb–Douglas with constant returns to scale.

15. The enforcement of tax law itself generates inequalities because tax evaders who are caught and evaders who get away with it are treated differently. This may have quite important implications for the design of penalties, for harsh penalties enforced with a low probability would cause considerable ex-post inequity (Skinner and Slemrod, 1985). See Chapter 8 for a fuller discussion of the design of optimal anti-evasion policy.
16. Both Weiss (1976) and Stiglitz (1982), however, claim that tax evasion might actually reduce the distortionary effect of a tax on wages. They argue that evasion increases the uncertainty of future income and that for some forms of the utility function this leads individuals to supply more labour than they otherwise would do.
17. The underground economy includes both the black economy and criminal activity. It is then necessary to assume how this output is divided between the two underground sectors, although this has relatively little effect upon the estimates of welfare cost.
18. These figures are obtained when (i) *all* elasticities of substitution are assumed to be − 0.5, and (ii) black output and criminal output are assumed to be 5 per cent and 10 per cent respectively more labour-intensive than legitimate output. The lower figure is obtained when the own-price elasticity of demand is assumed to be −0.5, whilst the upper

figure arises when the elasticity of demand is assumed to be -1.
19. The same conditions as described in note 18 apply.
20. Some of the private costs of hiding income from the tax authority may
    not be large. For example, simply failing to record part of one's income
    on the tax form does not impose any cost. However, restructuring one's
    bank accounts, e.g. by setting up an overseas bank account, may be
    somewhat more expensive. Evasion also leads to downstream costs for
    the criminal justice system – court time, fine administration and possibly
    prison costs. In addition, there may be costs imposed upon the honest
    taxpayer, i.e. the possible invasion of his/her privacy by revenue depart-
    ment auditors in their pursuit of evaders.
21. This is borne out by his finding that welfare cost is little affected by
    different assumptions about how underground output is divided be-
    tween black goods and criminal goods.

8   Policy issues

1. For example, Singh attempted to find the 'optimum level of the probability of detection such that tax evasion may be eliminated' (Singh,
   1973, p. 258). On the other hand Fishburn assumed 'the probability of
   detection as given and (sought) the "prohibitive penalty rate"' (Fishburn, 1979, p. 268).
2. This suggests that individuals faced by higher marginal tax rates should
   also be faced by higher penalties.
3. See, for example, Singh (1973) and Fishburn (1979). Singh uses a model
   based on the work of Srinivasan (1973) in which individuals are assumed
   to be risk-neutral and pay a penalty on the amount that income is
   understated in addition to paying all the tax due. In that case the
   'honesty boundary' is defined by

$$p = \frac{T^1(Y)}{\pi + T^1(Y)}$$

   Where $T^1(Y)$ is the marginal tax rate, p is the probability of detection
   and π is the penalty rate. A similar boundary can be derived for the
   'Yitzhaki case', where individuals pay a penalty on the amount of evaded
   tax, i.e.:

$$p = \frac{1}{1 + \pi}$$

   In all these cases it is clear that there is an inverse relationship between p
   and π, so that one policy instrument can be traded off against another.
4. For a discussion of the equity issues surrounding tax-enforcement policies see Scotchmer (1987). She argues that 'efficient' enforcement policies introduce a regressive bias into the tax code.
5. Baldry (1984), for example, has shown that a policy of complete enforcement will maximise expected tax revenues. However, an infinitesimally

small reduction in p (the probability of detection) will leave expected tax revenues unchanged, but reduce detection costs. This saving can then be passed on to consumers in the form of either tax cuts or increased public goods provision which will raise welfare. A policy of full compliance cannot then be optimal.

6. Calculating the marginal benefit of reducing tax evasion might be rather complicated. Recall our discussion in Chapter 7.

7. Interestingly Kolm has shown that an optimal choice of θ, π and p would imply that 'a public pound has a higher social value than a private pound' (Kolm, 1973, p. 269). However, provided that a public pound is less than twice as valuable as a private pound our conclusion will still apply.

8. It is fairly easy to show that in the Allingham–Sandmo model, for example, both $\partial EU/\partial p$ and $\partial EU/\partial \pi < 0$, evaluated at the optimal declaration $W > X > 0$. This assumes that the tax rate is fixed. If it is not, then it would seem to be sensible to enforce compliance, but also lower the tax rate at the same time (see Cowell, 1987, pp. 12–17). In addition, an alternative social welfare function would produce a rather different optimal policy. For example, Cowell shows that with a Rawlsian social-welfare function (which attaches most weight to the least-well-off members of society) an optimal policy would be to set p and π such as to 'terrify everyone into compliance' ibid, p. 25). The 'advantage' of that from an equity point of view, of course, is that because no one actually evades nobody pays the enormous penalties and there are no problems with ex-post inequality. Yet as Cowell concludes 'if the penalties are never actually applied, will they be believed?' (ibid, p. 32).

9. Even if an audit is undertaken it does not guarantee to provide the authority with perfectly accurate information. Accuracy can be improved by investing more resources.

10. However, they claim to have also analysed the case of proportional taxation and found the dominance of cut-off rules over random audits to hold.

11. For example, in the USA, Australia, UK and Israel penalties are related to the amount of evaded *tax* rather than the amount of undeclared income.

12. The public goods effect and the income effect of the tax change obviously work in opposite directions. If the public goods effect dominates then evasion will increase.

13. All that the Department would say was 'the figure was not a firm estimate but rather a broad judgement made in response to much higher figures suggested by others which were not considered realistic. It was a rounded figure using such information as the Inland Revenue had about evasion . . . making some fairly broad assumptions in arriving at the aggregate amount' (*Keith Report*, p. 772). A typically vague and unhelpful Civil Service phrase.

14. In the words of Note 41 'Our judgement is that so far the black economy has not seriously undermined the attitude of the general public . . . but further growth – or indeed the growing awareness of

the existing state of affairs – could well have such an effect' (*Keith Report*, p. 774).

15. For example, the recommendations that traders should keep detailed accounts and records relating to tax returns for at least six years and that third parties who provide information to tax authorities should inform taxpayers of what they have reported (and that the information is kept for at least three years).

16. This relates to the Inland Revenue's policy of reducing the frequency of issuing tax returns to people in the PAYE system in order to devote resources to investigations into the black economy!

17. 'As regards the use . . . of the power to search . . . for evidence of tax fraud, the few occasions on which it has been invoked since 1976 do not, in our view, amount to an oppressive exercise of power' (*Keith Report*, p. 7).

Bibliography

ACHARYA, S. (1983) 'The Underground Economy in the United States: Comment on Tanzi', *IMF Staff Papers*, vol. 31, pp. 742–6.

ADAM, M. C. and GINSBURGH, V. (1985) 'The Effects of Irregular Markets on Macroeoconomic Policy: Some Estimates for Belgium', *European Economic Review*, vol. 29. pp. 15–33.

ALLINGHAM, M. G. and SANDMO, A. (1972) 'Income Tax Evasion: A Theoretical Analysis', *Journal of Public Economics*, vol. 1, pp. 323–38.

ALM, J. (1985) 'The Welfare Cost of the Underground Economy', *Economic Inquiry*, vol. xxiii, pp. 243–63.

AMEMIYA, T. (1980) 'Selection of Regressors', *International Economic Review*, vol. 21, pp. 331–54.

ANDERSEN, P. (1977) 'Tax Evasion and Labor Supply', *Scandinavian Journal of Economics*, vol. 79, pp. 375–83.

ARROW, K. (1970) *Essays in the Theory of Risk-Bearing*, Amsterdam: North Holland.

BALDRY, J. C. (1979) 'Tax Evasion and Labour Supply', *Economic Letters*, vol. 3, pp. 53–6.

BALDRY, J. C. (1984) 'The Enforcement of Income Tax Laws: Efficiency Implications', *The Economic Record*, vol. 60, pp. 156–9.

BANK OF ENGLAND (1982) 'Recent Changes in the Use of Cash', *Bank of England Quarterly Bulletin*, vol. 22, pp. 519–29.

BECKER, G. S. (1968) 'Crime and Punishment: An Economic Approach', *Journal of Political Economy*, vol. 76, pp. 169–217.

BENJAMINI, Y. and MAITAL, S. (1985) 'Optimal Tax Evasion and Optimal Tax Evasion Policy: Behavioural Aspects', in Gaertner and Wenig (1985).

BHAGWATI, J. and HANSEN, B. (1973) 'A Theoretical Analysis of Smuggling', *Quarterly Journal of Economics*, vol. 87, pp. 172–87.

BLADES, D. (1982) 'The Hidden Economy and The National Accounts', *OECD Economic Outlook*, Occasional Studies, June, pp. 28–45.

BLOCK, M. K. and HEINEKE, J. M. (1975) 'A Labor Theoretic Analysis of Criminal Choice', *American Economic Review*, vol. 65, pp. 314–25.

BOWSHER, N. N. (1980) 'The Demand for Currency: Is the Underground Economy Undermining Monetary Policy', *Federal Reserve Bank of St Louis*, vol. 62, pp. 11–17.

BOYLE, G. E. (1984) 'In Search of Ireland's Black Economy', *Irish Banking Review*, March, pp. 32–42.

CAGAN, P. (1958) 'The Demand for Currency Relative to the Total Money Supply', *Journal of Political Economy*, vol. 66, pp. 303–28.

CARTER, M. (1984) 'Issues in the Hidden Economy – A Survey', *The Economic Record*, vol. 60, pp. 209–21.

CASSELL, D. (1984) 'The Growing Shadow Economy: Implications for Stabilization Policy', *Inter Economics*, September/October, pp. 219–25.

CHRISTIANSEN , V. (1980) 'Two Comments on Tax Evasion', *Journal of Public Economics*, vol. 13, pp. 363–73.

CHRISTOPHER, A. (1976) An Article in *Taxes*, pp. 210–11, quoted in O'Higgins (1980).

CLOTFELTER, C. T. (1983) 'Tax Evasion and Tax Rates: An Analysis of Individual Returns', *Review of Economics and Statistics*, vol. 65, pp. 363–73.

CONTINI, B. (1981) 'Labor Market Segmentation and the Development of the Parallel Economy – The Italian Experience', *Oxford Economic Papers*, vol. 33, pp. 401–12.

CONTINI, B. (1982) 'The Second Economy of Italy', in Tanzi (1982) pp. 199–208.

COWELL, F. (1985a) 'Tax Evasion with Labour Income', *Journal of Public Economics*, vol. 26, pp. 19–34.

COWELL, F. (1985b) 'The Economic Analysis of Tax Evasion', *Bulletin of Economic Research*, vol. 37, pp. 163–93.

COWELL, F. (1987) 'Honesty is sometimes the Best Policy', ESRC Programme on Taxation, Incentives and the Distribution of Income, Discussion Paper TIDI /107.

COWELL, F. and GORDON, J. (1986) 'Unwillingness to Pay: Tax Evasion and Public Good Provision', ESRC Programme on Taxation, Incentives and the Distribution of Income, Discussion Paper TIDI /103.

COX, D. (1984) 'Raising Revenue in the Underground Economy', *National Tax Journal*, vol. 37, pp. 283–9.

CRANE, S. E. and NOURZAD, F. (1986) 'Inflation and Tax Evasion: An Empirical Analysis', *Review of Economics and Statistics*, vol. LXVIII, pp. 217–23.

CROSS, R. and SHAW, G. K. (1981) 'The Tax Evasion–Avoidance Choice: A Suggested Approach', *National Tax Journal*, vol. 34, pp. 489–91.

CROSS, R. and SHAW, G. K. (1982) 'The Economics of Tax Aversion', *Public Finance*, vol. 37, pp. 36–47.

DEAN, P., KEENAN, T. and KENNEY, F. (1980) 'Taxpayers' Attitudes to Income Tax Evasion: An Empirical Survey', *British Tax Review*, pp. 28–44.

DE GRAZIA, R. (1980) 'Clandestine Employment: A Problem of Our Times', *International Labour Review*, vol. 119, pp. 549–63.

DEL BOCA, D. and FORTE, F. (1982) 'Recent Empirical Surveys and Theoretical Interpretations of the Parallel Economy in Italy', in Tanzi (1982) pp. 181–97.

DENISON, E. F. (1982) 'Is US Growth Understated Because of the Underground Economy? Employment Ratios Suggest Not', *The Review of Income and Wealth*, Series 28, pp. 1–16.

DILNOT, A. and MORRIS, C. N. (1981) 'What Do We Know about the Black Economy?', *Fiscal Studies*, vol. 2, pp. 58–73.

DREZE, J. and MODIGLIANI, F. (1972) 'Consumption Decisions Under Uncertainty', *Journal of Economic Theory*, vol. 5, pp. 308–35.

DUBIN, J. A., GRAETZ, M. J. and WILDE, L. L. (1987) 'Are We A Nation of Tax Cheaters? New Econometric Evidence on Tax Compliance', *American Economic Review*, vol. 77, pp. 240–5.

Economic Trends (1987) London: HMSO.

Family Expenditure Survey (1985) London: HMSO.
FEIGE, E. (1979) 'How Big is the Irregular Economy?', *Challenge*, vol. 22, pp. 5–13.
FEIGE, E. (1980) 'A New Perspective on Macroeconomic Phenomena: The Theory and Measurement of the Unobserved Sector of the United States, Causes, Consequences and Implications', mimeo, The Netherlands Institute for Advanced Study.
FEIGE, E. (1981) 'The UK's Unobserved Economy' *Journal of Economic Affairs*, July, pp. 205–13.
FEIGE, E. and MCGEE, R. T. (1983) 'Sweden's Laffer Curve: Taxation and the Unobserved Economy', Industrial Institute for Economic and Social Research, Working Paper no 95.
FISHBURN, G. (1979) 'On How to Keep Taxpayers Honest (or Almost So)', *Economic Record*, vol. 55, pp. 267–70.
FREUD, D. (1979) 'A Guide to Underground Economics', *Financial Times*, 9 April.
FREY, B.S. and POMMEREHNE, W. W. (1982) 'Measuring the Hidden Economy: Though This Be Madness, there is Method in it', in Tanzi (1982) pp. 3–27.
FREY, B. S. and POMMEREHNE, W. W. (1984) 'The Hidden Economy: State and Prospects for Measurement', *The Review of Income and Wealth*, Series 30, pp. 1–21.
FREY, B. S. and WECK, H. (1983a) 'Estimating the Shadow Economy: A "Naive" Approach', *Oxford Economic Papers*, vol. 35, pp. 23–44.
FREY, B. S. and WECK, H. (1983b) 'What Produces a Hidden Economy? An International Cross Section Analysis', *Southern Economic Journal*, vol. 49, pp. 822–32.
FREY, B. S. and WECK-HANNEMAN, H. (1984) 'The Hidden Economy As An "Unobserved" Variable', *European Economic Review*, vol. 26, pp. 33–53.
FREY, B. S., WECK, H. and POMMEREHNE, W. W. (1982) 'Has the Shadow Economy Grown in Germany? An Exploratory Study', *Weltwirtschaftliches Archiv*, vol. 118, pp. 499–524.
FRIEDLAND, N., MAITAL, S. and RUTENBERG, A. (1978) 'A Simulation Study of Income Tax Evasion', *Journal of Public Economics*, vol. 10, pp. 107–16.
GAERTNER, W. and WENIG, A. (eds) (1985) *The Economics of the Shadow Economy*, Berlin: Springer-Verlag.
GARCIA, G. and PAK, S. (1979) 'The Ratio of Currency to Demand Deposits in the United States', *The Journal of Finance*, vol. XXXIV, pp. 703–15.
GEEROMS, H. and WILMOTS, H. (1985) 'An Empirical Model of Tax Evasion and Tax Avoidance', *Public Finance*, vol. XXXX, pp. 190–209.
GORDON, J. (1987) 'Modelling Tax Evasion where Honesty may be the Best Policy', ESRC Programme on Taxation, Incentives and the Distribution of Income, Discussion Paper 102.
GORDON, R. J. (1981) *Macroeconomics*, Boston: Little Brown, 2nd edn.
GRAETZ, M. J. and WILDE, L. L. (1985) 'The Economics of Tax Compliance: Fact and Fantasy', *National Tax Journal*, vol. 38, pp. 355–63.
GRAETZ, M. J., REINGANUM, J. F. and WILDE, L. L. (1984) 'A Model

of Tax Compliance with Budget-constrained Auditors', California Institute of Technolgy, Social Science Working Paper no 520.

GREENBERG, J. (1984) 'Avoiding Tax Avoidance: A (Repeated) Game-Theoretic Approach', *Journal of Economic Theory*, vol. 32. pp. 1–13.

GUTMANN, P. M. (1977) 'Subterranean Economy', *Financial Analysts Journal*, November, pp. 26–7, 34.

GUTMANN, P. M. (1979) 'Statistical Illusions, Mistaken Policies', *Challenge*, November/December, pp. 14–17.

HARBERGER, A. C. (1962) 'The Incidence of the Corporation Income Tax', *Journal of Political Economy*, vol. LXX, pp. 215–40.

ILERSIC, A. R. (1979) 'Tax Evasion in the United Kingdom', *Canadian Tax Journal*, vol. 27, pp. 693–9.

ISACHSEN, A. J. and STRØM, S. (1980) 'The Hidden Economy: The Labour Market and Tax Evasion', *Scandinavian Journal of Economics*, vol. 82, pp. 304–11.

ISACHSEN, A. J. and STRØM, S. (1985) 'The Size and Growth of the Hidden Economy in Norway', *The Review of Income and Wealth*, Series 31, pp. 21–38.

ISACHSEN, A. J., KLOVLAND, J. T. and STRØM, S. (1982) 'The Hidden Economy in Norway', in Tanzi (1982) pp. 209–31.

KALDOR, N. (1982) *The Scourge of Monetarism*, Oxford: Oxford University Press.

KEITH REPORT, The (1983) *Committee on Enforcement Powers of the Revenue Departments*, Cmnd 8822, 9120 and 9440, London: HMSO.

KEMSLEY, W. F. F. (1975) 'Family Expenditure Survey: A Study of Differential Response Based on a Comparison of the 1971 Sample with the Census', *Statistical News*, no 31, pp. 16–22.

KENADJIAN, B. (1982) 'The Direct Approach to Measuring the Underground Economy in the United States: IRS Estimates of Unreported Income', in Tanzi (1982) pp. 93–101.

KIRCHGÄSSNER, G. (1983) 'Size and Development of the West German Shadow Economy', *Journal of Institutional and Theoretical Economics*, no 139, pp. 197–214.

KLOVLAND, J. T. (1980) 'In Search of the Hidden Economy: Tax Evasion and the Demand for Currency in Norway and Sweden', Norwegian School of Economics and Business Administration, Discussion Paper 18/80.

KLOVLAND, J. T. (1984) 'Tax Evasion and the Demand for Currency in Norway and Sweden: Is There a Hidden Relationship?', *Scandinavian Journal of Economics*, vol. 86, pp. 423–39.

KOLM, S-C, (1973) 'A Note on Optimum Tax Evasion', *Journal of Public Economics*, vol. 2, pp. 265–70.

KOSKELA, E. (1983) 'A Note on Progression, Penalty Schemes and Tax Evasion', *Journal of Public Economics*, vol. 22, pp. 127–33.

LANDSBERGER, M. and MEILIJSON, I. (1982) 'Incentive Generating State Dependent Penalty System', *Journal of Public Economics*, vol. 19, pp. 333–52.

LAURENT, R. D. (1974) 'Currency in Circulation and the Real Value of Notes', *Journal of Money, Credit and Banking*, vol. 6, pp. 213–26.

LAURENT, R. D. (1979) 'Currency and the Subterranean Economy',

Federal Reserve Bank of Chicago Economic Perspectives, vol. III, pp. 3–6.
LEWIS, A. (1979) 'An Empirical Assessment of Tax Mentality', *Public Finance*, vol. 34, pp. 245–57.
LEWIS, G. R. and ORMEROD, P. A. (1979) 'Policy Simulations and Model Characteristics', in S. T. Cook and P. M. Jackson (eds) *Current Issues in Fiscal Policy*, Oxford: Martin Robertson.
MACAFEE, K. (1980) 'A Glimpse of the Hidden Economy in the National Accounts', *Economic Trends*, February, pp. 81–7.
MCCALEB, T. S. (1976) 'Tax Evasion and the Differential Taxation of Labour and Capital Income' *Public Finance*, vol. 31, pp. 287–93.
MARTINO, A. (1981) 'Measuring Italy's Underground Economy', *Policy Review*, vol. 16, pp. 87–106.
MASON, R. and CALVIN, L. D. (1984) 'Public Confidence and Admitted Tax Evasion', *National Tax Journal*, vol. XXXVII, pp. 489–98.
MATTHEWS, K. G. P. (1982) 'Demand for Currency and the Black Economy in the UK', *Journal of Economic Studies*, vol. 9, pp. 3–22.
MATTHEWS, K. G. P. (1983) 'National Income and the Black Economy', *Economic Affairs*, July, pp 261–7.
MATTHEWS, K. G. P. (1984) 'The GDP Residual Error and the Black Economy: A Note', *Applied Economics*, vol. 16, pp. 443–8.
MATTHEWS, K. G. P., and RASTOGI, A. (1985) 'Little Mo and the Moonlighters: Another Look at the Black Economy', Liverpool Research Group in Macroeconomics *Quarterly Economic Bulletin*, vol. 6, no. 2.
MILLER, R. (1979) 'Evidence of Attitudes to Evasion From a Sample Survey', in A. Seldon (ed) *Tax Avoision*, London: Institute of Economic Affairs, Readings 22.
MIRUS, R. and SMITH, R. S. (1981) 'Canada's Irregular Economy', *Canadian Public Policy* vol. VII, pp. 444–53.
MORK, K. A. (1975) 'Income Tax Evasion: Some Empirical Evidence', *Public Finance*, vol. XXX, pp. 70–5.
NEVILE, J. W. (1984) 'Macro- Economic Effects of Tax Avoidance', in D. J. Collins (ed) *Tax Avoidance and the Economy*, Sydney: Australian Tax Research Foundation.
NORMAN, N. R. (1982) 'The Economics of Tax Evasion', paper presented to the 11th Conference of Economists, Adelaide; quoted by Carter (1984).
O'HIGGINS, M. (1980) *Measuring The Hidden Economy: A Review of Evidence and Methodologies*, London, Outer Circle Policy Unit.
O'HIGGINS, M. (1981) 'Aggregate Measures of Tax Evasion: An Assessment – I', *British Tax Review*, pp. 286–302.
O'HIGGINS, M. (1982) 'Assessing the Underground Economy in the United Kingdom', paper presented to an International Conference on the Unobserved Economy held at the Netherlands Institute for Advanced Study; quoted by Matthews (1984).
PARK, T. (1979) 'Reconciliation Between Personal Income and Taxable Income, 1974–77', mimeo, Bureau of Economic Analysis, Washington DC.
PEACOCK, A. T. (1983) 'The Disaffection of the Taxpayer', *Atlantic Economic Journal*, vol. 11, pp. 7–15.
PEACOCK, A. T. and SHAW, G. K. (1982a) 'Tax Evasion and Tax

Revenue Loss', *Public Finance*, vol. 37, pp. 269–78.

PEACOCK, A. T. and SHAW, G. K. (1982b) 'Is Tax Revenue Loss Overstated?', *Journal of Economic Affairs*, July, pp. 161–3.

PEACOCK, A. T. and SHAW, G. K. (1982c) 'Calculating the Revenue Loss from Evasion', *Journal of Economic Affairs*, July, pp. 222–6.

PENCAVEL, J. H. (1979) 'A Note on Income Tax Evasion, Labour Supply and Non-Linear Tax Schedules', *Journal of Public Economics*, vol. 12, pp. 115–24.

PERSSON, M. and WISSEN, P. (1984) 'Redistributional Effects of Tax Evasion', *Scandinavian Journal of Economics*, vol. 86, pp. 131–419.

PESTIEAU, P. (1984) 'Belgium's Irregular Economy, Measurement and Implications', in Gaertner and Wenig (1985).

PETERSEN, H-G. (1982) 'Size of the Public Sector, Economic Growth And The Informal Economy: Development Trends In The Federal Republic of Germany', *The Review of Income and Wealth*, Series 28, pp. 191–215.

PORTER, R. D. and BAYER, A. S. (1984) 'A Monetary Perspective on Underground Economic Activity in the United States', *Federal Reserve Bulletin*, vol. 70, pp. 177–89.

POTERBA, J. (1987) 'Tax Evasion and Capital Gains Taxation', *American Economic Review*, vol. 77, pp. 234–9.

PYLE, D. J. (1983) *The Economics of Crime and Law Enforcement*, London: Macmillan.

PYLE, D. J. (1984) *An Economic Analysis of Recorded Property Crimes in England and Wales*, unpublished PhD thesis, University of Leicester.

PYLE, D. J. (1987) *The Political Economy of Tax Evasion*, Edinburgh: The David Hume Institute, Hume Paper no 6.

REINGANUM, J. F. and WILDE, L. L. (1983) 'An Equilibrium Model of Tax Compliance with a Bayesian Auditor and Some "Honest" Taxpayers', California Institute of Technology, Social Science Working Paper 506.

REINGANUM, J. F. and WILDE, L. L. (1984) 'Sequential Equilibrium Detection and Reporting Policies in a Model of Tax Evasion', California Institute of Technology, Social Science Working Paper 525.

REINGANUM, J. F. and WILDE, L. L. (1985) 'Income Tax Compliance in a Principal–Agent Framework', *Journal of Public Economics*, vol. 26, pp. 1–18.

RICKETTS, M. (1984) 'On the Simple Macroeconomics of Tax Evasion: An Elaboration of the Peacock–Shaw Approach', *Public Finance*, vol. 39, pp. 420–3.

ROSS, I. (1978) 'Why the Underground Economy is Booming', *Fortune*, 9 October, pp. 92–5 and 98.

SANDMO, A. (1981) 'Income Tax Evasion, Labour Supply and the Equity–Efficiency Trade-off', *Journal of Public Economics*, vol. 16, pp. 265–88.

SHLICHT, E. (1985) 'The Shadow Economy and Morals: A Note', in Gaertner and Wenig (1985).

SCHNEIDER, F. (1986) 'Estimating the Size of the Danish Shadow Economy Using the Currency Demand Approach: An Attempt', *Scandinavian Journal of Economics*, vol. 88, pp. 643–68.

SCHNEIDER, F. and HOFREITHER, M. (1986–7) 'Measuring the Size of the Shadow Economy: Can the Obstacles Be Overcome?', *Economic Affairs*, December/January, pp. 18–23.

SCHNEIDER, F. and LUNDAGER, J. (1986) 'The Development of the Shadow Economies for Denmark, Norway and Sweden: A Comparison', University of Aarhus, memo 1986–1.

SCHWEIZER, U. (1984) 'Welfare Analysis of Excise Tax Evasion', *Journal of Institutional and Theoretical Economics*, no. 140, pp. 247–58.

SCOTCHMER, S. (1987) 'Audit Classes and Tax Enforcement Policy', *American Economic Review*, papers and proceedings, vol. 77, pp. 229–33.

SIMON, C. P. and WITTE, A. D. (1982) *Beating the System – The Underground Economy*, Boston: Auburn House.

SINGH, B. (1973) 'Making Honesty the Best Policy', *Journal of Public Economics*, vol. 2, pp. 257–63.

SKINNER, J. and SLEMROD, J. (1985) 'An Economic Perspective on Tax Evasion', *National Tax Journal*, vol. 38, pp. 345–53.

SLEMROD, J. (1985) 'An Empirical Test for Tax Evasion', *Review of Economics and Statistics*, vol. LXVII, pp. 232–8.

SMITH, J. D. (1985) 'Market Motives in the Informal Economy', in Gaertner and Wenig (1985).

SMITH, S. (1986) *Britain's Shadow Economy*, Oxford: Clarendon Press.

SMITH, S., PISSARIDES, C. A. and WEBER, G. (1986) 'Evidence from Survey Discrepancies', chap. 12 of Smith (1986).

SONG, Y-D and YARBROUGH, T. E. (1978) 'Tax Ethics and Taxpayer Attitudes: A Survey', *Public Administration Review*, vol. 38, pp. 442–52.

SPICER, M. W. and BECKER, L. A. (1980) 'Fiscal Inequity and Tax Evasion: An Experimental Approach', *National Tax Journal*, vol. 33, pp. 171–5.

SPICER, M. W. and HERO, R. E. (1985) 'Tax Evasion and Heuristics', *Journal of Public Economics*, vol. 26, pp. 263–7.

SPICER, M. W. and LUNDSTEDT, S. B. (1976) 'Understanding Tax Evasion', *Public Finance*, vol. 31, pp. 295–305.

SPROULE, R. A. (1985) 'Tax Evasion and Labour Supply Under Imperfect Information About Individual Parameters of the Tax System', *Public Finance*, vol. XXXX, pp. 441–55.

SRINIVASAN, T. N. (1973) 'Tax Evasion: A Model', *Journal of Public Economics*, vol. 2, pp. 339–46.

STIGLER, G. J. (1970) 'The Optimum Enforcement of Laws', *Journal of Political Economy*, vol. 78, pp. 526–36.

STIGLITZ, J. E. (1982) 'Utilitarianism and Horizontal Equity: The Case of Random Taxation', *Journal of Public Economics*, vol. 18, pp. 1–33.

STIGLITZ, J. E. (1986) *Economics of the Public Sector*, New York: Norton.

TANZI, V. (1980) 'The Underground Economy in the United States: Estimates and Implications', *Banco Nazionale del Lavoro*, no. 135, pp. 427–53.

TANZI, V. (ed.) (1982) *The Underground Economy in the United States and Abroad*, Lexington: Lexington Books.

TANZI, V. (1982) 'A Second (and more sceptical) Look at the Underground Economy in the United States', in Tanzi (1982) pp. 103–17.

TANZI, V. (1983) 'The Underground Economy in the United States: Annual Estimates, 1930–80', *IMF Staff Papers*, vol. 30, pp. 283–305.

TANZI, V. (1984) 'The Underground Economy in the United States: Reply to Acharya', *IMF Staff Papers*, vol. 31, pp. 747–50.

TUCKER, M. (1982) 'The Underground Economy in Australia', in Tanzi (1982) pp. 315–22.

US INTERNAL REVENUE SERVICE (1979) *Estimates of Income Unreported on Individual Income Tax Returns*, Washington, DC: US Government Printing Office.

WEISS, L. (1976) 'The Desirability of Cheating Incentives and Randomness in the Optimal Income Tax', *Journal of Political Economy*, vol. 84, pp. 1343–52.

WHITE, R. (1983) 'Keith: The Mouse that Roared', *British Tax Review*, pp. 332–9.

WITTE, A. D. and WOODBURY, D. F. (1983) 'The Effect of Tax Laws and Tax Administration on Tax Compliance', mimeo, Department of Economics, University of North Carolina.

WITTE, A. D. and WOODBURY, D. F. (1985) 'The Effect of Tax Laws and Tax Administration on Tax Compliance: The Case of the US Individual Income Tax', *National Tax Journal*, vol. 38, pp. 1–13.

YITZHAKI, S. (1974) 'Income Tax Evasion: A Theoretical Analysis', *Journal of Public Economics*, vol 3, pp. 201–2.

YITZHAKI, S. (1987) 'On the Excess Burden of Tax Evasion', *Public Finance Quarterly*, vol. 15, pp. 123–37.

Author Index

Subject Index

unemployment in official
economy 139–40

Family Expenditure Survey
participation in 59
used to estimate
income–expenditure
discrepancy 59–60, 68
Fisher's equation 27, 56

ghost, a definition 4
Gutmann method 25, 46

income–expenditure discrepancies
(*see also* initial residual
difference)
as indicator of the black
economy 57, 61–8
at the household level 7, 58
at the national level 69–73
income velocity of circulation in
black economy 14–15, 23–6
information bias and the black
economy 136–41
information uncertainty and
participation in the black
economy 103, 105–6
initial residual difference
defined 69
effect of inflation upon 71
effect of tax rates upon 72
as a measure of the black
economy 69–72
reasons for changes in UK after
1976 70–1

Keith Report 166–72

labour force participation rate
and measurement of the black
economy 7
falling in Italy 51
in Belgium's black economy 76
in Norway's black economy
75–6
low in Italy 74
studies of participation in the
black economy 74–8
labour supply

effect of wage rates on labour
supply to black economy 101
entry into the black economy
100
estimates of Italy's irregular
labour force 75, 77–8
models of labour supply in the
black economy 95–102

macroeconomic policy, effect of
black economy upon (*see also*
economic consequences) 10,
11
breakdown of macro policy in
late 1970s 136
effect of black economy upon
output, employment and
prices 141–4
effect of tax evasion upon size of
multiplier 144
information bias 136–41
moonlighting
definition 1
moonlighter 4

national income accounts data 68
as means of estimating size of
black economy 72–3

policy towards tax evasion and the
black economy 153–72
equity issues of 153, 157, 159,
178–9
failure of incremental approach
108
punishment, certainty and severity
of
and effect upon tax evasion
90–102, 118–21, 125, 127, 154,
155
differential audit
probabilities 160
investigative effort 157–8
limits to severity 155
trade-off between certainty and
severity 155
self-employed workers, and the
black economy 61–7
separability